LEVINAS, JUDAISM, AND THE FEMININE

Indiana Series in the Philosophy of Religion
Merold Westphal, general editor

Levinas, Judaism, and the Feminine

The Silent Footsteps of Rebecca

CLAIRE ELISE KATZ

INDIANA UNIVERSITY PRESS
Bloomington & Indianapolis

Publication of this book is made possible in part with the assistance of a Challenge Grant from the National Endowment for the Humanities, a federal agency that supports research, education, and public programming in the humanities.

This book is a publication of

Indiana University Press
601 North Morton Street
Bloomington, Indiana 47404-3797 USA

http://iupress.indiana.edu

Telephone orders 800-842-6796
Fax orders 812-855-7931
Orders by e-mail iuporder@indiana.edu

MANUFACTURED IN THE UNITED STATES OF AMERICA

Library of Congress Cataloging-in-Publication Data

Katz, Claire Elise, date
Levinas, Judaism, and the feminine : the silent footsteps of Rebecca / Claire Elise Katz.
p. cm. — (Indiana series in the philosophy of religion)
Includes bibliographical references (p.   ) and index.
ISBN 0-253-34302-X (cloth) — ISBN 0-253-21624-9 (paper)
1. Levinas, Emmanuel. 2. Femininity (Philosophy)—History—20th century. 3. Ethics, Modern—20th century.
4. Ethics, Jewish—History—20th century. I. Title. II. Series.
B2430.L484K38 2003
194—dc21
2003007798

1 2 3 4 5 08 07 06 05 04 03

For my daughter, Olivia Morgan Conway,
linked forever to the children of Israel as
שידי   אל יאודה

CONTENTS

PREFACE

I wrote the initial draft of this book well before my pregnancy and the birth of my first child. However, I undertook substantial revisions to the manuscript during my pregnancy and well into the first year of my daughter's life. My relationship with my newborn, who then became a crawling baby, and then finally a toddler, transformed the relationship that I have to Levinas's writings—it is not simply an intellectual endeavor or academic enterprise to engage his project, if it ever was simply that.

Levinas's distinction between erotic love and ethical love appealed to me intellectually, but it was not until I had a child of my own that the truth of this distinction became utterly apparent. My child claimed me in ways that I could never have imagined and that I had never experienced. Although the pain of childbirth has subsided and I can no longer remember for how many nights there were feedings every two hours, I know I experienced all of it. Of course, I also thought, "this too shall pass," only to realize that 2 A.M. feedings were far easier than keeping an eye on a toddler who is exploring the world. But with the loss of ease came the intensity of joy. This child is not simply my responsibility. She is the joy of my life. And the movement between joy and responsibility is wondrous. Levinas is right to name the parent-child relationship the ethical relationship par excellence. A parent's relationship to her child does not end; nor is it part of an economy of debt. My responsibility to my child is never finished, and my daughter is not responsible to me in return.

I do not mean to trivialize the intellectual pursuit either of philosophy in general or of Levinas's project in particular. But Levinas's writings are not simply intellectual exercises for those who read them. They speak to us—and they speak to each of us differently. I am sure that there are times in this book where Levinas's thought ends and my own begins, even if unacknowledged as such. One might argue that a more careful reading—and writing—would mean being clear about my exegesis of Levinas's writings and my use of them to advance my own philosophical position. But my task in this book does not exclude either of these ways of writing. My writing has a dual role. The first is to explicate Levinas's thought such that one can see three things: (1) what he means by the feminine; (2) what relationship the Jewish sources have to his writing; and (3) how this relationship influences his characterization of the feminine. The second role is to go beyond his writings and explore what they mean for both the past and the present, for reading the stories of the women of the Hebrew Bible and for women who live today. I embark on this second task always bearing in mind that going beyond his work does not mean leaving his work behind. Levinas's discussions of ethics, Judaism, the feminine, and maternity influenced how I think. The birth of my daughter deepened their meanings for me even further. I am grateful to be claimed by my daughter such that Levinas's writings can speak to me as they do. This book is dedicated to her.

ACKNOWLEDGMENTS

This book grew out of my dissertation, which I defended in 1999 at the University of Memphis. Although my fundamental interests in Levinas's use of the feminine and the role of Judaism and his Jewish writings in his philosophical thought have not changed, the project has changed dramatically. I thank the members of the philosophy department at the University of Memphis for the lively community they created in which to do graduate work. I extend my deepest gratitude to Tina Chanter and Robert Bernasconi, both of whom nurtured my initial interest in Levinas's thought. I am especially grateful to Tina for encouraging me to pursue my own project and to find my own voice in which to express it. Len Lawlor's continued support, personally and professionally, is always in the background of my philosophical life.

My community in Memphis still remains a vital part of my life, even from its distant location. I thank, in particular, Rabbi Micah Greenstein, whose support over these past ten years has been invaluable and whose life always serves as an example to me.

I am grateful to the many people with whom I have corresponded over the years about this project. I had the opportunity to present versions of several chapters at conferences, and the feedback that I received was invaluable. I am grateful to Eric Nelson, Kent Still, and Antje Kapust for including my paper on the Binding of Isaac in their conference "Addressing Levinas," hosted by Emory University. The reception of my paper at this conference indicated that my project indeed had an audience.

Earlier versions of this book were published or are forthcoming in the following places, and I wish to extend my gratitude to these publishers for permission to reprint this material. Two different versions of chapter 8 are forthcoming: one as "The Responsibility of Irresponsibility: Taking Another Look at the *Akedah*," in *Addressing Levinas,* edited by Eric Nelson, Kent Still, and Antje Kapust; and the second as "The Voice of God and the Face of the Other," in *The Journal of Textual Reasoning.* An earlier version of chapters 3 and 9 is forthcoming as "From Eros to Maternity: Love, Death, and the 'Feminine' in the Philosophy of Emmanuel Levinas," in *Women and Gender in Jewish Philosophy,* edited by Hava Tirosh-Samuelson. An earlier version of chapters 4 and 6 appeared as "Re-Inhabiting the House of Ruth," in *Feminist Interpretations of Emmanuel Levinas,* edited by Tina Chanter. An earlier version of chapter 5 appeared as "'For Love Is as Strong as Death': Taking Another Look at Levinas on Love," in *Philosophy Today.* I am grateful to the Chagall estate, the Artists Rights Society, and Art Resource for permission to use the cover image.

The people I would like to thank at Penn State are too numerous to name. However, I do wish to name a few. Susan Welch, the dean of the College of Liberal Arts, supported my research. The Institute for Arts and Humanities awarded me a grant to bring this project to completion. The Jewish studies program provided me with generous financial support, and I would like to thank in particular Alan Block and Caroline Eckhardt. I would also like to thank the Penn State Philosophy Department for its generous support. I am particularly grateful to have had the good fortune to work with John Stuhr, the former head of the philosophy department. In addition to benefiting from his administrative talents, I am grateful for the support that he has given me over these last few years, which helped make it possible for me to complete this book. I wish to thank Emily Grosholz for her support and for her own work in poetry that led me to Eleanor Wilner's poems. Thanks also go to Greg Recco, Erin Jones, and Joshua Miller, whose admirable proofreading talents helped advance the manuscript to its final stage.

The people at Indiana University Press have been a joy to work with. I thank Janet Rabinowitch for seeing the initial promise of this project and Dee Mortensen for helping to bring it to completion. Dee is what all first-time authors hope for—a firm but gentle presence. She has been a true supporter during the final stages of this project. I would like to thank Merold Westphal, whose generosity as a reader allowed him to see a place for my book in his series. I would like to thank Jane Lyle, Miki Bird, and Tony Brewer for handling the project on its way to production. And I wish to thank the book's designer, Sharon Sklar, for her work on the cover. I extend a special thanks to Käthe Roth for her extraordinary (in every sense of the word) copy-editing talents. Her patience, conscientiousness, and good humor turned an otherwise tedious task into something (almost) enjoyable! The mistakes that remain are, of course, my own.

My students are a constant source of inspiration. I wish to thank those I taught at Salisbury University, Washington College, the University of Memphis, and Pennsylvania State University for allowing me to test new ideas in the classroom.

I am grateful for the friendship, both personal and professional, of several people who read earlier drafts of this manuscript and whose comments and discussions with me only helped to improve this book: Leora Batnitzky, Bettina Bergo, Robert Gibbs, Sandor Goodhart, Martin Kavka, Kelly Oliver,

Jill Robbins, and Anthony Steinbock. Their Levinasian generosity will always serve as an example to me. I am grateful for the people who have come together to form the Levinas Research Seminar, which has blossomed into quite a group—too many to name. I wish to thank Diane Perpich for our many discussions over the years and for the patient way she explains very difficult concepts. I also wish to thank Jim Hatley, who first introduced me to Levinas's work. I have benefited tremendously from our conversations about Levinas, Judaism, teaching, and all things both philosophical and non-philosophical. My research on Levinas and Judaism introduced me to wonderful people whose scholarship has been important to my own thinking. In particular, I am grateful to Oona Eisenstadt for her critical comments, her support of my project, and the work she has already accomplished in this field. Thanks also to Steven Kepnes and Zachary Braiterman for their support of my work and for welcoming me into the community of Jewish philosophy. I am indebted to Hava Tirosh-Samuelson and Norbert Samuelson for their generous hospitality and the opportunities they provided me to participate in their conferences.

There are too many friends who need to be thanked; no doubt if I tried to list them all, I would unintentionally forget to name someone. I thank Katie Hustad for her companionship and support during that first year of balancing motherhood and careers in the academy. My deep thanks to Anne Rose and Susan Harris, for including me in their Chavura organized around the topic of women and Judaism, and for their ongoing support and astute advice. I also enjoyed the pleasure of Miriam Bodian's friendship and many extraordinary and priceless conversations about Judaism and Jewish history. Her suggestions for translations of several Hebrew words remain invaluable. And I thank Cara Johnson, Debbie Snow, Gigi Moore, Valérie Loichot, Lynette Wright, and Pam Roth for their sustained friendship and encouragement. And I thank Andrea Motyka and Tamara Smith for always feigning interest.

Finally, my deepest gratitude goes to my family—my husband, Daniel Conway, and our daughter, Olivia Conway. Olivia is still a bit young to care much about philosophy. But during the course of this writing she nonetheless taught me many things—about flowers, and balloons, and fish, and hippos, and dancing. Thank you, Dan—for your "ughs" and kisses, for popcorn and wine, for the Dairy and the Mockingbird, for the *NYT* crossword and "L & A," but most of all I thank you for "little O," for through her you have taught me about magic.

LIST OF ABBREVIATIONS

References to the following works by Emmanuel Levinas are made by abbreviation within the body of the text. Complete references may be found in the bibliography. For reprinted essays, references will be made to the most recent publication. Standard English translations will be quoted.

AE	*Autrement qu'être ou au-delà de l'essence*
AT	"Aimer la Thora plus que Dieu"
BG	"The Bible and the Greeks"
BeG	"La Bible et les Grecs"
BTW	"Between Two Worlds"
DCF	"Et Dieu créa la femme"
DDF	"Damages Due to Fire"
DEE	*De l'existence à l'existant*
DF	*Difficult Freedom*
DFo	"Dying For"
DL	*Difficile Liberté*
DMT	*Dieu, la mort et le temps*
DP	"Dieu et Philosophie"
DPF	"Les dommages causés par le feu"
EDM	"Entre deux mondes"
EE	Existence and Existents
EI	*Ethics and Infinity: Conversations with Philippe Nemo*
EeE	"Éthique et Esprit"
EeI	*Éthique et Infini*
ES	"Ethics and Spirit"
GCW	"And God Created Woman"
GDT	*God, Death, and Time*
GP	"God and Philosophy"
IR	*Is It Righteous to Be?: Interviews with Emmanuel Levinas*
JF	"Judaism and the Feminine"
JeF	"Le judaïsme et le féminin"
JP	"On Jewish Philosophy"
JRS	"On the Jewish Reading of the Scriptures"
LJE	"De la lecture juive des Ecritures"

LT	"Loving the Torah more than God"
MP	"Mourir Pour"
NP	*Les Noms Propres*
OTB	*Otherwise than Being, or Beyond Essence*
PJ	"Sur la philosophie juive"
PN	*Proper Names*
PP	"Peace and Proximity"
PeP	"Paix et proximité"
RA	"A Religion for Adults"
RdA	"Une religion d'adultes"
RJT	"Revelation in the Jewish Tradition"
RTJ	"La Révélation dans la tradition juive"
TA	*Le Temps et l'autre*
TdT	"La tentation de la tentation"
TeI	*Totalité et infini: Essai sur l'exteriorité*
TI	*Totality and Infinity: An Essay on Exteriority*
TO	*Time and the Other*
TT	"The Temptation of Temptation"

LEVINAS, JUDAISM,
AND THE FEMININE

Introduction

In a 1982 radio interview with Emmanuel Levinas and Alain Finkielkraut, Shlomo Malka refers to Levinas as the "philosopher of the 'other.'"[1] This designation accurately describes Levinas and his philosophical project, which focuses on responsibility to the other. Levinas's philosophy demonstrates a radical shift in the portrayal of the other. We can see in the French existential tradition, and more generally in modernity, the portrayal of the other as a threat to one's subjectivity and freedom—indeed, a threat to everything that one may have and want. Instead of viewing the other as occupying a lower status in the zero-sum "fight" for subjectivity, Levinas views the other as having priority in the relationship between the 'I' and the Other. In Levinas's view, in fact, the response to the other founds subjectivity. The other not only does not threaten my subjectivity, but is also necessary for my subjectivity. This shift in thinking alters not only the status of the other, but the relationship between an 'I' and an Other. It also reveals that we are not the isolated, independent atoms that are described in much of the history of Western philosophy. Rather, we are always already connected to the other through our ethical obligation to the other.[2]

The traditional understanding of 'the other,' particularly in the Western philosophical tradition, further complicates how we view the status of the feminine throughout Levinas's project. Since Levinas gives priority to ethics over ontology, the position of the other as an ethical other grants it a privileged status. Therefore, the feminine, insofar as it occupies the position of the other, also occupies a privileged position. This does not mean that the feminine is an unproblematic term in Levinas's writing. Quite to the contrary, what he means by the other, and even the feminine, is often not clear.

The common understanding of the other in Levinas's writings is as an ethical other, the other to whom I am responsible. In *Time and the Other,* a long essay published in the 1940s, Levinas had not yet named the ethical relationship. But in this essay he defined the feminine not only as the Other, but also as the absolutely other. In his first major book, *Totality and Infinity*—published in the 1960s—the ethical relationship, now named, excluded the feminine. The feminine appeared to play a transcendental role, providing the conditions that make the ethical relationship possible, while not participating in the ethical relationship itself. The status of the feminine and its relationship to the ethical in these two early writings is already at issue. And from the questionable status of the feminine emerge several other problems.

Due in part to the way that Levinas uses his terms, there is first a problem identifying the relation that the feminine has to the ethical. The 'other' connected to the definition of my subjectivity is conflated with the 'other' who is the feminine—the other who sits on the margins of a system, the other who, according to *Time and the Other*, will make the ethical possible via the experience of alterity, and who, according to the argument in *Totality and Infinity*, provides the means by which the ethical can occur. One cannot simply assume that the feminine is part of the ethical relation, at least not in his writings prior to *Otherwise than Being*. In no event can one assume it unproblematically. He regularly conflates the two conceptions of 'other' at work in his discussion.

Second, Levinas's use of the feminine to mark stereotypically feminine traits—for example, hospitality, generosity, welcoming—leads one to conclude that the feminine functions as something more than a metaphor, and the scholarly debate over this term centers on whether it also refers to concrete women. Additionally, Levinas often vacillates in several of his writings between using "le féminin" and "la femme," further complicating its referent.[3] In both *Totality and Infinity* and "Judaism and the Feminine," for example, he interchanges "le féminin" and "la femme." Additionally, in "Judaism and the Feminine," he lists several attributes that he calls feminine, but then he specifically names female figures in the Hebrew Bible as people who exemplify those traits. Whether the feminine functions simply as a metaphor, referring to the stereotypical feminine traits that may be shared by all people, or whether it refers to empirical women is unclear. If the feminine refers to concrete women, then does this mean that women are also outside the ethical relation? If they are, are they excluded categorically? If not categorically, then what role are they likely to play in the ethical? In light of Levinas's own descriptions, his own writing, and his own lack of precision when using these terms, we must ask after the relation between the feminine and woman.

Third, in *Otherwise than Being*, Levinas reconceives the feminine, and so the ethical relation, as maternity.[4] In this book, the feminine plays a substantial role in the ethical relation. But this image opens up new questions for the feminine, and so for ethics as a whole, in Levinas's project. What does it mean to base an ethics on the image of maternity? What does Levinas's ethics, which praises the possibility of one sacrificing his or her life for an other, mean for women? The imagery that we find in *Otherwise than Being* is striking insofar as it refers to maternity, or the maternal body, as the ethical relation par excellence. This book is also striking in that references to the Hebrew Bible—for example, to Isaiah and Lamentations—are ubiquitous.

The fourth problem emerges from the complex relationship that Levinas's philosophical writings have to his writings on Judaism. His move away from ontology corresponds to a movement toward both the feminine *and* the Hebrew Bible as illustrations of the ethical. There is a sense in which his efforts recover both Judaism and the feminine. Thus we can ask what role Judaism and the accompanying Jewish sources play not simply in his philosophy but, more specifically, in his evolving conception of the feminine.

In *Levinas, Judaism, and the Feminine,* I disclose the connections between Levinas's philosophical project, his conception of the feminine, and the Judaic sources that influence his philosophical thought. With these connections in mind, I offer a different perspective on his work from those that we have seen thus far. I demonstrate that by reading Levinas against the backdrop of Jewish themes, we gain a richer understanding of his project and of the deeper themes that guide that project. By placing his description of the feminine in the context of the Jewish influences on his intellectual thought, we arrive at a more comprehensive understanding of the feminine and his conception of the ethical. My discussion demonstrates that the feminine is a dynamic structure—on which he depends throughout his project, and thus one that changes as his conception of the ethical matures. By synthesizing my discussions of the problems addressed above, I argue that the feminine does indeed play a dual role as both metaphor *and* as referent to empirical women, and that in this dual role the feminine serves as both the interruption of virility and the model for the ethical.

Finally, by illuminating the themes both from Judaism and from Levinas's religious writings that are already present in his philosophical writings, and by incorporating consideration of key biblical figures into my discussions of both his philosophical and his confessional writings, my argument opens a space for appreciating his description of the feminine as positively inflected. I take seriously his claim that he uses his references to biblical verse not to serve as proof. Likewise, I too do not cite the Bible as proof; nor do I wish to disregard his reasons for keeping these writings separate. Like Levinas, I attempt instead to use the discussions of these figures to broaden our conception of his feminine and of the biblical figures themselves. And with respect to Judaism, I endorse Levinas's observation that "Judaism is not the Bible; it is the Bible seen through the Talmud, through rabbinical wisdom, interrogation, and religious life" (IR 76).

What Levinas wants us to see in Judaism is not that virility is absent, since it is not absent. Rather, he sees Judaism as valuable in the way that it attempts to balance the tensions between virility and femininity, between justice and mercy, and between politics and ethics. As I mentioned earlier, the feminine serves as both the interruption of virility and the model for the ethical. If we remember that the original other is the feminine and that the other is also my teacher, then it is from the traits of the feminine that we must learn. The Greek (philosophical) tradition, by silencing the feminine, also silenced mercy, and thus silenced ethics.

Although my concern lies elsewhere, I wish to remark briefly on the debate over the status of Levinas's confessional writings, especially with respect to his philosophical writings. Levinas makes numerous remarks about this relationship in several interviews. He is clear that Judaism and Jewish sources serve as pre-philosophical experiences that inspire his philosophical thought. I discuss this point in more detail in chapter 1. But my point here is to indicate that the task of my book is not to offer proof of the relationship between the two bodies of writings—a number of recent books accomplish this task effectively. Rather, I wish to demonstrate how the two bodies of thought can work together to aid our understanding of Levinas's project—in particular, his conception of the feminine. This reading of Levinas's two bodies of work as related to each other is not contrived, but is evinced by the similarity of themes between the two. My position, then, negotiates these poles that unfortunately divide Levinas scholarship between those who read him with Jewish sources in mind and those who do not. My argument in this book is two-fold: (1) I claim that the feminine in Levinas's work is rooted in a distinctly Jewish conception of the feminine; and (2) I claim that we can understand more clearly how the feminine functions in his project and what use his description of the feminine may be to us today, if we understand it in this light.

I realize that bringing Levinas's use of the feminine to bear on the discussion of his relationship to Judaism may raise more questions than it answers. For all of its wonderful traditions, Judaism is regrettably limited with regard to its treatment of women, both textually and in practice. I am aware of, and indebted to, the abundance of feminist literature on Judaism and its ambivalent treatment of women.[5] This literature is indispensable to anyone who wants to take women and Judaism seriously. Even so, I advance a positive reading of Levinas and Judaism with regard to the feminine. By reading the feminine in this way, I refocus our attention on Levinas's critique of the Western philosophical tradition that gives priority to a Greek-influenced Christianity under the veil of fraternal atheism and/or secularism. My book is not intended to be an apology for either Levinas or Judaism. I offer a different perspective on Levinas's work so that philosophers and non-philosophers might have an alternative interpretation of his project.

In spite of my reservations about Judaism, I nonetheless argue in this book that it is Judaism that offers us a different way—a positive way—of reading Levinas's conception of the feminine. Levinas's critique of Western philosophy is implicitly a critique of the Western construction of masculinity as virility, and he is using a Jewish conception of the feminine as the image of its interruption.[6] There is much at stake here: What, if anything, can feminism glean from his work? How do we understand the contribution that a patriarchal religion such as Judaism can make to this conversation? What does a "Jewish reading" of Levinas mean for his philosophical project?

I am not the first to raise such questions. However, this book offers a new approach to understanding the relationships among Levinas, Judaism, and the feminine in order to see the complexity that defines these relationships. The goal of this book is to help its readers hear the silent footsteps of the feminine.

OUTLINE OF THE CHAPTERS

In chapter 1, I take up the question of the relationship between Levinas's Jewish writings and his philosophical writings by examining his own comments about this relationship and his understanding of Jewish holy texts. This chapter demonstrates that Levinas sees a relationship between the two modes of writing, even though he maintains that we ought to respect the differences in their respective argumentative styles. This chapter concludes with an examination of the role of midrash in the interpretation of Jewish holy texts. The midrash is fundamental to the exegesis of these texts, since it reveals the obscured meanings hidden in the written words.

In chapter 2, I examine the first half of *Time and the Other* in light of the biblical story of creation. Similar to the commentary on this story, *Time and the Other* emphasizes the leitmotif of separation and individuation throughout Levinas's book, a theme that is significant for his discussion of alterity and the relationship to the other. One cannot be in a relationship unless one is separate from the other person.

In chapter 3, I consider the discussion of the feminine in *Time and the Other* in light of the creation of the sexes in the biblical story of creation. I also examine the feminine in light of Levinas's talmudic essay "And God Created Woman." I argue that Levinas's conception of the feminine and the creation of the sexes in the story of creation reveal the relationship between the inauguration of sexual difference and the originary experience of alterity.

In chapter 4, I explore the discussion of the feminine in *Totality and Infinity*. The discussion first considers the description of the feminine in this book in light of Levinas's description of the feminine in his essay "Judaism and the Feminine." Although the descriptions are found in the two separate modes of writing—religious and philosophical—they are uncannily similar. The discussion of the feminine in this chapter then explicates Levinas's description of love in "The Phenomenology of Eros."

In chapter 5, I interrogate two influential critiques of Levinas's description of the feminine: those offered by Luce Irigaray and by Jacques Derrida. Both critiques focus on the role of sexual difference in Levinas's philosophy. Irigaray's concern is that Levinas neglected the significance of sexual difference, while Derrida's concern is that sexual difference may actually define, and so limit, Levinas's ethics.

In chapter 6, I consider Levinas's project in light of the influence on him of Franz Rosenzweig's distinctly Jewish references to love and fecundity. Reading Levinas in light of Rosenzweig provides an alternative to how we might understand the themes he employs. Thus, we may reconsider the critiques offered by Irigaray and Derrida in light of this influence. This chapter ends with a discussion on the Book of Ruth, a story that unites the themes of love and fecundity and demonstrates the way that the feminine, as Levinas describes it, may actually disrupt its own status as that which is outside the ethical relation.

In chapter 7, I analyze Levinas's account of the ethical relation and his concern about the power of virility in light of the story of Cain and Abel. This story illuminates several of his themes: the face-to-face; the Other; the "thou shalt not kill"; and human fraternity. Thus we see in the biblical figure of Cain a person who has not yet attained subjectivity. Cain is completely detached from human fraternity.

In chapter 8, I approach Levinas's conception of subjectivity in light of the biblical figure of Abraham. I examine the movement of subjectivity from Cain, who could not admit to his responsibility, to Abraham, whose "here I am" reveals his profound responsibility. The *Akedah*—the Binding of Isaac—tells the story of Abraham, who raises a knife to his son. I return to this story in light of Søren Kierkegaard's interpretation of Abraham in *Fear and Trembling*. I interpret Abraham as a figure who, in this story, begins by not responding to the other, but who ultimately realizes that responsibility to God is expressed through responsibility to the human other.

In chapters 9 and 10, I turn to *Otherwise than Being* and its image of maternity as the ethical relation par excellence. These chapters consider the implications of such a concept for both women and ethics. For example, if the feminine in the figure of maternity names the ethical relation par excellence, then how do we understand the violence that women commit against their own children? If Levinas describes the ethical in terms of the possibility of sacrificing one's own life for another, then what are the dangerous implications for women? How do we understand a maternity that is viewed in terms of responsibility? What role, if any, can eros have? Finally, how do we understand the relationship between enjoyment and responsibility such that Levinas escapes the charge that he is simply an ascetic thinker?

Unless otherwise indicated, all translations of the Hebrew Bible are from the Jewish Publication Society translation.

ONE

Judaism and the Ethical: Recovering the Other

> The verses of the Bible do not here have as their function
> to serve as proofs; but they do bear witness to a tradition
> and an experience. Do they not have a right to be cited
> at least as equal to that of Hölderlin and Trakl?
> —Levinas, "No Identity," *Collected Philosophical Papers*

In his essay "The Bible and the Greeks," Levinas writes,

> What is Europe? It is the Bible and the Greeks. The Bible: an ontological in-
> version? The original perseverance of realities in their being—the inertia of
> material objects, the enrootedness of plants, the struggle between wild ani-
> mals, the war among "owning and interested" men, as Bossuet calls them—
> is inverted in the man announced to humanity in Israel. Thus, for being
> dedicated to being, for being that has no other purpose than to be, the
> human self might also signify the possibility of interrupting its *conatus es-*
> *sendi*, the possibility of answering for the other, who is "none of my busi-
> ness," who is nothing to me. "Thou shalt not kill," that is to say, "thou shalt
> love thy neighbor." This is an odd recommendation for an existence sum-
> moned to live at all costs. (BG 133/BeG 155)

According to Levinas, the "Greek" signifies the prevailing emphasis on being, on our *conatus essendi,* on the will to survive, on self-preservation. The
Bible, he maintains, signifies the possibility of something other than the
drive to exist, the possibility of interrupting our *conatus essendi,* the possibility of something greater than that will to survive. The above quotation
underscores Levinas's belief that there is the possibility of a responsibility
for the alterity of the other person. We reveal the interruption of the *cona-*
tus essendi when we provide the material conditions for one who is hungry

or thirsty, for the nakedness of the defenseless mortal, for "in that fragile uniqueness outside the extension of the concept, the face is commanded, and from that moment forth, in this self persevering in being, there emerges mercy and the overturning of being's tautology of pure 'being *qua* being'" (BG 133/BeG 155).

Levinas refers to the biblical story of Rebecca at the well, in which Rebecca offered water to Abraham's servant and to the camels of the caravan. Levinas believes that Rebecca's actions exemplify the ethical response to the other, the kindness shown to another, "a responsibility exceeding the demand heard by myself in the face of the other" (BG 134/BeG156). But the face-to-face, the response to the other, is always accompanied by a third party, and the third party is also a neighbor. The presence of the third party, who also requires a response, complicates the simple response to the other. With the entry of this third party we can ask, Who speaks first? Where does the priority lie? A decision must be made. Along with the original imperative in the face of the other comes the need for judgments, for knowledge, for verification, and for objective science; there is a desire to reach a conclusion; and "there must be judgments, the state, political authority" (BG 134/BeG 156).[1] Levinas observes that the Bible recognizes this need for justice. Thus, in his view, the original violation of mercy—the move to a community, to this place where judgments must be made and where the face of the other, the uniqueness of the other, is sacrificed or lost—is also an unavoidable violation.

By "Greek," Levinas does not mean only the grammar and vocabulary of the Greek language. He also means the "manner in which the universality of the West is expressed, or tries to express itself—rising above the local particularism of the quaint, traditional, poetic or religious. It is a language without prejudice, a way of speaking that bites reality without leaving any marks" (BG 134–135/BeG 156). Thus, when Levinas identifies Greek as the inevitable discourse recommended by the Bible itself, he is referring to the language of justice and the response to the other that we find in the Bible. The move to the universal, to justice, is warranted by the "original imperative in the face of the other" (BG 135/BeG 157). This is what Levinas believes the West has lost. We are concerned with the universal and with justice, but we have forgotten why. The original saying of the Bible necessarily does not translate into Greek. Thus, the particularity of the face and our responsibility to the other, both of which give justice meaning, have become obscured.

Levinas explains that "the humanity of the human must be set back within the horizon of the universal. Oh, welcome messages from Greece! To become educated among the Greeks, to learn their language and their wisdom. Greek is Europe's inevitable discourse, recommended by the Bible itself" (BG 134/BeG 156). The tension between universal and particular, maintained in the Judaic, is lost when the Greek translates the Bible and places the message of Judaism into the language of the universal. The Greek focus on the universal covers over the individual. But Levinas sees the relationship as involving a tension. He is not advocating the loss of the universal. The Bible, he believes, reminds us that this tension cannot be resolved. On the one hand, he sees the translation of the Bible into Greek—the message of the Bible, a message expressed in the voice of particularity—as necessary. On the other hand, the justice put forth by the Greek cannot be allowed completely to annihilate, or universalize, the uniqueness of the other; it is this biblical message that Levinas intends to recall for us.

For Levinas, the Bible is Judaism and the Greek is philosophy. The passages quoted above thus reveal the complicated relationship between his philosophical writings and his writings on Judaism. These passages also raise questions about how his readers are to understand these apparently disparate modes of expression. He separates these two modes of writing for good reason, and the debate surrounding this relationship arises in part from his own comments on this topic.

In a frequently cited statement from an interview, Levinas told his interlocutor that he wished to keep his confessional writings separate from his philosophical writings and that he even used separate publishers for each.[2] But nowhere does he say that his religion has not been an influence on his work. In fact, he says the opposite.[3] In an interview with Philippe Nemo, he admits, "I did not have the impression early on that philosophy was essentially atheist, and I still do not think it today. And if, in philosophy, verse can no longer take the place of proof, the God of verse can, despite all the text's anthropological metaphors, remain the measure of Spirit for the philosopher" (EI 23/EeI 18). Later in this same interview, in response to the question of whether he intended to harmonize the two modes of thought, biblical and philosophical, Levinas replies,

> I have never aimed explicitly to "harmonize" or "conciliate" both traditions. If they happen to be in harmony it is probably because every philosophical thought rests on pre-philosophical experiences, and for me reading the Bible has belonged to these founding experiences. It has thus played an essential role—and in large part without my knowing it—in addressing all mankind. . . . At no moment did the Western philosophical tradition in my eyes lose its right to the last word; everything must, indeed, be expressed in its tongue; but perhaps it is not the place of the first meaning of beings, the place where meaning begins. (EI 24–25/EeI 19)

And what are we to make of passages like those that we find in his essay "On Jewish Philosophy," in which he tells us that "philosophy is derived from religion" (JP 173/PJ 204) or when he says that "the relation to God is already ethics; or as Isaiah 58 would have it, the proximity to God, devotion itself, is already devotion to the other man" (JP 171/PJ 202)? Certainly, we can concede that Levinas has two different styles of writing. But his intention for keeping these styles separate does not appear to be primarily about the relationship that the themes in each have to the other. Rather, he suspects, and probably rightly so, that he will be taken less seriously as a philosopher if his readers confuse his religious writings with his philosophical writings. His confessional style does not offer a philosophical argument and should not be judged in the same manner as we would judge a philosophical argument. His philosophical writings do offer an argument and should be judged on that basis.

Levinas's characterization of the subordinate position of philosophy to religion cannot easily be dismissed. He frequently quotes from the Book of Isaiah and uses other expressions from the Hebrew Bible in his philosophical work. Although he is clear that he does not cite these passages to serve as proof, he does cite them as examples or illustrations (IR 62). These passages, found in his "Jewish writings," rehearse themes that we also find in his philosophical writings. My point here is not to reduce Levinas's philosophical project to "merely" religious musings. Rather, reading his Jewish writings as complementary to his philosophical writings enriches our appreciation of his philosophy by aiding us in understanding the difficult themes that he discusses in his project. Levinas concedes that the putting into question is philosophical, even if the inspiration for it is religious. He observes that the verse often displays a philosophical accent, in which case he draws that verse into his philosophical writing. When he does so, however, he stays true to its original formulation in verse. The Bible renders the Greek necessary and Europe comprises both the Bible and the Greek (IR 64).

References to Jewish writings and the reliance on the Jewish tradition do not undermine the universal nature of Levinas's philosophical arguments. For him, the ethical message of the Hebrew Bible applies to everyone, even if in a particular way for each. Thus, Levinas asserts that philosophy is derivative of religion, the latter of which he equates with ethics. He sees the inseparability of God and Torah as fundamental to the Judaic faith. And he understands Torah as the ethical, the recognition of the other person. Thus, Levinas explains,

> The Jewish Bible I quote is not the originality of an ethnic particularism, no more so than is the Hellenic rationality of knowledge. The Bible signifies for all authentically human thought, for civilization *tout court,* whose authenticity can be recognized in peace, in *shalom,* and in the responsibility of one man for another. "Peace, peace, to him that is far off and to him that is near. . . ." [Thus what Levinas] calls wisdom is a thought guided by the care for objectivity and truth, but a thought in which, in this care, there is no

loss of the memory of the justice that gave rise to them; justice that relates back to the original right of the neighbor, and to responsibility of the neighbor. (JP 171–172/PJ 202)[4]

In fact, Levinas believes that the commandment "Thou shalt not kill" "is not simply the prohibition against murder. It becomes a fundamental definition or description of the human event of being, a permanent prudence with respect to the violent and murderous acts against the other which are perhaps the very assertion of being, as if the very imposition of a being's existence were already to jeopardize someone's life" (IR 62).

For Levinas, the biblical commands that enjoin the 'I' to respond to the Other exemplify the ethical relationship that one has to another: "Thou shalt not kill"; "Thou shalt love the stranger"; and "Thou shalt love thy neighbor as thyself." The biblical commands require that the ego project out of itself toward the other. The Bible, then, illustrates the origins of human subjectivity: "The Bible teaches us that man is he who loves his neighbor, and that the fact of loving his neighbor is a modality of meaningful life, of a thinking as fundamental—I would say more fundamental—than the knowledge of an object, than truth as knowledge of objects" (IR 64). The Bible renders the Greek necessary because the human begins in religion or, "if you will, the subject begins, starting from its relation, its obligation with regard to the other" (IR 64). Judaism means, for Levinas, this responsibility to the other, a responsibility that is nontransferable, a surplus of responsibility, a responsibility for the other's responsibility, a responsibility that is not chosen, but rather that has chosen me. The Bible, Judaism, marks the time of election, the time of chosenness. The Bible reflects the responsibility of a time before memory and before choice itself.[5]

BEFORE THE TIME OF CLOCKS

What, then, does it mean to have and describe a responsibility that is anarchical and yet claims me prior to my choice in that claim? *Otherwise than Being; or, Beyond Essence,* Levinas's most mature work, begins by asking what would it mean "not *to be* otherwise, but to be otherwise than being" (OTB 3/AE 13, emphasis added). This completely other sense of "otherwise than being" is how he understands transcendence. It is what marks the very separation of being and nothingness, the very difference between being and beyond. That is, "otherwise than being" is not to be understood in terms of death, nothingness, or any kind of negation or privation. It is the difference between these things.

In *Otherwise than Being,* Levinas distinguishes his version of subjectivity from a traditional conception of subjectivity. Modern philosophy viewed subjectivity as a clash of egos, in which competing drives ultimately find themselves at war. Levinas observes that in this conception there exists a "multiplicity of allergic egoisms which are at war with one another and are thus together" (OTB 4/AE 15). And this view understood peace as that condition in which reason reigns. Thus, modern philosophers believed that reason suspended the clash of beings. It makes sense to wonder if we can characterize this peace, wherein the "allergic intolerance of their persistence in being" (OTB 4/AE 15) persists, as an otherwise than being. Levinas thinks it cannot. Commerce, exchange, mediation, calculation, and politics characterize this kind of peace.

We find a similar account of peace in Levinas's essay "Peace and Proximity." Here, Levinas tells us that truth forms the basis for peace, as it has arisen from the Greek tradition. Rather than maintaining the alterity of the other, peace assimilates the stranger into the Same (PP 162/PeP 339). In the traditional conception, peace rests on the needs of the state. Peace, therefore, means maintaining a democracy, even if doing so overrides the uniqueness of the individual.[6] The conflict that characterizes the relationship of ethics to politics announces itself in the pursuit of peace. This pursuit violates the alterity of the other, in the name of the needs of the community.

In *Totality and Infinity,* Levinas defined the ethical relation as the face-to-face, a relation of two. Although the term "face-to-face" is absent from his discussion of responsibility in *Otherwise than Being,* the ethical remains a relationship between two people. In both books, politics, viewed as a mode of equalization or leveling, emerges with the entry of a third party. The entry of the third party requires that goods be distributed fairly. Thus, what Levinas calls politics refers to the traditional conception of ethics found in modernity. And in his view, the political—which coincides with the traditional understanding of the ethical—obscures the ethical as he describes it. Moreover, the ethical as he understands it makes the political possible. His task in *Otherwise than Being* is to recover what cannot be recovered directly. He views the ethical as that which is "immemorial." It precedes memory, "the time of clocks," and the time of history. The ethical, for Levinas, is "anarchical." He uses this term in its literal sense—anarchical, without an *arché*. He does not intend to recover a first principle. The ethical precedes any first principle that we could define, or "discover"; the ethical, in fact, makes possible any idea of a first principle to which we might appeal. To use Llewelyn's phrase, Levinas's ethics is a proto-ethics;[7] it is the *before* of any ethical system that we have come to understand as ethical. For example, an ethical system such as Kant's, which employs the categorical imperative to determine how one will act in a given situation, and which calls for equality, formalization, and universalization, belongs to what Levinas calls the "political." The response to the other that defines the ethical relation ultimately makes necessary rules to govern our behavior toward the other.

The ethical theories to which Levinas responds operate at the level of ontology. He distinguishes his version of ethics from the ethical theories of others by his characterization of the relationship between ethics and ontology. For Levinas, ethics precedes ontology; that is, ethics has priority over ontology and gives it meaning. As a result, terms such as "freedom" and "commitment" do not apply to Levinas's account of responsibility, since these concepts are ontological. We are *elected* to responsibility. Responsibility is not freely chosen. Responsibility claims the subject before memory can capture that moment, and the claim comes from outside of our conventional understanding of time. It is not that memory is incapable of remembering the choice, since that would imply that memory is simply flawed. Rather, one is always already responsible.

Levinas recognizes the philosophical problem that attends his efforts to talk about an *otherwise than being*. In particular, he acknowledges that the verb "to be" already seems to encompass everything. Any attempt to discuss that which is outside of being only serves to emphasize being. This problem is not new to Levinas, and *Otherwise than Being* can be read as a response to Derrida's essay "Violence and Metaphysics," which raises this question in response to *Totality and Infinity*. In this essay, Derrida calls attention to the problem of how one talks about a "beyond ontology" without using the language of ontology. In Levinas's terms, how does one discuss a saying without thematizing it and turning it into the said? This problem haunts him in *Otherwise than Being*. We see evidence of his awareness of this problem when he wonders if "'otherwise' does not inevitably refer to the verb 'to be'" (OTB 4/AE 14). His work in *Otherwise than Being* endeavors to inaugurate such a discussion. He emphasizes the possibility of a non-being, not simply a negation of being (which would indicate only nothingness or death). His discussion of the saying and the said aids him with this task.

A clarification of the relationship of the said to the saying might help explain the "inescapable fate in which being includes the statement of being's other" (OTB 5/AE 16). Levinas tells us that "the proximity of the one to the other, as the responsibility of the one for the other, as the commitment of approach" defines the saying (OTB 5/AE 17). And he explains that "the original or pre-original saying, what is put forth in the forward, weaves an intrigue of responsibility" (OTB 5–6/AE 17). Thus, since he equates language with the said, we are to understand the saying as that which precedes language. And he warns us that we should understand that any proposed correlation between the saying and the said is really a subordination of the saying to the said (OTB 6/AE 17), and thus a betrayal of the saying. Levinas's examination in this book reveals the deception of language.

Similarly, theory and thought, which are being's contemporaries—and, so, also the contemporaries of language—are actually "motivated by the pre-original vocation of the saying, [motivated] by responsibility itself" (OTB 6/AE 18). Thus, Levinas sees that language permits us to talk about the otherwise than being, even if its place in the realm of ontology also betrays this utterance.[8] With regard to this paradox, Levinas observes, "We have been seeking the *otherwise than being* from the beginning, and as soon as it is conveyed before us it is betrayed in the said that dominates the saying which states it" (OTB 7/AE 19). We thus arrive at Levinas's stated methodological problem:[9]

> [W]hether the pre-original element of the saying (the anarchical, the non-original, as we designate it) can be led to betray itself by showing itself in a theme (if an an-archeology is possible) and whether this betrayal can be reduced; whether one can at the same time know and free the known of the marks which thematization leaves on it by subordinating it to ontology. Everything shows itself at the price of this betrayal, even the unsayable. In this betrayal the indiscretion with regard to the unsayable, which is probably the very task of philosophy, becomes possible. (OTB 7/AE 19)

Who is the philosopher Levinas speaks of in the passage quoted above, and what is the philosopher's task? As we typically understand him or her, the philosopher seeks and expresses truth. As such, ontology plays a central role in the philosopher's mission. His or her concern is truth as the exhibition of being, with *what* shows itself in truth. According to Levinas, the philosopher raises these concerns and then investigates even before establishing the distinction between being and entities. To address these issues in terms of the "what" indicates that one remains at the level of ontology. The guiding force of being defines the philosopher's quest. If "what" lies at the origin of all thought, then "all research and all philosophy go back to ontology, to the understanding of the being of entities, the understanding of essence" (OTB 24/AE 44). Truth, as a progression that takes place in several moments, reveals the appearance of being. What being signifies, what is important in being, is its own manifestation, its own appearing. Levinas focuses on a "past which was never present and whose anarchical antiquity was never given in the play of dissimulations and manifestations, a past whose *other* signification remains to be described, signifies over and beyond the manifestation of being, which thus would convey but a moment of this signifying signification" (OTB 24/AE 45). He refers to this past as a past that is more ancient than any present. And it lies outside the ontological framing of the world.

Levinas, then, takes as his tasks to both say and not say what he is trying to express. In order for entities and phenomena to be shown or to appear, the said must continually absorb the saying. Philosophy is therefore a primary culprit in the thematization of the saying. Levinas often refers to the thematization of the saying as a violence done to its particularity. Thus, if Cain's killing of Abel physically expresses the virile—the attempt to destroy the alterity of the other—then philosophy, one might say, is an intellectual expression of the virile. Philosophy's search for truth and knowledge obscures the ethical responsibility to and the alterity of the other. Thus, the "otherwise than being" must be stated but also left unsaid. Levinas must express the saying both directly and indirectly. He must extract the otherwise-than-being from the said in such a way that we can receive it as otherwise-than-being, not as a being otherwise.

The said begets another said. Language begets language; vocabulary begets more vocabulary. And the stratification of the layers of the said further buries the saying. The static character of the said exemplifies the passivity of the saying, whereby the saying collapses under the weight of the said. Derrida's criticisms in "Violence and Metaphysics" penetrate to the center of the problem that Levinas faces in *Totality and Infinity*, when he tries to express that which is not ontological. Levinas realizes that the movement of language consists in an alternation between the saying and the said. He nonetheless must distinguish between the saying and the said in order for us to see clearly the role that each plays. His problem, as he himself is well aware, is how to draw this distinction within language. How does one use language, the said, to disclose the saying, which is itself neither revealed in light, nor static, nor ontologized, nor language?

Levinas defines the saying as both an affirmation and a retraction of the said (OTB 44/AE 75). The saying is an interruption of the said and of essence. By disclosing an otherwise than being, Levinas also exposes the ontological said that it interrupts. In spite of this, one can reach the saying only through the said. One can get there only through the reduction of what shows itself.

To be sure, Levinas does not intend this reduction to imply a metaphysical transition from the merely apparent world to a real world. This is not the movement from non-truth to truth. It is not a movement to an entity beyond. Ontology operates at the level of the said. To enter into being and truth is to enter the said. It is to enter language, the spoken, *logos.* Thus, the reduction in question is the reduction beyond language, beyond the said, to the unspoken. It is a movement beyond the categories of true and non-true, for non-true still implies the priority of language and being. It is the reduction to signification, to the one-for-the-other involved in responsibility (or, more exactly, in substitution) (OTB 45/AE 77). It is the reduction to literal rest-less-ness. The subjective and the good cannot be understood outside of ontology. On the contrary, if we start with subjectivity in the form of the saying, the signification of the said will be interpretable. It will be conceivable to show that there is a possibility of the said and of being only because there is the priority of the saying.

What, then, is the relationship that responsibility has to the saying and the said? Responsibility for the other is, in Levinas's words, a past that is more ancient than any representable origin. This past signals a lapse of time that does not return. It cannot be remembered and it cannot be recalled. Thus, time must be understood not as an essence, nor as ontological, nor as historical, nor as inside language; rather, it must be shown as a saying. But how do we utter the saying? We cannot accomplish this task in a linear movement. This "diachronous pre-original" cannot be recuperated by memory and history. We must find another way. Levinas names this way "responsibility for the other," a responsibility that does not begin in my own freedom, in my commitment, or in my decision (OTB 10/AE 24).

To make the claim that responsibility for the neighbor defines this relationship is to recognize the infinite debt, or infinite responsibility, which in "the memory of man" has never been contracted. It is not simply that it has not been chosen. As mentioned above, responsibility lies outside the category of choice. It has not been chosen because it is not something that *can* be chosen. This responsibility was always already—it is a past more ancient than history and a passivity more passive than any passivity. This is an extreme passivity, which is not assumed but was already there. This responsibility cannot be in the memory of an individual, for it is out of such a contract, out of this subjectivity, that consciousness arises. It is at this point that we return to the question of subjectivity, whereby the subject remains irreplaceable in its uniqueness. This uniqueness, this inability to cast off responsibility, is the subjectivity of the subject. Levinas names the supreme model of responsibility "passivity."

THE SAYING OF JUDAISM

In his interview with François Poirié, Levinas tells us that "Judaism is not the Bible; it is the Bible seen through the Talmud, through the rabbinical wisdom, interrogation, and religious life" (IR 76). In an interview published under the title "On Jewish Philosophy," Levinas tells his interlocutor, "it seems to me essential to consider the fact that the Jewish reading of Scripture is carried out in the anxiety, but also the hopeful expectation, of midrash" (JP 169/PJ 199). Levinas goes on to name Rashi's commentary in particular as that which brings the *Chumash* to light: "the Pentateuch—*Chumash*—never comes to light without Rashi" (JP 169/PJ 199).[10] To ap-

proach the Torah Jewishly, then, is precisely to approach it through the rabbinic commentary on it. Thus, midrash keeps the Torah alive by preventing
its easy thematization. And it prevents this thematization by posing questions and offering alternative readings of the text. The interpretative model
of midrash is similar to Levinas's saying insofar as the saying is an excess,
that which lies beyond the said. In Levinas's words, the saying opens me to
the other (GP 74/DP 121). The saying expresses the infinite of the other
person.

But the midrash is not simply rabbinic commentary on the Torah. Because of the problems inherent in the Biblical Hebrew—for example, the
absence of punctuation and vowels (although there are vowel aspira-
tions)—midrash exposes the problems while providing only a "plain" reading of the narrative. But midrash is also not simply a tool for reading a
story. The Bible is a holy text, and the rabbis believe that through midrash—that is, through their interpretative process—the holy voice of God
as alterity opens itself up to us. Levinas also holds this view. Midrash opens
up the voices in the Torah that are muted in the text, either because they are
explicitly absent from the narrative structure or because the narrative structure lacks clarity. Midrash lifts these voices out of the text and then brings
them to bear on the narrative. By enabling our access to these others, midrash brings us closer to the ethical and, thus, closer to God.

David Stern writes, "[S]ince interest in the midrash was first expressed
some fifteen years ago, scholars have been trying to find in midrash an alternative to the various 'logocentric' hermeneutical traditions . . . that have
dominated Western literary culture since antiquity. As a result, the urge to
define the hermeneutics of midrash has been invested almost from the
beginning with a desire to locate in Rabbinic exegesis a hermeneutic em-
bodying Otherness."[11] The hermeneutic method involved in midrash demonstrates an interpretative process that allows for polysemy without indeterminacy.

One reading of midrash by Stern tells us,

> [T]he Torah is conceived as the instrument God used in creating the world,
> as His blueprint, or the way the Rabbis themselves looked into the Torah
> as the blueprint for the existence they constructed for themselves. Torah,
> then, is not identical with God; its relationship to Him is, one might say,
> metonymic rather than metaphoric, a matter of extension rather than re-
> semblance. The study of Torah, the activity of midrash, does not therefore
> constitute an act of directly interpreting God as though the text itself were
> literally divine. Instead, one could almost call midrash the interpretation of
> Torah as a figure or trope standing in for God.[12]

And Stern recounts that another reading of midrash claims that the study
of Torah—in other words, midrash—is as much a path to holiness as is fol-

lowing Halakhah. Levinas echoes this point when he tells us, "[I]t is worth noting that the study of the commandments—the study of the Torah, that is, resumption of the rabbinical dialectic—is equal in religious value to actually carrying them out. It is as if, in this study, man were in mystical contact with the divine will itself" (RJT 141/RTJ 170).

Levinas discusses the relationship to God in terms of our relationship to the other: to respond to the other *is* to respond to God. He reiterates this view in his claim that to follow the "Most-High is also to know that nothing is greater than to approach one's neighbor, than the concern for the lot of the 'widow and orphan, the stranger and poor' and that to approach them with empty hands is not to approach them at all" (RJT 142/RTJ 171–172). And this is an ethical message already found in the Bible. Referring to the midrash on Nehemiah 10:39 and Malachi 3:10, Levinas asks, "Do not such 'proofs' imply the inspired origin of the whole biblical canon? Does it not present the notions of height and transcendence as established, and the very idea of god as clear and distinct?" (JRS 108–109/LJE 134–135). And again, referring to midrash, Levinas says, "No less remarkable is the second text in which the epiphany of God is invoked in the human face. The face of the other, irreducible difference, bursting into all that gives itself to me, all that is understood by me and belongs to my world" (JRS 112/LJE 139). In his reference to the rabbinic reading that brings together Ruth 2:4 and Judges 6:12, he attests to a "transcendence, both in the text in which exegesis finds more than the written seems to say, and in the ethical content, the message, which is thus revealed" (JRS 112/LJE 139). Certainly he sees many instances of the response to the other in the Bible itself, but the midrash adds a new dimension to these events. For example, he cites the story of Rebecca at the well as an example of a response to the other. And the midrash on this story affirms what we believe to be the events of the story. But the midrash not only confirms this observation, it embellishes it. The midrashim that Levinas recounts tell us that "as soon as Rebecca came out to meet [Abraham's servant] the waters in the deep rose above their natural level" (BG 134/BeG 155). In this commentary, the rabbis imply that Rebecca's response to the other was anticipated by God.

Thus, Levinas sees the figures in the Torah not simply as literary figures, and for him, the interpretative practice of midrash cannot be reduced simply to literary theory. It is not simply that God is present in the Torah. The words of the Torah express the *ethical law*—they express our relationship to the other. In his retelling of the story of Yossel ben Yossel, Levinas emphasizes Yossel's discovery: to love the Torah more than God is to love this God—the God *of* the Torah. As Oona Ajzenstat states, "Yossel, alone, has no opportunity to turn to the other, but according to Levinas, he shows us that this is the meaning of Judaism and its book. Words, ethics, Torah— these are the meaning of God."[13] Thus, God's presence in the Torah and midrash separates these writings from a distinctly literary genre—for example, Shakespeare's oeuvre and the interpretative practices that examine it. This is not to say that Shakespeare's oeuvre and its accompanying commentaries are not instructive. They are instructive, even for Levinas, but we can now see that when he cites from Scripture, the instructive force is different for him.

Levinas realizes that in addition to the midrash, "[t]he oral reading of Talmud remains inseparable from the Old Testament" (RJT 136/RTJ 166). The Talmud

> orientates its [the Torah's] interpretation. . . . The entire prescriptive part of the Torah is "reworked" by the rabbinical scholars, and the entire narrative part is expanded and clarified in a specific way. In such a way that it is the Talmud that allows the Jewish reading of the Bible to be distinguished from the Christian reading or the "scientific" reading of the historians and philosophers. Judaism is definitely the Old Testament, but through the Talmud. (RJT 136/RTJ 166)

Nonetheless, it is the Jewish commentaries on the Bible that distinguish the Torah as Torah, as the Jewish Scripture. One might say, then, that the Jewish style of questioning the Bible and of writing in response to the Bible, a style that renews the text and keeps it alive, is exemplary of the saying that refers to responsibility before memory. This may be why Levinas sees the need to translate the Bible (Judaism, ethics, religion) into Greek (philosophy, ontology). Although the Hebrew Bible appears to be too particular to be translated into a universal language, Levinas views the ethical message in Judaism as a message that applies to all. As Robert Gibbs observes, "While Levinas has been extremely hostile to the tradition of Western philosophy earlier in his writings, in this latter stage he begins tacitly to refer to his own project as this kind of translation of a Jewish saying into Greek language."[14] Thus, Levinas's goal is twofold: (1) the continued interpretation of Jewish texts; and (2) the continued translation of those texts into Greek.[15] Gibbs maintains that "the Greek interrogation, the demand first to know, is A NECESSARY TRIAL FOR THE TORAH. If reading of Scripture with the Oral Torah opens up the possibility for the text to reveal, then the translation into Greek opens up the possibility to become known. Both readings are, according to Levinas, essential to the Torah."[16]

David Lachterman makes a similar point when he claims that to be Greek is not to be located or confined to a particular place; thus the universal that is associated with Greek thinking is also without place.[17] It applies to everyone. Yet, to be Jewish is precisely to be located in a particular place, attached to a particular people. Any so-called truths arising from Judaism are seen as particular and parochial, as applying only to the Jewish people.

Levinas sees Judaism's particularity. But particularity is not its sole defining feature. And universality is not always positive. As mentioned earlier, Levinas observes that the benefits of Greek universality are counterbalanced by its inability to produce a saying (BG 134–135/BeG 156). As we saw above, not only does Judaism work to balance the particular and the universal, but the motivation for the Greek to express the universal, to express justice, comes from the Bible itself (BG 134/BeG 156). As Gibbs also notes, when the Greek translates the Bible there is a risk that the Bible will lose its particular meaning—a story of and about Judaism. Levinas sees the peculiar nature of Judaism that renders it both particular and universal at the same time. Gibbs astutely comments on this point:

> Levinas makes his task, therefore, the translation of what the Jewish texts say into the idiom of the university [as opposed to the Jewish Yeshiva]. But here [in the passage from "The Bible and the Greeks" cited above] he explicitly indicates the limitations of that idiom. Its very absence of bias makes it sometimes NAÏVE, and more important, the absence of bias leaves it LACKING SOMETHING. Its naiveté is that it cannot see the indirection of rabbinic interpretation, the indirection necessary to say what can never become a said.[18]

Levinas thus realizes that "the most one can do is TRY to speak the Greek language because exactly what manages to become said in Greek necessarily will not be what the Torah says. The open question is to what extent it is possible for Greek to harbor a saying. . . . The risk Levinas takes is to invite the university into the tent: into the Jewish study-houses where the Torah is studied."[19] Levinas's philosophical project is not simply to recover the ethical; it is to reclaim the ethical as Jewish while also translating the Hebrew into Greek. It is to render the saying into a form that all can understand. And it is in this joint endeavor that we find the significance of Levinas's description of the feminine.

TWO

The Time of Creation

In the beginning God created the heaven and the earth—
the earth being unformed and void, with darkness over the
surface of the deep . . . and God said, "Let there be light";
and there was light . . . and God separated the light
from the darkness . . . and it was Good.
—Genesis 1:1–4

Levinas's critique of Heidegger in *Time and the Other* lays the foundation for a philosophical framework that assigns priority to the intersubjective relationship rather than to *Dasein*'s solitary relation to its own death. Levinas's goal in this collection of lectures is to demonstrate that time is "not the achievement of an isolated and lone subject, but that it is the very relationship of the subject with the Other" (TO 39/TA 17). His project, then, differs from Heidegger's in *Being and Time*. Levinas considers disturbing the view of the subject that Heidegger presents in *Being and Time* in that this relationship with the other seems to lack practical import in the "drama of being" (TO 40/TA 18).

Levinas's topic in this first section is the "time" before existents, and his focus is on the point before the solitude of existing, the point before subjectivity took hold. That is, Levinas wants to go back to the event by which the existents contracted their existing, what he calls the *hypostasis* (TO 43/ TA 22–23). As Levinas reminds us, perception and science always begin with existents in their private existence. He wants to interrogate the possibility of going back to the hypostasis. But what produces the hypostasis? What prompts the existent to contract existence? Initially, it cannot be the existent that pulls itself into existence. The initiation of the hypostasis must be heteronomous rather than autonomous. If Levinas wants to claim that subjectivity arises in the ethical relation—that is, in the claim that the other makes on me—and if the movement out of the hypostasis is the movement toward subjectivity, then the flight from the hypostasis cannot be made by the existent alone. It must be accomplished in relation to another. The existent cannot become a subject prior to the encounter with another. This chapter illustrates the fundamental role of the "there is" (*il y a*), the impersonal existence, in order to demonstrate its relationship to the feminine. My claim is that the relation to the feminine, conceived as radical alterity, is the means by which subjectivity is first constituted. Levinas himself states that the feminine is the first experience with alterity. So it is out of this experience that the existent initially contracts subjectivity.

THE SILENCE BEFORE CREATION

The ambiguity of Heidegger's analysis—that the "tragic character of solitude" (TO 40/TA 19) could be derived by nothingness itself or from the privation of the Other through death—compels Levinas to go beyond Heidegger's analysis, "to go beyond the definition of solitude by sociality and of sociality by solitude" (TO 40/TA 19). In particular, Levinas wants to show that the primary relationship with the other should not be characterized by the "with." The "with" indicates reciprocity, and the relationship with the other should not be characterized in terms of reciprocity, of being one with another. Levinas reconceives this relation as being one for the other. He intends his analysis to reveal where solitude can be exceeded. In so doing, he quickly points out what this excess will not be: it will not be a "knowledge," because through knowledge the object is absorbed by the subject and the duality of subject and object disappears. It will not be an ecstasis because, conversely, the subject is absorbed in the object and "recovers itself in its unity" (TO 41/TA 19). Both relationships, that of knowledge and that of ecstasis, result in the disappearance of the other.

The analysis in the first section of *Time and the Other* focuses on the solitude of the ego. Levinas uses Heidegger's notion of *Geworfenheit* to illustrate what he means by an existence prior to an existent. Like the English translators of *Being and Time,* Levinas translates this term as "thrownness," as "the 'fact of being thrown in' . . . existence" (TO 45/TA 25).[1] For Levinas, Heidegger's term indicates for the first time an existing that occurs without us, without a subject (TO 45/TA 25). "Thrownness" implies a thrower who cannot be named or known. This existing before existents Levinas calls the "there is" (*il y a*) (TO 46/TA 26). He describes the "there is" as a complete absence, a void, a silent murmur—it is anonymous and ". . . impersonal like 'it is raining'" (TO 47/TA 26). The "it" in the previous sentence does not have a direct reference, as it does in the sentence "It is a cat." But Levinas distinguishes this void, signaled by a non-referential "there is," from the indeterminate ground typically found in philosophical texts, in which being is in place but needs to be carved out and defined by science and perception. We typically understand such nothingness as an indeterminacy of being rather than as *not* being. For Levinas, the latter, the lack of determinacy that motivates science, still signals a something, even if that something remains undefined or indeterminate, rather than a nothing. For science, the existence of substance is assumed; we bring to substance our way of looking at the world. As a result, we carve up the world in a manner that coheres with how we think the world works, or our perception indicates to us foreground and background against the backdrop of a horizon. However, both of these modes of looking at something still indicate something already in existence—for example, substance that, by definition, has presence. The nothingness to which Levinas refers is not yet substantive, is not yet attached to being, but is itself "the very work of being" (TO 48/ TA 26). Thus, he refers to it as anonymous (TO 48/TA 26). He compares existing without existents to the absolute nothingness before creation, to an inability to escape into sleep (EI 48/EeI 46). By means of his comparison of the anonymity of the *there is* with the silence before creation of the universe, we see more clearly how the anonymity of the *there is* refers to all being even though it is not yet attached to any particular being.

Consciousness, which Levinas defines as the power to sleep (TO 51/TA 30), is the rupture of the anonymous existence—of the *il y a*. Levinas sees consciousness as the power to escape the vigilance of insomnia. Although consciousness participates in this vigilance, it cannot deliberately withdraw into sleep; insomnia prevents consciousness from escaping itself. The insomnia of which Levinas speaks is "vigilance without end" (TO 48/TA 27). There is no real past—that is, no past distinguished from the present. For Levinas, even a memory would be a welcome interruption, as it would mark a distinction in both time and consciousness. This consciousness would signify a subject, and the positing of such a subject would indicate a rupture in the anonymous *there is*.

The hypostasis is the event by which the existent contracts existence; it is "the freedom of the existent in its very grip on existing" (TO 54/TA 34). It is the interruption of the *il y a* and the moment when the existent becomes an existent, when it attains subjectivity. Subjectivity belongs to that which is a subject, to that which has "detached itself from the anonymous rustling of the *there is*" (EE 87/DEE 149). The subject is a particular being, a particular existent that can at once be in consciousness and also withdraw from consciousness; that is, it is a particular being that can withdraw from itself. Levinas explains that "[c]onsciousness, position, the present, the 'I' are not initially—although they are finally—existents. They are events by which the unnameable verb *to be* turns into substantives. They are hypostasis" (EE 83/ DEE 141–142). Thus, there is a moment, an event, that marks the movement from the *there is* to the hypostasis, the movement from anonymity to particular subjectivity. We have, then, the movement out of the silence before creation, out of chaos, to a world of separation and individuation.

SEPARATION AND INDIVIDUATION

Rashi employs the theme of separation and individuation to explain how the story of creation cannot be reduced to a chronological retelling of creation itself. Rashi's reading emphasizes the significance of separation rather than creation, and his claim is that the nothingness before creation is actually the nothingness before separation.[2] Before turning to Rashi's interpretation, however, I want to revisit the first version[3] of the story of creation as found in the Torah.[4]

> 1] When God began to create the heaven and the earth—2] the earth being unformed and void, with darkness over the surface of the deep and a wind from God sweeping over the water—3] God said, "Let there be light"; and there was light. 4] God saw that the light was good, and God separated the light from the darkness. 5] God called the light Day, and the darkness He called Night. And there was evening and there was morning, a first day.
> 6] God said, "Let there be an expanse in the midst of the water, that it may separate water from water." 7] God made the expanse, and it separated the water which was below the expanse from the water which was above the expanse. And it was so. 8] God called the expanse Sky. And there was evening and there was morning, a second day. (Genesis 1:1–8)

To summarize the rest of the story: On the third, fourth, and fifth days, God created, respectively, vegetation, the stars, and the living creatures that "creep," fly, and live in the water. On the sixth day, God created the land animals, such as cattle, and the first human being. God said,

> 26] . . . "Let us make man[5] in our image, after our likeness. They shall rule the fish of the sea, the birds of the sky, the cattle, the whole earth, and all the creeping things that creep the earth." 27] And God created man in His image, in the image of God He created him; male and female He created them . . . 2] On the seventh day God finished the work which God had been doing and ceased on the seventh day from all work which God had done. 3] And God blessed the seventh day and declared it holy, because on it God ceased from all the work of creation which God had done. (Genesis 1:26–27; Genesis 2:2–3)[6]

Many translations, and indeed many of us, recall the first words of the story of creation as, "In the beginning God created . . ." However, it is significant that the story is translated as it appears above. Rashi claims that the text would have been different in Hebrew had its primary purpose been to teach the order in which creation transpired.[7] For example, somehow the presence of water, which is introduced without any mention of its creation, disrupts the chronology and needs to be explained. According to Rashi, this disruption of the flow of the text exposes the gaps that need to be explained. It signals to him that the story of creation is not primarily concerned with establishing the actual chronology of the creation of the world. Rather, this story is meant to teach us something else: (1) the separation and individuation that is so important to man's relationship with God; and (2) the issue of finding a place on which to stand when the foundation is disrupted by this separation and individuation. What is the relationship between these two themes?

In her book *The Beginning of Desire: Reflections on Genesis,* biblical scholar Avivah Zornberg tells us that Rashi argues that the "main business of [the second day] was the radical transformation of reality from the encompassing oneness of God to the possibility of more than one."[8] The first day was not called the first day. Rather, the text says, "one day," perhaps implying God's oneness, aloneness.[9] The "silence before creation" is the time before separation and individuation and, according to Rashi, the story of creation is about finding a place to stand. Let us recall that in the story of creation the heavens are separated from the earth, light from dark, the sea from the land, the moon from the sun. In Hebrew, the term for separation is *havdalah,* and it is also the name of the service that ends the Sabbath. The movement of separation, though, often leaves one without a ground. By its very definition, to be individuated is to be separated from something. In this case, the separation may be separation from God and all that that separation means. Rashi thus writes,

> "*The* sixth day": the definite article [*heh*] is added here to teach that God had made a condition with all the works of the beginning, depending on Israel's acceptance of the Five [the numerical value of *heh*] Books of the Torah. Another reading: All the works of the beginning are suspended (lit., hanging and standing) until *the* sixth day of Sivan, which is destined for the Giving of the Torah.[10]

And Rashi's source reads as follows: "The definite article is not necessary. Resh Lekesh taught: God made a condition with the works of the Beginning—If Israel accepts the Torah, you will continue to exist; if not, I will bring you back to chaos [*tohu va-vohu*]."[11] The acceptance of the Torah at Sinai reprises the Judaic theme "to do and to hear." This expression is typically understood in English as "To do and *then* to hear," or "To do and *then* to understand." Why is this significant? The acceptance of the Torah, without knowing what the Torah is, demonstrates faith. More precisely, it is by living an ethical life that one understands what an ethical life is and the necessity of living life as such. But this acceptance is not merely a blind faith. Zornberg writes,

> "[T]o be or not to be" is a question that is "suspended or standing" till Mount Sinai. . . . The world, till Sinai, awaits its true creation. . . . This is not simply a matter of a shotgun commitment being demanded of the people at Mount Sinai. Their standing at the mountain is an experience *in extremis* of the instability, the terror, not only what would have happened had Israel not stood before Mount Sinai but also emphasizing the relationship between God and Israel: "Earth and all its inhabitants dissolve: 'it is I who keeps its pillars [*amudeha,* standing supports] firm' (Psalms 75:4). The world was in the process of dissolving. Had Israel not *stood* before Mount Sinai and said, 'All that [God] has said, we will do and obey' [lit., we will do and we will listen (Exodus 24:7)] the world would already have returned to chaos. And who made the world stand firm? The 'I' made the pillars of it stand firm."[12]

So, according to rabbinic interpretation, it is the "standing at Sinai" that affirms what God is to create (has created) and also saves the world. The face to face with God is connected to finding a foundation. Individuation separates, and it is the commitment to the ethical that puts these early inhabitants back into relationship to God. Thus, the giving of the Torah at Sinai necessitates, as recounted in Deuteronomy 5:4,[13] the ability to stand "face to face"[14] with God. To be able to stand in this way with God, "who alone exists and whose *anokhi* emerges from a vast silence, is to take that immensity of the *anokhi* immediately within oneself."[15] To stand "face to face" requires one to be separated, to be individuated. The following passage by Zornberg powerfully illustrates this relationship between standing and separation, and the terror of returning the world to the chaos and emptiness before creation:

> "You have been shown to know that the Lord alone is God; there is none beside Him" (Deuteronomy 4:35). Rashi's comment emphasizes the visual-mystical experience of de-realization: "When God gave the Torah, he opened the seven firmaments, upper and lower worlds were torn apart and they saw that He is alone; that is why it says, '[lit.] you were *shown*.'" In other words, what the people overwhelmingly see is that there is nothing, nothing to stand on. "If you do not accept the Torah, I shall return the world to chaos and emptiness."[16]

According to Rashi, the story is about the birth of separation and individuation—of identity, if you will.[17] As an example, he tells us that the water as always created, or rather as not created, distinguishes it from all other physical objects. The Throne of Glory (*Ruah Elohim*) was hovering over the water, "even though Scripture had not yet revealed when the creation of the water took place. Thus, you learn from this that the [creation of the water] preceded that of the earth. . . . Therefore, you must say that Scripture did not [intend to] teach anything about the sequence of the earlier and later [acts of Creation]."[18] The water, we could say, stands as a metaphor for that which is wholly different from the other objects of creation. Thus, the hierarchy has been established, and it cannot be said that each physical object stands in an equal or reciprocal relation to all others. With Rashi's interpretation we see an original moment of alterity and asymmetry. The land in the midst of the water signifies the separation of land from water, such that land and water are individuated.

Rashi's recognition that the water is not created leads him to believe that land and water fall into two categories: created and not created, or created and always already there. His reading serves as a reminder of the asymmetry with which we enter into relationships. The water, like God, serves as the radically other, the absolute other. If we think of Thales's claim that all the world is water, we immediately see the difference between the Greek and the Jew. Where Thales, and those who followed in the footsteps of the Western philosophical tradition, looked for the one substance on which the world was based, the Jewish reading of creation emphasizes difference, separation, and individuation, and thus underlines the significance of being able to be in a relationship with another. Thales is looking for the one thing that will subsume everything else, even if everything else differs in appearance. Rashi's reading allows us to see the possibility that there is not a stuff that makes everything the same, or at least that there is another possibility for how to understand what the world means to us.[19]

Abraham Heschel offers an interpretation of the Sabbath that is commensurate with Rashi's explanation of creation. For Heschel, the Sabbath is not about finding a place, per se, to stand. Rather, it is about finding a way to exist in time, which, for Heschel, includes finding a way to relate to God. Among other things, the "creation" of the Sabbath marks time. But it does not simply mark time; it marks it in a meaningful way. The Sabbath is "holiness in time."[20]

Heschel explains that by observing the Sabbath, we transcend place. This means that we transcend material culture, technical civilization, and all of those things to which we have become slaves the other six days of the week. To observe the Sabbath is to realize that we are not owned by these things, and it is also to realize that we are more than our ability to master the tools that we manufacture. Our focus on things blinds us to that which is not merely a thing; it blinds us to that which exists in time and not space. In Heschel's words, the Bible is more concerned with time than with space.

Heschel thus reminds us that the Sabbath is the only Jewish holiday that originates in creation and that is unrelated to the moon. It is not dependent on events in nature, and it is the only act of creation that God declared holy: "And God blessed the seventh *day* and made it *holy*." As Heschel observes, "Judaism is a *religion in time* aiming at *the sanctification of time*."[21] After proclaiming the holiness of time, God proclaimed the holiness of humanity: "You shall be unto me a holy people." And after proclaiming the holiness of humanity, God proclaimed the holiness of space, when the Tabernacle was created by Moses. God first hallowed time. According to Heschel, the essence of the Sabbath is that it is completely detached from space. On the Sabbath we are called to share with each other in time. And we are called to turn our attention from the results of creation, those material things that we enjoy, to the mystery of creation, "from the world of creation to the creation of the world."[22]

The Sabbath marks the difference between space and time. It is a day that allows us to reflect on what it means to be human and what it means to be in relationship to that which is eternal in time, whether we understand that to be God, love, the ethical, or something else. Therefore, in order to resist the deification of the law, the rabbis declared that saving a life takes precedence over the observance of the commandment not to work on the Sabbath. To keep the Sabbath holy might mean precisely that one is called to save the life of another.[23] That is, the spirit of the Sabbath is to be kept intact without turning one into a slave to the Sabbath itself. The intent behind its creation and the commandment to keep it holy is to allow oneself the opportunity to enjoy the company of humanity, to visit with friends, to eat a festive meal, to engage in sexual fulfillment with one's spouse, to transcend oneself as merely an object in material space. The Sabbath is to be a delight.

According to rabbinic tradition, the Sabbath as a holy day was created on the seventh day. After the six days of creation, the world still lacked something; it lacked rest. Thus, one interpretation maintains that rest was created on the seventh day.[24] We could interpret the entire story of creation, from day one to day seven, as a story of separation and individuation, as a story of the evolution of the process of creation itself. The story is not linear but cyclical, repetitive, and dynamic. The rabbinic interpretation of the story of creation also has a normative component. It is not simply that the people at Sinai have a place on which to stand. They have a place so that they can accept the Torah, or, rather, so that they can be in relationship to

God. Or from Heschel's view, they have a place on which to stand so that God can be in relationship to humanity.

If we incorporate into Rashi's reading of creation Heschel's beautiful reading of the Sabbath, our picture of creation develops even further. We find in the story of creation a multitude of separations: the holy and the mundane; space and time; day and night; land and water; and the heavens and earth. And each aspect of the separation is defined in terms of itself, not in terms of the negation of the other. Separation and individuation exist, but not as negations of each other. The story of creation unfolds as a story about the relationship we have to what is eternal in time; it is the story of our relationship to others. The Jewish reading of the Sabbath offers a view of creation in which the ego is invited to transcend itself, to suspend itself as an ego, to be interrupted.

In "The Temptation of Temptation," Levinas gives his own reading of standing at Sinai. Not unlike Rashi's, Levinas's interpretation presents the temptation of temptation as the temptation of knowledge (TT 34/TdT 74). It was their willingness to take a risk—to do and then to hear—that distinguished those who accepted the Torah at Sinai. According to Levinas, the priority of knowledge and, more specifically, of philosophy is the "temptation of temptation." Knowledge allows us to weigh our decisions, to balance pros and cons. It does not leave the other in its otherness. The priority of knowledge is the first step in subsuming the other into the realm of calculation (TT 35/TdT 77). Finally, the temptation of temptation is a temptation to reduce risk, to eliminate the possibility of danger. Thus, Levinas contrasts the temptation of philosophy, the temptation of knowledge, with the actions of those who stood at Sinai.

To support his point, Levinas comments on Rav Abdimi bar Hama's interpretation of the events at Mt. Sinai. Levinas wonders if the rabbi's reading is trying to tell us something about the relationship between Israel and the mountain at the time of the covenant. According to Rav Abdimi, Israel is placed below the mountain (Sinai) as if it would be crushed by the weight of the mountain, or as if the weight of the mountain threatens it, should Israel refuse to accept the gift of the law (TT 37/TdT 81).[25] The Israelites have just been set free from Egypt, and they are now about to have the Law imposed on them. The freedom, then, is a freedom of responsibilities. So Levinas asks, "Is one already responsible when one chooses responsibility? Does [the rabbi] think that the choice for responsibility is made under threat and that the Torah would not have been chosen freely?" (TT 37/TdT 81). Certainly we can ask if the reception of the Torah was voluntary or compelled. And we can ask after the implications of each possibility. But the Torah says no to unwarranted violence. It would be odd, then, if the Torah, which outlines a path to the ethical, was imposed through violence on the Israelites. Instead, the events leading up to the reception of the Torah appear to indicate that if the Torah is not accepted, "you [the Israelites] will not leave this place of desolation and death. . . . You will not be able to begin history, to break the block of being stupidly sufficient unto itself. . . . Only the Torah, a seemingly utopian knowledge, assures man of a place" (TT 39/TdT 85). Thus, we see again the relationship between separation and individuation, and we see again what it means to have a place. Here, Levinas's reading also indicates the relationship between ethics and ontology.

> The unfortunate universe also had to accept its subordination to the ethical order, and Mount Sinai was for it the moment in which its "to be" or "not to be" was being decided. The refusal of the Israelites would have been the signal for the annihilation of the entire universe. How does being realize its being? The question of ontology will thus find its answer in the description of the way Israel receives the Torah. This way consists—such is the thesis we are upholding—in overcoming the temptation of evil by avoiding the temptation of temptation. (TT 41/TdT 90–91)

SOLITUDE, TIME, AND THE OTHER

As a story of creation, *Time and the Other* presupposes a conception of time that resonates with Heschel's view that time is privileged over space. The first of Levinas's lectures in *Time and the Other* ends with a discussion entitled "Solitude and Materiality," in which he ultimately claims that "solitude is an absence of time" (TO 57/TA 38). Here, he takes up the solitude of the existent, the way in which the existent is occupied with itself (TO 55/TA 36). The relationship that one has to oneself in this solitude is the enchainment that one has to oneself. The being, occupied with itself, is concerned for itself. Thus, the paradox of freedom: "[A] free being is no longer free because it is responsible for itself" (TO 55/TA 36).

For Levinas, in contrast to Heidegger, the material character of the present does not result from anxiety about the future. Rather, it is concerned with the present in the present. In other words, in contrast to Heidegger's view that being toward death, or the "mineness" of death, founds solitude, Levinas posits that it is the existent's preoccupation with the materiality of its own existence that defines solitude. This existing in the present, for the present, turns into materiality (TO 56/TA 37). And this materiality expands the existing into an ontological event. Thus, for Levinas, "the freedom of the Ego and its materiality go together" (TO 57/TA 38). The existent is sealed unto itself, locked into itself.

In other words, Levinas asserts that the present is not a fall from authenticity; nor is it to be trivialized. The concern for one's own life, which some would see as "base materialism" or "animality," is not frivolous. If one accepts Heidegger's analysis in *Being and Time,* then death is precisely that which confirms one's solitude; death is that which is most my own. But in Levinas's view, death does not lead to this kind of solitude; rather, the mystery of death comes to me, or jars me, precisely because it is ungraspable. My solitude, according to Levinas, is broken by death. Thus, to shatter the "enchainment" is to shatter the hypostasis, to be pulled out of that moment; it is to be given in time (TO 57/TA 38). Time is what jars the existent out of its solitude. For Levinas, this movement is described by the relationship with the other. That is, the relationship with the other is a relationship in time.

So, contrary to Heidegger, Levinas believes that the tragedy of solitude is not the absence of the other per se. Rather, the tragedy of solitude is that the existent is shut up within itself, because it is matter (TO 57/TA 38). And whereas for Heidegger death signifies freedom, for Levinas, death is immobilizing. It is precisely because death is ungraspable, unpredictable, and comes at the existent from nowhere, and always too soon, that death is overwhelming and renders the existent passive. We cannot grasp death precisely because it marks the end of life. Alterity, then, in Levinas's account, is not death as a possibility, as in Heidegger's, but the mystery of death.

The move that Levinas makes to link solitude and materiality is far more radical than many have realized. This move allows him to acknowledge pain and suffering—for example, the suffering of those who do not have enough food to eat—while not ascribing to them the redemptive quality of "finding meaning in suffering." To seek this kind of meaning not only trivializes suffering, but also makes suffering necessary for further "enlightenment."[26] Levinas writes, "I do not believe that the oppression that crushes the working classes gives it uniquely a pure experience of oppression in order to awaken in it, beyond economic liberation, the nostalgia for a metaphysical liberation" (TO 61/TA 43). For Levinas, the "authentic" existence to which we are to ascend has assumed a normative position, and with it an "ostrich-like" (TO 61/TA 43) position in which, with its head in the sand, it avoids the gaze of those who suffer around it. By linking solitude with the subject's materiality, Levinas allows for the possibility that death confronts us all, although not as something we avoid in "inauthentic activities" of existence. Rather, death confronts us as something that comes from outside us and that is ungraspable by all of us. By connecting solitude with materiality, he enables us to see how it is that the bond between Ego and self is loosened. One moment in which we can see this loosening is in enjoyment.

Although the existent in the hypostasis is concerned with what it needs for its everyday existence, there is also the possibility of enjoyment (*jouissance*), of not eating simply to live, but also living to eat. There is the possibility of strolling, not to get somewhere but simply to enjoy the fresh air (TO 63/TA 45–46). We use tools for our own survival, but it is possible to have another relationship with these instruments. Enjoyment is both an absorption of the object and a distancing from it (TO 63/TA 46). Levinas thus writes, "The morality of 'earthly nourishments' is the first morality . . . it is not the last, but one must pass through it" (TO 64/TA 46). In essence, he has exchanged the "morality" of authenticity for the "first morality" of enjoyment, the first moment of being called outside oneself. Enjoyment offers the subject liberation from itself insofar as it enjoys without the necessity of the object. The subject is then able to exist at a distance from itself. But even here there is a return to the same since the object is experienced by light. Light, or illumination, allows me to experience the object as other than myself, but since "the object is illuminated, one encounters it as if it came from us. It does not have a fundamental strangeness. Its transcendence is wrapped in immanence" (TO 64–65/TA 47). So, for Levinas, the "exteriority of the light does not suffice for the liberation of the ego that is the self's captive" (TO 65/TA 47). Since "life could only become the path of redemption if, in its struggle with matter, it encounters an event that stops its everyday transcendence from falling back upon a point that is always the same" (TO 66/TA 49), there must be something other than these objects, other than enjoyment, that lends a real exteriority to the exterior world (TO 66/TA 49). Levinas refers to this event as the encounter with an other.

For Levinas, the very fact that we lose our mastery in death indicates that there is a way in which an event can happen that we cannot assume, without us having anything "a priori." Death is the first instance of this event, but it is the approach of death that indicates that we are in a relationship with something absolutely other. This is not as something that "we can assimilate through enjoyment, but as something whose very existence is made of alterity" (TO 74/TA 63). We recognize the other's being as exterior, but not merely exterior, for that would signify being in a place. Rather, the other is constituted by its alterity.[27] But even though death breaks my solitude, it is not yet time. In order for the future to become an element of time, it must also enter into a relationship with the present (TO 79/TA 68). The relationship with the future, "the presence of the future in the present" is accomplished in the face-to-face with the Other (TO 79/TA 68).

The above interpretations offered by Rashi, Heschel, and Levinas focus on the relationship between the ego and interruption of the ego. For Rashi, the significance of this interruption is revealed after first recognizing the importance of separation and individuation, which allow for the experience of alterity. For Heschel, the Sabbath is not simply an interruption of the work week. The interruption of work is significant, since it allows us to transcend ourselves by freeing ourselves from our mundane tasks. Thus, we are brought into relationship with that which is holy. For Levinas, too, time takes precedence over space. It is the movement out of the hypostasis that brings the existent into relation with another. And for Levinas, it is the feminine as the absolutely other that accomplishes this movement.

THREE

The Inauguration of Sexual Difference

Bone of my bones and flesh of my flesh. This shall be
called Woman [*Isha*], for from man [*Ish*] was she taken.[1]
—Genesis 2:23

Male and female He created them.
—Genesis 1:27

Femininity . . . appeared to me as a difference
contrasting strongly with other differences,
not merely as a quality different from all others,
but as the very quality of difference.
—Levinas, in the preface to *Time and the Other*

In a footnote to her introduction to *The Second Sex,* Simone de Beauvoir
takes Levinas to task for what she sees as his attempts, allegedly like those
of preceding philosophers, to posit woman as Other. The footnote, including the passage that she cites from *Time and the Other,* reads as follows:

E. Levinas expresses this idea most explicitly in his essay *Temps et l'Autre.* "Is
there not a case in which otherness, alterity [*altérité*], unquestionably marks
the nature of a being, as its essence, an instance of otherness not consisting
purely and simply in the opposition of two species of the same genus? I
think that the feminine represents the contrary in its absolute sense, this
contrariness being in no wise affected by any relation between it and its correlative and thus remaining absolutely other. Sex is not a certain specific difference . . . no more is the sexual difference a mere contradiction. . . . Nor
does this difference lie in the duality of two complementary terms, for two
complementary terms imply a pre-existing whole. . . . Otherness reaches its
full flowering in the feminine, a term of the same rank as consciousness but
of opposite meaning."

I suppose that Levinas does not forget that woman, too, is aware of her
own consciousness, or ego. But it is striking that he deliberately takes a man's

point of view, disregarding the reciprocity of subject and object. When he writes that woman is mystery, he implies that she is mystery for man. Thus his description, which is intended to be objective, is in fact an assertion of masculine privilege.[2]

Thus, even Levinas's positive transformation of the other, from a threat to the very ground of my subjectivity, employs a conception of the feminine as other that does not escape de Beauvoir's attack. But to understand de Beauvoir's criticism of Levinas, one must realize that she understands this relationship of subject/other in its most disparaging form. To be 'other' to the male subject is to be incidental, to be inessential to the essential.[3] De Beauvoir takes issue with what she sees as Levinas's disregard for reciprocity and his attempt to disguise his masculine privilege as an objective position. According to de Beauvoir, Levinas assumes a masculine privilege when he maintains the subject/object dichotomy. He, qua male, occupies the position of subject, until the feminine, the "mysterious" feminine, occupies the position of object. As we saw in de Beauvoir's note, the mystery is not any mystery: the feminine is a mystery *for men*.

In a translator's note to *Time and the Other,* Richard Cohen defends Levinas by claiming that de Beauvoir has misunderstood his analysis and simplified the relationship between the subject (he) who is absolute, and the feminine other. Cohen's defense reminds us that, for Levinas, the other has priority over the subject. Thus, de Beauvoir was too quick to chastise him. However, each of these notes—de Beauvoir's criticism, which assumes the other as antagonistic, and Cohen's defense of Levinas—represents an extreme view, between which we may more faithfully situate Levinas's work. De Beauvoir does not see the positive implications of alterity, and Cohen does not allow that de Beauvoir's intuition may have some merit.

De Beauvoir is right to pose this question to Levinas—that is, she is right to ask how he conceives of the feminine. However, by attacking him for blithely casting woman as other, she reveals her misunderstanding of what he means by the other, and of the priority he assigns to the position that the other holds in his analysis.[4]

Levinas first introduces the concept of the feminine in his work of the 1940s: *Existence and Existents* and *Time and the Other.* Both are short books that do not usually receive the attention given to *Totality and Infinity* or *Otherwise than Being.* But these early books lay the foundation for what is to follow. Although the discussion of the feminine in these books is brief, it is both dense and illuminating. In *Existence and Existents,* Levinas tells us,

[T]he plane of *eros* allows us to see that the other par excellence is the feminine, through which a world behind the scenes prolongs the world. . . . Eros, when separated from the Platonic interpretation which completely fails to recognize the role of the feminine, can be the theme of a philosophy which, detached from the solitude of light, and consequently from phenomenology properly speaking, will concern us elsewhere. (EE 85/DEE 145)

Although the discussion of eros briefly resumes a few pages later, the feminine is not mentioned again. Like *Time and the Other, Existence and Existents* ends with the mention of the birth of the son. In both books, the feminine is defined (implicitly in the earlier text) as the originary experience of alterity.

Although Levinas's conception of the feminine needs to be explored and is not without flaws, de Beauvoir's specific attack reveals her misunderstanding of Levinas's project, which radically departs from the Western philosophies that precede his.[5] It is not the feminine as other that is the problem. Rather, what is in question in Levinas's work is the distinct role that the feminine plays and what it means, specifically, for the feminine to be other. We need to be fair to de Beauvoir on two counts. First, we need to bear in mind that the ethical relation is not named in *Time and the Other;* thus, the positive status of the other (*autre* and *autrui*) may not be as obvious as it could be. Second, we should bear in mind what informs her position on the other and, more generally, on the conception of woman that has been cast as such. Like Sartre, de Beauvoir is indebted to Hegel's analysis of lordship and bondage, which is demonstrably the struggle for self-consciousness. In fact, she refers to it in *The Second Sex,* in conjunction with Sartre's pessimistic existentialism, to offer a deflationary account of the relationship between men and women.[6] It is natural, then, that she would receive any conception of the feminine cast in terms of the other with suspicion and concern. Still, de Beauvoir helps us to see exactly what Levinas means to do—and not to do.

This chapter focuses on these two early books, *Existence and Existents* and *Time and the Other,* because they set the stage for the treatment of sexual difference in Levinas's philosophy. It is worth noting that these early philosophical writings appeared shortly *before* Levinas encountered Mordechai Shushani, the mysterious and brilliant sage who inspired Levinas to explore Talmudic and other rabbinic texts. They also inaugurate the discussion of the Other, a term that Levinas appropriates positively. I pair the discussion of these two books with an interrogation of Levinas's talmudic essay "And God Created Woman." This pairing reveals the continuity between his philosophical and Talmudic writings. An examination of the similarities between his treatment of alterity and the biblical story of the creation of Adam and Eve—and specifically, his reading of this story—helps to disclose the role of the feminine in his early philosophical project.

Feminist biblical scholars such as Phyllis Trible argue that there is little, if any, evidence in the straightforward reading of the story to justify the subordination of women to men. The arguments that claim to find such a justification are founded on a patriarchal bias that contaminates how these scholars read the story and what they think is present in the story.[7] Trible argues, as I also argue in this section, that sexual difference and humanity are derived simultaneously. Or, more specifically, the creature, sexually undefined, becomes sexually defined only when woman (*Isha*) is created. It is only with the creation of woman that man qua male being is created. Levinas asserts that sexual difference is secondary to the creation of humanity, and he does so because he believes that ethics is prior to sexual difference. His intention is to create an ethics that includes everyone.

This chapter focuses on the relationship between, and the implications of, these two accounts of creation and sexual difference. By revisiting the story of creation in Genesis 1 and then reading it back into *Time and the Other,* we can understand the role that the theme of separation and individuation plays in this early book. In particular, we find an interesting parallel in the separation and individuation that occur in both the story of creation and the "creation" of sexual difference—namely, both are "good." So, by employing themes that we find in the Hebrew story, we may be in a better position to understand the difficult concepts that we encounter in Levinas's work.

ALTERITY IN THE GARDEN OF EDEN

In the last part of *Time and the Other,* Levinas explains what he means by a relation with the other. Before we turn to his discussion, I need to note that Levinas's inconsistent use of *other* (*autrui*) and *other* (*autre*) often makes the referent for each term unclear.[8] Does the former term indicate a human other, while the latter term indicates death? Or is this problem simply the result of a lack of rigor on Levinas's part? With this complication in mind, I will proceed with the exegesis. For Levinas, the other is not defined in terms of a future; rather, the future is defined by the other: "the very future of death consists in its total alterity" (TO 82/TA 74). Here, Levinas claims that if a relationship is to be truly intersubjective, it cannot be reciprocal. For Levinas, alterity already characterizes the intersubjective relationship: "The Other is what I myself am not" (TO 83/TA 75). The alterity of the other thus prohibits a reciprocal relation. It is not simply that the relationship with the other, as Levinas conceives it, is impossible if the two participants are symmetrical to each other.[9] The relationship is impossible because there is no other; they are the same, they could each be other. To assume symmetry indicates a misunderstanding of the nature of such a relation.

Simply by being other, that is, simply by being not me, the other is alterity. The intersubjective space is asymmetrical insofar as the other is characterized as those who are most vulnerable, while I am the rich and powerful. The asymmetry has less to do with the space that separates than it does with the actual relation that the subject has to the other, for the relationship with alterity is neither spatial nor conceptual. Who is the other, and what does the other become, precisely, in the face of the subject viewing it?

For Levinas in the 1940s, eros, characterized by the feminine, is the original form of this alterity.[10] He characterizes the feminine, the creation of woman as exemplified in Eve's relationship to Adam, as the "absolutely contrary contrary [*le contraire absolument contraire*], whose contrariety is in no way affected by the relationship that can be established between it and its correlative, the contrariety that permits its terms to remain absolutely other" (TO 85/TA 77). The feminine is the example in which "the alterity of the other appears in its purity" (TO 85/TA 77). For Levinas, the formal structure of sexual difference precludes one sex from being assimilated into the other; as such, sexual difference defies the Parmenidean notion of the one, and instead maintains a reality of multiples, or twos (TO 85/TA 77).

The separation and relation discussed in the previous chapter does not take into account the relationship between human beings; nor does it take into account the separation and individuation of man and woman. Zornberg reminds us of Rambam's[11] view that "man as alone and autonomous is 'not good,' because he would live a static, unchanging, and unwilled life. Man needs to live face-to-face with the Other, dancing to the choreography of his own freedom."[12] Yet this splitting off of man is accomplished only when "man himself comes to recognize the pains of solitude."[13] The biblical reading—in particular, Rashi's commentary—can help us here. Although Rashi focuses on the creation story generally, his understanding of separation and individuation as the underlying theme of the story of creation can also be applied to the question of sexual differentiation. As we recall from the discussion in the preceding chapter, although the presence of water is mentioned, there is no reference to the creation of water in Genesis 1. Rashi thus concludes that Genesis 1 cannot be considered a chronological retelling of the events of creation; it must have a different meaning and purpose. For Rashi, the story is about separation and individuation; that is, it is a story about identity. These themes reappear in an examination of the question of sexual differentiation.

For Levinas, the feminine, wearing the veil of radical alterity, accomplishes the break in Parmenidean unity; it breaks the totality. That is, the feminine allows for separation and individuation, but in a positive sense. Levinas thus believes that there is a sense of alterity that is not merely the "reverse side of its [the other's] identity" [TO 85/TA 77]. He believes that there is a sense of alterity that is not characterized as merely the opposition of two species of a genus. This elusive alterity, for Levinas, is the feminine. By making this claim, he does not cast the feminine as simply the "opposite" sex; nor does he define the feminine as a negation. It is, instead, contrariety. The feminine is an alterity that serves as an interruption.

With this characterization, Levinas has set the stage for the indispensable role that the feminine plays and will continue to play in his work. In its capacity as interruption, the feminine is fundamental to the I's originary experience of alterity. Because Levinas has defined the feminine in such a peculiar manner, it is not clear that anything else could play its role, should the feminine be removed. The feminine serves the function that it does precisely because of how it is defined by Levinas. It is how we understand the meaning of the feminine that gives rise to any metaphorical meaning that it would then hold.[14] In other words, it is not clear that the feminine is simply a named placeholder, which can be removed and replaced by a term that is less provocative. The "feminine" satisfies this role *precisely* because of the meaning that it has for us, even though this meaning alerts us to the potential problems and stereotypes that accompany it.

In Levinas's view, it is the feminine that provides the break in the unity, and thus makes possible multiplicity. So, we could say that the feminine is the transcendental condition of reality as multiple. We can see, then, how Levinas's view of love contrasts with the view we find in Aristophanes's speech in Plato's *Symposium*.[15] According to Aristophanes, the angry gods punish the humans, who were originally joined to their lovers, by splitting the creatures in half. The creatures are left wandering the Earth, searching eternally for their "other halves."[16] According to Aristophanes, love arises from a lack. In contrast, Levinas insists that sexual difference is not the result of a duality of two complementary terms, "for two complementary terms presuppose a preexisting whole" (TO 86/TA 78). Love, according to Levinas, is not to be posited as a previously existing fusion that must be renewed.[17]

But from this view of love, the following implications emerge. On the one hand, Levinas can be criticized for once again characterizing woman as "mystery." On the other hand, by emphatically rejecting the Aristophanic model, Levinas grants the feminine a separate identity. In Aristophanes's speech, and in other accounts of love that resemble this version, woman is characterized as the "opposite of man." More specifically, she is often defined in terms of what man is not. Woman is rarely, if ever, characterized in a positive sense. By portraying the feminine as alterity and by defining the feminine with a positive reflection, Levinas has unwittingly changed how the feminine can be discussed. The mystery of which he speaks is not the mystery of simply being feminine, as is found, for example, in chivalry or literature. Rather, it is the mystery of the other, a mystery that accompanies all manifestations of alterity. The feminine slips away from the light—from comprehension—as does the Other.

Levinas reiterates this point in his 1960 essay "Judaism and the Feminine,"[18] when he says that "if woman completes man, she does not complete him as a part completes another into a whole but, as it were, as two totalities complete one another—which is, after all, the miracle of social relations" (JF 35/JeF 58).[19] Thus, for Levinas, this distinction between a possible initial fusion and the originary existence of two separate beings joined together is crucial. Rather than seeing the separation of the two as a punishment, as in Plato's recounting of Aristophanes's speech, Levinas, like Rashi and Maimonides, sees the separation as "worth more than the initial union."[20] Levinas thus takes issue with Aristophanes's view that the initial fusion is more perfect than the separation that follows it. He also rejects the idea that love is a lack that can be or could have been sated, merely by finding or having been joined to one's complementary "other half." For Levinas, love is both need and desire, but neither of these can be simply fulfilled. There is always an alterity in the other that eludes me. This relationship to alterity appears to be derived from the originary event of sexual differentiation. The sexual differentiation to which Levinas refers necessitates that another can never be completely joined with me. It is only in a relation of separation that I can have a relation with absolute alterity.

Levinas takes up this issue again in his talmudic reading "And God Created Woman." He mentions that the split of the human into two distinct beings, as illustrated by the creation story, reveals the response to a radical alterity. This response furthermore signifies the inauguration of an ethical response to the other. Yet the two stories of creation present us with slightly different accounts of the creation of woman. In the first version—"God created him, man and woman"—humanity is created after everything else. And, the story implies, man is created simultaneously with woman, or at least with the idea of woman. The second version of the creation story found in Genesis is slightly different from the first. This change not only helps us understand what Levinas refers to when he compares existing without existents to the absolute emptiness before creation, but also emphasizes the relationship between separation and the creation of the sexes. In this version, man is created first, before anything else. Thus, the focus on separation and individuation reappears, although here the separation is of humanity into man and woman.[21]

The story of the creation of man and woman in Genesis 1 reads as follows:

> [24] God said, "Let the earth bring forth every kind of living creature: cattle, creeping things, and wild beasts of every kind. . . ." [26] And God said,

Let us make man in our image, after our likeness. . . . [27] And God created Man in His image, in the image of God He created him; male and female He created them. [28] God blessed them and God said to them "Be fertile and increase . . . "

And from Genesis 2:

[15] The Lord God took the man and placed him in the garden of Eden, to till it and tend it. [16] And the Lord God commanded the man saying, "Of every tree of the garden you are free to eat; [17] but as for the tree of knowledge of good and bad [meaning 'everything'] you must not eat of it; for as soon as you eat of it, you shall die [you shall become mortal]."
[18] The Lord God said, "it is not good for man to be alone; I will make a fitting helper for him." [19] And the Lord God formed out of the earth all the wild beasts and all the birds of the sky, and brought them to the man to see what he would call them; and whatever the man called each living creature would be its name. [20] And the man gave names to all the cattle and to the birds of the sky and to all the wild beasts; but for Adam no fitting helper was found. [21] So the Lord God cast a deep sleep upon the man; and while he slept, He took one of his ribs and closed up the flesh at that spot. [22] And the Lord God fashioned the rib that He had taken from the man into a woman; and He brought her to the man. [23] Then the man said "this one at last / Is bone of my bones / And flesh of my flesh. This one shall be called Woman [Isha], / For from man [Ish] was she taken." [24]—Hence a man leaves his father and mother and clings to his wife, so that they become one flesh.

What does it mean to say that God created him, male and female? In light of such a statement, what does it mean to say that God created woman? Does this mean that sexual difference, or at least the concept of it, existed prior to the creation of woman—that is, prior to the existence of both man and woman as such? Did it exist prior to God's creation of 'Man',[22] who embodies both male and female? And how do we account for two different stories of creation found in the book of Genesis? We at least need to note the very real problem of biblical interpretation. There are two different conceptions of God at work in the story, revealed by the Adonist and the Elohim traditions. How does the presence of two different conceptions of God, possibly the result of two different storytellers, change or influence our interpretation? My present focus is on Levinas's interpretation of the passages. His discussion of this passage begins with a question about the Hebrew. In the Hebrew text, the word *vayyitzer* ("made"), when referring to the formation of "man," is written with two *yods*. But when the word is used to indicate the creation of other things—for example, animals—it is written with only one *yod.* One rabbi speculates that this discrepancy signals the difference between the creations: humanity incorporates an element of the divine, and this is differentiated from the other things that God made. Another interpretation suggests that *yetzer* indicates inclination; thus, man was created with two inclinations, toward good and evil. According to Levinas, however, this interpretation cannot be correct, for *yetzer* means "creature," not "inclination." He cites Isaiah 29:16[23] as his evidence. Finally, Levinas offers the interpretation that suggests that the two *yods* indicate the dual sexual dimension of 'Man,' or the sexual dimension of the creature in its initial creation. Thus, this view underscores the sexual dimension of humanity itself: "He created him, male and female." In some translations this line reads, "He created him, man and woman" or "He created them, man and woman." Midrash indicates that "even Adam's physical creation was twofold, male and female in one body. In front he was a man, but attached to him in back was a woman."[24] Rabbi Jeremiah b. Leazar tells us, "When the Holy One blessed be He, created Adam, He created him an hermaphrodite [bisexual]. . . .";[25] and Rabbi Samuel b. Nahman says, "When the Lord created Adam he created him double faced."[26] Here Levinas ventures a possible explanation of the odd doubling of the *yods.* For him, this line suggests a creature with two faces, a being who is open and exposed, a being who indicates the end of interiority, the end of the subject (GCW 167/DCF 132).

Yet, for Levinas this passage also suggests something else. Woman is not yet an issue. The feminine face does not appear until later, and, contrary to how this verse is normally understood, woman is not created from man. Rather, woman and man are created from what is human (GCW 168/DCF 132). Thus, according to Levinas, the face is not marked even by sexed characteristics. Although one can see why Levinas would need to adopt this position, especially in light of his own emphasis on separation and individuation, it is nonetheless peculiar that he would take such a stance. If it is the individuation of both man and woman, male and female, that allows them to participate in a relationship with each other—the first relationship between human beings—then their ability to participate in such a relationship is contingent on their being sexed.[27] Certainly, we could say that it is not necessary that they be sexed in order to be in a relationship. But in this case, the separation that allows for two beings to be in a relationship is also the separation of the sexes as such.

Derrida focuses on Levinas's claim that the face is not marked by sexual difference. It is this claim that Levinas advances as his defense against the potential danger of an ethics marked by sexual difference. But in spite of Levinas's own attempts at a defense, Derrida reveals the problematic feature of the claim in question. Derrida's contention that there are now "two" created from what is/was "one" is correct.[28] That is, two beings are created from what was/is already human. However, Levinas's claim—namely, that this interpretation shows that sexual difference is secondary to what is human—is not obviously true. Nor is it evident that the distinction between the creation of humanity and the creation of sexual difference is a sign of Levinas's own impartiality with regard to the sexes—even though he claims the contrary. It is not clear that Levinas's ethics are neutral with regard to sexual difference, in spite of his insistence that sexual difference derived from humanity.

With regard to the first point, that sexual difference derived from the creation of humanity, the conclusion actually appears to be precisely the opposite. The biblical story reads, "God created him, male and female." Both the text itself and the midrashim on the text indicate that the birth of sexual difference occurred at the same moment as the creation of what is human. If what is human is created simultaneously with male and female, then how can we establish a priority, ontological or otherwise? If humanity is created as male *and* female, then humanity is always already marked by sexual difference.

The simultaneity of the creation of humanity and sexual difference undermines any attempt that Levinas might make to claim that sexual difference is secondary to "being human." This description of the relationship between sex and humanity gives the impression that our sex could be scraped off like a layer of peeling paint to reveal the underlying wood. That is, just as paint is merely incidental to the wood to which it adheres, so, according to Levinas, our sexuality is something that merely adheres to our humanity. That is, his claim indicates that sexual difference is not constitutive of our humanity but instead could be separated from it.

The second version of the creation of woman from man, the fashioning of the rib into woman, suggests a more complex understanding of this act than is normally assumed. For Levinas, the contribution of the rib to the creation of the face of another exemplifies the "for the other," since it indicates the loss of one's skin to another. Interestingly, the contribution of the rib is a "for the not-yet" other. That is, it is in the giving of the skin, the giving of the rib, that the other is actually created. But we must bear in mind that the commentary on the text depicts God creating woman from man's rib, not the other way around. The relationship is not interchangeable. Levinas asks whether this non-interchangeable relation in fact marks the difference between the sexes (GCW 168/DCF 133).

In any event, Levinas insists that while woman is not herself secondary, the relationship of man to woman, as woman, is secondary. This point is underscored when he says, "Fundamental are the tasks that man accomplishes as a human being and that woman accomplishes as a human being. They have other things to do besides cooing, and, moreover, something else to do and more, than to limit themselves to the relations that are established because of the differences in sex" (GCW 169/DCF 135). The sexual relation is incidental to being human: "[C]ulture is not determined by the libido" (GCW 172/DCF 140). Although Levinas insists that sexual difference be understood in practice as secondary to what is human, he nonetheless maintains the priority of the position of the male in the order of the creation of sexual difference. He claims that the presence of the creature prior to sexual difference signifies the priority of what is human over the relationship between the sexes. But in this essay, he also affirms the need for the hierarchy (GCW 175–177/DCF 143–148).

Additionally, there is a textual discrepancy concerning the order of the creation of the sexes. Hebrew vocabulary—*ish*/man, shortened from *isha*/woman—suggests that man was created after, or from, woman. Even more interesting is the fact that after this creation, regardless of the initial order, men (future humans) do indeed issue from women! If nothing else, the story depicts an inversion of the biological truth. We need only look at what woman is called to see this point clearly. In the second story, that of Adam and his mate, woman is named "Eve." In Hebrew, this name is *Chava*, which means "life."

Nonetheless, the fact that in the story woman is *created from* man's side means that woman is created second. But what does this mean for her status in relation to man? What is this so-called non-sexed humanity? Even among feminist biblical scholars who have grappled with this story, there is no clear "feminist" interpretation. Judith Plaskow, in her seminal work *Standing Again at Sinai*,[29] remains unconvinced that the story can be interpreted as anything other than an affirmation of patriarchy. For Plaskow, that Eve was created second confirms this view.[30] Plaskow is responding to Trible's argument that Eve not only is not inferior, but may in fact be Adam's equal, if not his superior.

According to Trible, the fact that Eve repeats God's prohibition demonstrates both that Eve knows or understands what is forbidden and that her act of defiance demonstrates will, autonomy, and thoughtfulness. She had to make sense of what God asked, and then she had to decide to obey or disregard what she was told. Adam, however, blindly obeyed Eve's suggestion to eat the fruit. Trible claims that even if Eve was created second, that need not indicate inferiority. In fact, it may suggest the opposite. Throughout the Bible, it is often the second who is superior and who is favored—for example, Jacob and Joseph. And, Trible reminds us, Adam played no role in the creation of Eve. Adam was asleep. He was neither a participant nor an observer. Thus, Trible concludes, he did not have any control over Eve or her creation. She is the creation of God just as Adam is. Finally, the term used to refer to Eve as a helpmate is the same Hebrew word, *erev*, that is used to refer to the relationship of God to Israel and the animals to Adam. Thus, "helpmate" does not carry an intrinsic positional property. Eve cannot be said to be inferior to Adam simply by virtue of the reference to her as a helpmate. Trible thus concludes that the animals are inferior to Adam; God is superior to Adam; and Eve is equal to Adam.[31]

The question of equality or superiority is not as easily settled for the rabbis as it may be for others. Derrida's worry that there is still a priority of male over female is not without warrant. As he points out, there is the assumed privilege of male neutrality in the issue of humanity. This implicit privilege results from the attempt to whitewash the secondariness of woman: rather than merely say that woman is secondary to man, the relation is reframed so that it places sexual difference secondary to what is human. But this refocusing does not change the order of male to female in the story of creation.

Nonetheless, in spite of this attempt to establish equality, it is still possible to interpret the division between the sexes, the order of the creation of man (male) and woman (female), and the "fact" that woman is created from man, as illustrating an explicit priority of male over female. Levinas cites Rav Abbahu, who claims that God originally wanted two beings—not man issuing from woman or woman issuing from man. God wanted two separate, equal beings. But Rav Abbahu believed that this equality could not be sustainable, for there would be war. Equal beings would compete for control. He thought that to create a world that would not self-destruct, one being must be subordinated to the other. There had to be a difference that did not compromise equality or affect how justice was distributed with regard to what it means to be human. Once again, humanity is detached from sexual difference. According to these rabbis, sexual difference, including the priority of one sex over the other, was created in order to prevent a war.[32]

These points, however, are contestable. First, returning to Trible's essay, we find a different interpretation. Humans were equal to each other in the garden, and then equality began to deteriorate. One possible interpretation of the story is that it is meant to teach us a lesson about how to treat each other. This interpretation assumes that our goal should be to try to return to the garden, which is a metaphor for the restoration of equality. Second, the claim that sexual difference is secondary to humanity is simply false. To begin with the latter point, we need only return to the biblical text: "God created him, man and woman." Sexual difference, at least as it appears in this phrasing, is not secondary to humankind—they were created simultaneously. Rather, God created male and female, but God placed them within one being. Moreover, if we take as our point of departure the midrash commentary on the two *yods,* then we must ask, "What kind of creature remains after woman is fashioned from man?" If the two *yods* indicate sexual difference, man and woman within one creation, then what is man after woman is taken from him? Is he the same creature? Even if we grant that woman is created "after" man, is it not the case that when woman is created, man and woman—as we understand each—are created simultaneously? Is it not the case that the focus on the creation of woman obscures the description of the event as the creation of both man and woman as such? To be sure, the creature that was initially created by God cannot be the same creature following the separation of the female. If "God created him, male and female," then whatever remains after the separation of the female from the creature is not the same creature that God initially created. One might say that it is only after the creation of woman—or, rather, after the removal of woman from the creature—that man exists qua male being.

In her book *Lethal Love,* Mieke Bal makes a similar point and takes the argument one step further. According to Bal, the creature *needs* to be separated from itself. She writes, "It needs to be divided over-against itself in order to have a fit companion. The creature is lonely; 'the animals are unfit' and the different human being is not unfit because, according to Bal, it is the tension between the *same* and the *different* that creates sexuality. The earth-being has to be severed, separated from part of itself, in order for the 'other half' of what will then be left to come into existence."[33] Several of Bal's points bear further elaboration. First, she reminds us that it is not God who names the creature *Adam,* but the narrator.[34] Second, even if it is true that woman was created second, it is not clear that this is sufficient to justify the subordination of woman to man. Finally, it is worth repeating Bal's insight that it is the *tension* between the same and the different that creates sexuality.

This insight underscores my point about Levinas's discussion of the feminine in *Time and the Other.* Bal's discussion also helps us to understand why the face of the Other must be a human face. In this case, the animals are too different. The creation of woman from man—that is, the presence of woman—is the first experience with alterity.[35] While it is the case that the sexes as separate entities were created after the initial creation of the earth creature, this creation seems to have occurred only because Adam was lonely. According to the Torah, God brought all the animals before Adam but none of them was adequate. Then woman was created, and Adam recognized immediately the difference between woman and the other creatures that God had previously paraded before him. Woman, by virtue of being removed from that to which she was once attached, is the radical other to man.

But while Levinas speaks of the feminine as "other," he insists that his conception of the feminine should not be confused with romantic notions of woman as other, or woman as mystery, misunderstood and unknown (TO 86/TA 78). He admits, nonetheless, that the feminine, the essentially other, is a mystery to him (TO 86/TA 78). Not only is the feminine in its alterity not assimilated into the same, but it also provides *the* condition for any relation with alterity.[36] This alterity, which characterizes the difference between the sexes, informs Levinas's view of love such that "it [love] is a relationship with what always slips away" (TO 86/TA 78). The feminine, conceived as eros itself, withdraws into its mystery (TO 86/TA 78).[37] In love, the alterity of each is not neutralized, but preserved (TO 86/TA 78). Thus, if we return once again to the biblical verse "He created him, male and female," we can see that there were always two beings present. There was not a previously existing whole, or fusion. Rather, there were always two beings, two totalities attached as one, two who were always marked by their relation to sexuality.

The feminine, in Levinas's view, is a mode of being that slips away from the light of publicity and, consequently, from reason and knowledge.[38] The feminine is characterized by modesty, as it hides from light. The mystery of the feminine and, therefore, the mystery of the other constitute alterity. However, Levinas wants to avoid the trap of the Hegelian master-slave dialectic, wherein the struggle for freedom and recognition results in the consciousness becoming the slave to the other, who becomes master.[39] For Levinas, alterity does not arise out of an initial characterization of the other as freedom. The other is other simply because she is not me.

Alterity is not a function of ontic characteristics, such as hair color, race, and so on. Thus, it is in the absolutely original relationship that we find alterity not characterized as a power struggle. Male and female have separate roles to play. In the relation between man and woman, each is indispensable to the other. His role is to become a subject and hers is to help bring about that subjectivity. The 'I' and the other are different: "The existent [the 'I'] is accomplished in the 'subjective' and in 'consciousness'" (TO 88/TA 81). But "alterity is accomplished in the feminine . . . the feminine is not accomplished as a *being* [*étant*] in a transcendence toward light, but in modesty" (TO 88/TA 81).

This same theme had already been noted in *Existence and Existents,* in which Levinas says, "[T]he plane of *eros* allows us to see that the other par excellence is the feminine" (EE 85/DEE 145). The feminine's transcendence is puzzling, for it consists in its withdrawal. In struggling for an appropriate term, Levinas can find no word suitable to characterize the relationship to the feminine other than "mystery" (TO 88/TA 81). His aim in this characterization of eros is to illustrate what eros is not. By showing that eros differs from power and possession, he reveals that it is neither "a struggle, a fusion nor a knowledge" (TO 88/TA 81). It is a relationship with the very dimension of alterity, with the future. So even in the face of death, where all possibles are impossible, the subject is still a subject through eros (TO 88/TA 81).

The voluptuousness of the erotic differs from all other pleasures because it is not solitary. And the account of voluptuousness that Levinas advances illustrates the role of the feminine and its alterity—namely, that it precludes its absorption into the same. Even more profound is Levinas's insight that one seeks the caress not because it is a simple pleasure in itself, as Freud—at least as Levinas interprets him—would have us believe. Rather, one seeks the caress because it is directed toward the future; it is the anticipation of a "pure future [*avenir*]" (TO 89/TA 83). The feminine is not synonymous with the pure event. Rather, the feminine makes possible this pure event, which Levinas names *paternity* (see TO 84–85, 90–91/TA 77, 85).

Eros, characterized in opposition to fusion, power, and grasping, is a transcendent event that Levinas calls "victory over death" (TO 90/TA 84). How is this possible? The victory over death is paternity, described as a relationship with a stranger—a son, who is both same and other. The son is not his possession. Rather, he is his son (TO 91/TA 86). In the relation between father and son, in the fulfillment of becoming a father, time is accomplished. So, in response to the question "How is victory over death possible?" Levinas writes that the birth of the son defies death. But his conception of love and its relation to paternity remains unclear. Moreover, the role that the feminine plays in bringing about subjectivity remains obscured by the apparent significance it has in bringing about paternity and the birth of the son.[40]

Levinas mentions explicitly the transcendental function of woman, which he broadens in *Totality and Infinity*. The feminine is not the pure event; rather, it makes this pure event possible.[41] The feminine provides the physical means by which paternity takes place. On another level, the feminine provides the first contact with an alterity so radical that it (the feminine) will not be able to be the ethical other. The feminine will be before and beyond the ethical, but the feminine cannot partake in the ethical. We can see this point more clearly in Levinas's quotation of the last chapter from Proverbs: "[S]he makes possible the life of men; she is the home of men. But the husband has a life outside the home: He sits on the Council of the city; he has a public life; he is at the service of the universal; he does not limit himself to interiority, to intimacy, to the home, although without them he would be incapable of anything" (GCW 169/DCF 135, translation modified). Although he wants to claim that the relationship to woman as woman might be secondary in terms of the libido, the passage makes clear that it is not secondary with regard to the very functioning of society.

Regardless of how we finally decide that matter, it is clear that once the sexual division takes place, a division of labor follows. Moreover, the division of labor along the lines of sexual difference is fundamental to the very manner in which men function both in and outside the home. The "other" tasks men have, besides "cooing" to their lovers, are still defined in terms of, and made possible by, women, empirically existing women, not merely the metaphorical feminine. This, I maintain, shows that sexual difference plays a fundamental role in the drama of existence. One could say that the fact that man and woman, as such, were created after the initial appearance of the "earth creature" indicates the priority of what is human over that which pertains to the marked characteristics of sex. This interpretation of the order of creation would allow Levinas to maintain that his ethics is not marked by sexual difference. However, Levinas's discussion assumes a division of labor that makes possible those tasks that he claims are fundamental to being human. He enforces this division of labor and then gives priority to the male experience of participating in the ethical.

EROS, DEATH, AND THE FEMININE

As we saw in the previous chapter, the *there is* characterizes the 'before' of subjectivity; it is what is prior to the existent contracting its existence. And we have seen that it is radical alterity housed in the feminine that enables the movement from the *there is* to the hypostasis. We will now turn to Levinas's characterization of the feminine as the future and investigate what that means for the relationship of the feminine to ethics. In doing so, however, we need to bear in mind that his conception of the future remains complicated, since he also defines the future in terms of death.

Death reveals itself as that which cannot take place in the light. When in a relationship with death, the subject encounters something that does not come from itself (TO 70/TA 56). Levinas calls this relationship "being in relationship with mystery" (TO 70/TA 56). Whereas for Heidegger, death is the event of freedom, the revelation of the virility of the subject, for Levinas, death is the limit of the possible. Death is never present. Insofar as I am master of my existence, master of the possible, death is not: "Death is never now" (TO 72/TA 59). I cannot be virile in relation to death—not because I am nothingness, but, according to Levinas, because I cannot grasp it (TO 72/TA 59).

Although Heidegger deems being-toward-death as an authentic mode of *Dasein,* Levinas illustrates through his reference to *Macbeth* that heroes seize the last chance before death, not death itself. Even the hero hopes that he will not die: death just comes. And while suicide presents a contrary example, for in suicide one brings about one's death, Hamlet's "To be or not to be" reveals the impossibility of annihilating oneself. It would seem that when one commits suicide, the subject is assuming that the "mastery" involved in taking one's own life carries over to the "other side." But Levinas insists that this is not the case. With the onset of death, the subject is no longer "*able to be able* [*nous ne 'pouvons plus pouvoir*]" (TO 74/TA 62).

That death is the impossibility of having a project (TO 74/TA 62) indicates that we are in relation with something that is other, "something whose very existence is made of alterity" (TO 74/TA 63). So, contrary to Heidegger, Levinas does not believe that death confirms my solitude. The "mineness" of death does not secure the "mineness" of my being; rather, death breaks my solitude (see TO 74/TA 63).

What, then, is the relationship between death and eros? Death's hold on my existing is mysterious; in this sense, the relationship with death is a relationship with a Mystery (TO 75/TA 63). And eros, which, Levinas claims, is as "strong as death," provides us with a way to understand the relationship with mystery. It is in his discussion of eros that he characterizes the feminine as both mystery and absolute other. He writes, "The other is the future. The very relationship with the other is the relationship with the future" (TO 77/TA 64). However, if Levinas categorizes both death and the feminine as possible others, to which other does this passage refer: death or the feminine? With regard to death as other, as that which crushes my solitude, he asks, "How can a being enter into relation with the other without allowing its very self to be crushed by the other?" (TO 77/TA 65). This question reveals the problem of preserving the ego in transcendence.

If the escape from solitude is meant to allow the subject to remain a subject independent of the object toward which it is projected, that is, not to be absorbed by the object, and if the subject cannot assume death, how can there be a reconciliation between death and the ego (TO 78/TA 66)? How does one remain a self in the face of death? For Levinas this reconciliation takes place in the face-to-face encounter with the Other, an encounter with a face that at once both reveals and conceals itself. For Levinas, "The other 'assumed' is the Other" (TO 79/TA 67). In order for "the future that death gives" to be time, the future must enter into a relationship with the present (TO 79/TA 69). This relationship between present and future occurs in the intersubjective face-to-face relationship, and "the condition of time lies in the relationship between humans, or in history" (TO 79/TA 69). I wish to make two points about the face-to-face relationship that Levinas establishes, the second being contingent on the first.

First, we see here the anticipation of the ethical relation with which Levinas will concern himself in the works to follow. Levinas employs the expression "face-to-face," which he later uses to signify the ethical relation. But who takes part in this face-to-face relation? Who is subject—'I'—and who is other, or Other? A common mistake in reading this series of lectures, especially in light of Levinas's later work, is to assume that the feminine occupies the place of the ethical other. This misreading arises because Levinas, in this early work, refers to the feminine as the absolutely other (*absolument autre*), while in his later work the absolutely other refers to the ethical other. It is not clear that *Time and the Other* can support such a reading.

I propose that the face-to-face relationship—at least as understood in terms of the ethical relation—initially excludes the feminine. However, this point does not preclude the feminine from playing any role at all or from playing a significant role. Rather, I suggest that the relation with the feminine provides the initial experience of present and future. The feminine, conceived as eros and in relation to fecundity, provides the means by which the 'I' can encounter the face-to-face. In a conversation with Bracha Lichtenberg-Ettinger, Levinas explains,

> The feminine is the future. The feminine in its feminine phase, in its feminine form certainly may die bringing life into the world, but—how can I say to you?—it is not the 'dying'; for me, the 'dying' of a woman is certainly unacceptable. I am speaking about the possibility of conceiving that there is meaning without me. I think the heart of the heart, the deepest of the feminine, is dying in giving life, in bringing life into the world. I am not emphasizing dying but, on the contrary, *future*. . . . Woman is the category of future, the ecstasy of future. It is that human possibility which consists in saying that the life of another human being is more important than my own, that the death of the other is more important to me than my own death, that the Other comes before me, that the Other counts before I do, that the value of the Other is imposed before mine is.[42]

Among the many points of interest raised in this exchange, I wish to focus on two.[43] First, there is a shift from the feminine to woman, without explanation, as if the two are interchangeable. Although Levinas argues, earlier in the conversation and in other places in his writing, that the feminine serves as a metaphor, in this response we can begin to see his vacillation between the feminine and woman. In the above passage, he not only uses these terms interchangeably, he also uses the term "feminine" to refer to the actions of empirically existing women. It is woman who bears the child, the son; it is woman who creates the home; it is woman who is the future. And it is the woman who may die in childbirth. Thus, it should be clear that the feminine is not simply a metaphor; it also refers to empirically existing women.

Second, Levinas's comments in this passage also help to reveal the function that the feminine—that is, woman—plays in *Time and the Other:* she helps to fulfill the future. If love, as we see later in Levinas's analysis, is a return to the self, then it is in the birth of the son that this return is rendered incomplete. If his conceptions of alterity, time, the future, and love are contingent on the erotic relationship and how that relationship unfolds in fecundity, then Levinas needs sexual difference. It provides the foundation for his philosophy.[44] The birth of the son ensures that the movement is directed toward an other, toward the future, but not a future that means being-toward-death, as Heidegger would have us believe. For Levinas, the future means a life characterized by life.[45]

Levinas tells us explicitly in *Existence and Existents* what role eros plays in his argument: "Intersubjectivity is not simply the application of the category of multiplicity to the domain of the mind. It is brought about by eros, where in the proximity of another the distance is wholly maintained, a distance whose pathos is made up of this proximity and this duality of beings" (EE 95/DEE 163). A few lines later, he tells us that "the reciprocity of civilization—the kingdom of ends where each one is both end and means, a person and personal—is a leveling of the idea of fraternity, which is an outcome and not a point of departure, and refers back to everything implicated in eros. For the intermediary of a father is required in order that we enter into fraternity, and in order that I be myself the poor one, the weak and the pitiful" (EE 96/DEE 164). It is in this passage, and the immediately following one, that we find an answer to our question regarding the relationship between the feminine and alterity, between eros and sexual difference. He says, "[I]n order to postulate a father, who is not simply a cause or a genus, *the heterogeneity of the I and the other is required*" (EE 96/ DEE 164, emphasis added). He continues,

> *This heterogeneity and this relationship between genders, on the basis of which society and time are to be understood,* brings us to the material to which another work will be devoted. . . . The peculiar form of the contraries and contradictions of eros has escaped Heidegger, who in his lectures tends to present the difference between the sexes as a specification of a genus. It is in eros that transcendence can be conceived as something radical, which brings to the ego caught up in being, ineluctably returning to itself, something else than this return, can free it of its shadow. To simply say that the ego leaves itself is a contradiction, since, in quitting itself the ego carries itself along. Asymmetrical intersubjectivity is the locus of transcendence in which the subject, while preserving its subject, has the possibility of not inevitably returning to itself, the possibility of being fecund and having a son. (EE 96/ DEE 164–165, emphasis added)

The above passage reveals how Levinas understands the issue of sexual difference. It is no accident that the 'I' has the appearance of being male, that the feminine appears as radical alterity, and that to be fecund is to bear not only a child, but a son. Levinas defines asymmetrical intersubjectivity in terms of transcendence, as that "which has the possibility of not inevitably returning to itself" (EE 96/DEE 165). Fecundity is the means by which this return is rendered incomplete. In this account, then, to bring about the birth of the son, the relation with eros must be the relationship of a man to a woman. The feminine is understood in relationship to the future and to the birth of a child.

Although Levinas insists that sexual difference is secondary to "humanity," it is sexual difference that provides the means for the ethical relation to occur. It is fundamental to the movement of subjectivity. Eros, as the feminine, provides the means by which there is an originary experience with alterity, by which the existent contracts its existence. In other words, alterity via the relationship to the feminine in eros is the means by which the existent becomes a subject. This relationship is therefore marked by transcendence without a complete return to the self, owing to the birth of a son. But because of the birth of the child, this experience with alterity is also the means by which both man *and* woman escape the trap of totality, a concern that de Beauvoir also has. The child interrupts the closed relationship and opens the couple onto the world. This is a discussion that Levinas expands in *Totality and Infinity.*

FOUR

The Hospitality of the Feminine

If, however, there is a needy person among you . . .
do not harden your heart and shut your hand against
your needy kinsman. Rather you must open your hand
and lend him sufficient for whatever he needs.
—Deuteronomy 15:7–8

A man's home is his wife (The house is Woman).
—The Talmud

We saw in the previous chapter that in *Time and the Other,* the feminine, conceived as eros, is the originary experience of alterity. We also saw that sexual difference informs the theme of separation and individuation and establishes the conditions for the ethical relation, even though the ethical is not yet named in this book. In *Totality and Infinity,* Levinas tells us that in order for the ethical to arise, there must be an intimacy—a familiarity or an enjoyment—that is disrupted. In habitation, the 'I' takes pleasure in the handling of a tool (over and against the mere instrumentality of tools, as we see in Heidegger). However, habitation also provides the space from which the man "enters" the world. The man goes into the world as someone who is at home with himself and who can return to his home. The home, which provides the place to which the man can return for enjoyment, is thus characterized by intimacy. Hence, the man has a life that is both inside (enjoyment) and outside (the ethical) the home. And the role that woman plays in making possible man's transcendence extends beyond the dwelling and into the erotic relationship. In this chapter, we see that the role of the feminine is doubled: it functions both as the welcoming in the dwelling and as the access to fecundity via the erotic relationship. Thus, we can raise questions not only about how Levinas understands the erotic relationship—that is, the love relationship between the man and woman—but also about how his conception of eros has been understood by his commentators.

THE DWELLING

The gentleness of habitation is the feminine presence.[1] The relation of the I to the Other in the face-to-face is identified by language, and the face, though always eluding my grasp, is not hidden. In contrast to the Other, woman, who is "discreetly absent" and "silent" (TI 155/TeI 128), accomplishes the task of making the home hospitable; woman makes possible the "condition for recollection . . . and inhabitation" (TI 155/TeI 128). Levinas tells us, "The Other who welcomes in intimacy is not the *you [vous]* of the face that reveals itself in a dimension of height, but precisely the *thou [tu]* of familiarity: a language without teaching, a silent language, an understanding without words, an expression in secret" (TI 155/TeI 129).[2]

The confusion that arises from Levinas's use of the feminine has its roots in its ambiguous reference: Does the feminine refer to empirically existing women, or does it describe metaphorically what might be interpreted as stereotyped feminine attributes such as gentleness?[3] Certainly, one could argue for the latter alternative, namely, that Levinas's account of the feminine is merely metaphorical. And comments by both Levinas and his readers support this position. In *Totality and Infinity,* Levinas avows his reliance on metaphor: "Need one add that there is no question here of defying ridicule by maintaining the empirical truth or counter-truth that every home *in fact* presupposes a woman? . . . [T]he empirical absence of the human being of the feminine sex in a dwelling nowise affects the dimension of femininity which remains open there, as the very welcome of the dwelling" (TI 157–158/TeI 131). And in *Ethics and Infinity,* Levinas says, "Perhaps all these allusions to the ontological differences between the masculine and the feminine would appear less archaic if, instead of dividing humanity into two species, they would signify that the participation in the masculine and the feminine were the attribute of every human being. Could this be the meaning of the enigmatic verse of Genesis 1:27: 'male and female created He them'?" (EI 68–69/EeI 71). Commentators often claim that Levinas uses the feminine only metaphorically. Adriaan Peperzak, for example, does so, and he concludes that Levinas does not exclude woman (or women) from the ethical relationship.[4] However, Peperzak arrives at this conclusion by substituting "man, woman, and child" for Levinas's references to "the stranger, the widow, and the orphan," respectively. Peperzak thus interprets Levinas as using the triplet to encompass all human beings.

However, there is evidence to suggest that Levinas's use of the feminine is not only, or simply, metaphorical. To interpret the feminine metaphorically, rather than opening up possibilities, actually occludes the nuance of the text. It hides the role that "real" women play in this relation. Additionally, we need to ask after the relationship of the metaphorical to the empirical. How does a metaphor become effective? One possible answer to this question is to suggest that interpreting the feminine as a metaphor can have purchase only because it ultimately refers to the empirical. Thus, to ignore the possibility that the feminine refers to empirical women actually undermines its effectiveness as a metaphor.

Stella Sandford's comments on this point in *The Metaphysics of Love* are worth repeating. She writes, "Presumably [Peperzak] would not be foolhardy enough to argue that, as a metaphor, the trope of the feminine has no connection whatsoever, no linguistic or cultural reference at all, to empirically existing women, as this would deprive the metaphor not just of its rhetorical force, but of its very sense: of any possibility of it functioning with any intended meaning at all."[5] Sandford also reminds us that "an insistence on the metaphorical status of the feminine is also forced to overlook the fact that Levinas speaks just as often of *la Femme*."[6] Levinas himself employs other terms for the feminine, and his use of *la femme* is at best ambiguous, referring to both wife and woman, neither term being used metaphorically.

In spite of what Levinas might tell us or what he might wish to be the case, his books might tell us something different. Although he tells us that "the I-Thou in which Buber sees the category of interhuman relationship is not with the interlocutor but with feminine alterity," he also tells us that "the other whose presence is discreetly an absence, with which is accomplished the primary hospitable welcome which describes the field of intimacy, is the Woman [*la Femme*]. The woman is the condition for recollection, the interiority of the Home, and inhabitation" (TI 155/TeI 128). He also refers to the feminine in this same section as silent and as one whose "footsteps reverberate the secret depths of being" (TI 156/TeI 129). The confusion, and the ensuing criticisms, can be attributed to his own vacillation between the literal and the metaphorical.

Certainly one could say that this interpretation of Levinas is too literal. However, my interest is to investigate the claim that the feminine is *merely* a metaphor, or that it is a simple metaphor. I contend that a closer examination of Levinas's use of the feminine reveals a more complex image: whereas the feminine ultimately functions as a metaphor, this is so only because empirical women inspire Levinas's image of the feminine. More specifically, Levinas derives his image of the feminine from the women of the Hebrew Bible. If we are to see the richness of Levinas's image of the feminine, we must take into account the roles that men and women play in the Hebrew Bible.

In the books of Malachi and Job, and elsewhere, references are made to "the stranger, the widow, and the orphan"—a reference that Levinas appropriates to identify those who are most helpless and exposed to injury. The widow (husbandless) and the orphan (fatherless) have in common a similar lack: neither is connected to a man. To map the biblical triplet—"the stranger, the widow, and the orphan"—onto generic man, woman, and child is to overlook a unique feature that binds together the stranger, the widow, and the orphan. In the Jewish tradition, references to "the stranger, the widow, and orphan" are not simply metaphorical. These individuals require our attention because of their very real circumstances—they lack protection and support of any kind. Thus, they uniquely represent those who are most in need. If these individuals are mapped onto "man, woman, and child," the instantiation will cover over the nuance of the biblical expression. The biblical reference implores us to look after not merely men, women, and children, but those who are the *most* vulnerable, those who are the most in need. This is not to say that we are to look after only these people. Rather, to understand the force behind the imperative in Levinas's ethics, we need to keep the biblical expression in mind. Thus, if we accept Peperzak's substitution, the biblical resonance is lost. Levinas's use of the feminine—at least in this philosophical work—is not merely metaphorical; its reference to concrete women, and the implications that arise from this reference, must be acknowledged and addressed.

Limiting our investigation to the section of *Totality and Infinity* called "The Dwelling" may not yield the definitive answer that we seek. And Levinas's own vacillation in this section contributes to the problem. However, we can identify statements of a more determinate position in his essays on Judaism. The view of the feminine, or woman, in "The Dwelling" is strikingly similar to the view that he gleans from the rabbinic tradition, and which he recounts in his essay "Judaism and the Feminine."[7]

Here, Levinas tells us that "[t]he characteristics of the Jewish woman are fixed thanks to charming feminine figures of the Old Testament" (JF 31/JeF 52). After listing the various wives of the patriarchs—Sarah, Rebecca, Rachel, and Leah—and prophetesses such as Ruth, Miriam, and Esther, Levinas claims, "But the world in which these events unfolded would not have been structured as it was—and as it still is and always will be—without the *secret presence, on the edge of invisibility,* of these mothers, wives and daughters; without their *silent footsteps* in the depths and opacity of reality, drawing the very dimensions of interiority and making the world precisely inhabitable" (JF 31/JeF 53, emphasis added). Moreover, the characteristics that Levinas recites and applauds are not the usual, stereotypical traits of women; they are as diverse as the women themselves. He reminds us that without Rebecca's ruse, Esau would have ruled Israel; without Miriam's creativity, Moses might have died; without Tamar's stubbornness, Ruth's faithfulness, and Bathsheba's political genius, David would not have been possible (JF 31/JeF 53). These are not women who sat on the sidelines and watched while the men made history. These women were engaged in the very act of making history. Or as Levinas believes, history and, more importantly, the sacred history of Judaism would not have been made without them.

Throughout this essay, just as in *Totality and Infinity*, the vacillation between the "feminine" and "woman" suggests that the feminine is not simply a label for feminine traits. It also signifies the female sex. Here, as in *Totality and Infinity*, woman is described as a "strange flow of gentleness" and as "the one 'who does not conquer'" (JF 33/JeF 55). Citing the Talmud, Levinas also claims that "[t]he house is woman" (JF 31/JeF 53), and that "Proverbs tells us it is through woman as a keepsake of the hearth that the public life of man is possible" (JF 32/JeF 53). Talmudic law, which excludes women from being judges and witnesses,[8] in effect prevents women from participating in the public realm. Women are considered keepers of the home, not of the courts. And yet, he points out, it is in Judaism that we find one of the earliest signs of respect for the dignity and legal status of women.

Levinas cites the passage from the rabbinic reading of the Book of Numbers, in which a decision about a woman accused of adultery is removed from the "heatedness" of her jealous husband and moved to the arbitration and judgment of the priests, a third party and a public power (JF 34/JeF 56–57).[9] The more orthodox traditions of Judaism affirm the public-man/private-woman opposition as preserving the traditional historical roles of men and women. Men are assigned roles dealing with public life, while women are confined to roles associated with the home.[10] In Judaism, this split between public and private, between man and woman, is so pronounced that women are exempted from the positive precepts—that is, the timed commandments that must be observed during certain times of the day, such as the prayers in the morning—which may interfere with their obligations to the home.[11] Women are the keepers of the hearth; men, the keepers of the law.[12]

Neither Levinas nor Judaism disparage home life. Rather, it is the home that makes the ethical possible. In fact, Levinas says, "The last chapter of Proverbs, in which woman, without regard for 'beauty and grace,' appears as the genius of the hearth and precisely as such, makes the public life of man possible, can, if necessary be read as a moral paradigm. But in Judaism the moral always has the weight of an ontological basis: the feminine figures among the categories of Being" (JF 32/JeF 53). The view of the feminine, or woman, that Levinas draws from the rabbinic tradition is so remarkably similar to the description he gives of the feminine in "The Dwelling" that it is worth quoting at length:

To light eyes that are blind, to restore to equilibrium, and so overcome an alienation which ultimately results from the very virility of the universal and all-conquering *logos* that stalks the very shadows that could have sheltered it, should be the ontological function of the feminine, the vocation of the 'one who does not conquer.' Woman does not simply come to someone deprived of companionship to keep him company. She answers to a solitude inside this privation and—which is stranger—to a solitude that subsists in spite of the presence of God; to a solitude in the universal, to the inhuman which continues to well up even when the human has mastered nature and raised it to thought. For the inevitable uprooting of thought, which dominates the world, to return to the peace and ease of being at home, the strange flow of gentleness must enter into the geometry of infinite and cold space. Its name is woman. (JF 33/JeF 55)

Thus, woman fills a place of companionship for man that even God cannot fulfill. If we recall the story of creation, Adam, the earth creature, was alone. It was a single creature uniting both man and woman.

For Levinas, the return of self takes place in the interiority of "the House," "the reverse of which would be place [*l'endroit*], but for the essential moderation of feminine existence living there, which is habitation itself" (JF 33/JeF 55). Although it is the man who brings home the corn and the flax, it is the woman who transforms them into bread and clothing. As he explains, "The wife, the betrothed, is not the coming together in a human being of all the perfections of tenderness and goodness which subsists in themselves. Everything indicates that the feminine is the original manifestation of these perfections, of gentleness itself, the origin of all gentleness on earth" (JF 33/JeF 55–56). According to rabbinic tradition, it is the woman who makes a life for the man, who makes life worth living, and who contributes to his life what is required for his soul. Without her, "man knows neither good, nor succour, nor joy, nor blessing, nor pardon. . . . Nothing which transforms his natural life into ethics, nothing which permits living a life, not even the death that one dies for another" (JF 33–34/JeF 56).

In her book *Menstrual Purity*, Charlotte Fonrobert responds to the above passage. She tells us that this view "entails Levinas's inability to conceive of 'these' (biblical) women as other than by their relationship to the men in their lives, as 'mothers, wives, and daughters.'"[13] Fonrobert's charge is accurate as far as it goes. All of the actions that Levinas mentions were conducted in relationship to sons, fathers, and husbands—except in the case of Ruth, whose action was initially directed at her mother-in-law. He works within the framework given to him by the Bible; it was not chosen by him.

Levinas specifically names Ruth, Esther, Sarah, Rebecca, Miriam, et al. as his examples of the feminine. In his view, it is precisely because these women are limited by the roles that define them that their actions are so extraordinary. He demonstrates that in spite of the roles that limit and define them, these women actually advance the dramatic movement of the biblical stories in question. Their actions actually enable them to exceed the passive roles that they were assumed to have had. On the one hand, we could say that it is not Levinas who constrains these women, but the Hebrew Bible itself. On the other hand, however, we could say that the array of women that Levinas includes in his description allows for significant differences among women. Thus, even the Hebrew Bible accounts for a variety. In any event, Levinas offers an image of the feminine that refers to a number of different women.[14] The women that he names participate in activities that range from faithfulness to deception.[15] These women serve as models for what Levinas calls "the feminine."[16]

THE PHENOMENOLOGY OF EROS

According to Levinas, the erotic, conjugal relationship between a man and woman is not an end in itself: "The meaning of love does not, then, stop with the moment of voluptuousness, nor with the person loved" (JF 36/JeF 60). He says, furthermore, "This dimension of the romantic in which love becomes its own end, where it remains without any 'intentionality' that spreads beyond it . . . is foreign to Judaism" (JF 36–37/JeF 60). This view of the erotic relation follows the treatment found in the Talmud. Judaism places a positive emphasis on sexual pleasure. But fecundity is important insofar as it also signifies the continuation of the Jewish people.[17]

While the language of justice opens the ethical relationship to the other, the language of eros turns to cooing and laughter. The language that marks the ethical relation is absent from the erotic. Levinas identifies the love relationship as a return to the same. This characterization is distinctly different from his characterization of the ethical relation. He echoes the description of the structure of love that we find in Sartre's *Being and Nothingness* when he describes the love relationship as one in which what the lover wants is not simply to love the other, but to have the beloved love him back.[18] The erotic relationship is not a relation of infinity in itself: The erotic fulfills the ethical, the reaching out toward infinity, through fecundity—specifically, through the birth of a son.[19] The erotic, or the relationship with "the Other as feminine, is required in order that the future child come to pass from beyond the possible, beyond projects" (TI 267/TeI 245). Since, for Levinas, the erotic relationship culminates in fecundity, and since he, as the writer, assumes the position of the 'I,' one must conclude that the other is the "feminine sex"—that is, a woman.

In light of his complaint that Heidegger overlooks the enjoyment of things as ends in themselves, it is ironic that in his phenomenology of love he gestures toward love as something directed toward a future (albeit a future that is "not yet"). One might assume that he would insist that love be valued solely as an end in itself. Although he does allow for the presence of pleasure—"voluptuosity"—for the sake of itself, he nonetheless emphasizes the futural aspect of the relation. And yet, as we will see, even this position is more complex than is usually allowed. What, then, is the connection between an erotic relationship that focuses on pleasure for the sake of itself, something that Levinas allows for explicitly, and the priority of the love relation that ends in fecundity? Feminist readers of Levinas are divided on the best way to interpret his analysis of love: on the one hand, he should be lauded for recognizing the pleasurable element of eros; but on the other hand, the priority he gives to the erotic relation, which ultimately ends in the birth of a son, appears to eclipse the pleasurable aspects of eros. Thus, it appears that pleasure in eros is only a means to an end. A closer examination might yield a different view.

For Levinas, ambiguity characterizes the erotic. The relation with the other in love turns into a relation of need, while also transcending such a relation. Love both presupposes the exteriority of the other, the beloved, while also exceeding this exteriority of the other (TI 254/TeI 232). He develops his discussion of love in *Time and the Other,* where he again refers to Aristophanes's speech in Plato's *Symposium.* He still disagrees with the implication of Aristophanes's story—namely, that fusion is desirable.[20] What he develops in this discussion is his view that love is a mixture of immanence and transcendence (TI 254/TeI 232). He finds compelling the ambiguous notion of love as a relation in which there is both a return to the self and a transcendence of self.

Levinas tells us that love "is an event situated at the limit of immanence and transcendence" (TI 254/TeI 232). The face of the other, of the beloved, reveals within it what it is not yet. It reveals the future that is never future enough, a future that is "more remote than possible" (TI 254–255/TeI 232–233). The ambiguity of love lies, finally, in the possibility for the Other to appear as an object of need, and yet still retain its alterity:

> [T]he possibility of enjoying the Other, of placing oneself at the same time beneath and beyond discourse—this position with regard to the interlocutor which at the same time reaches him and goes beyond him, this simultaneity of need and desire, of concupiscence and transcendence, tangency of the avowable and the unavowable, constitutes the originality of the erotic which, in this sense, is *the equivocal* par excellence. (TI 255/TeI 233)

It seems clear that the feminine in the dwelling could be equated with the beloved. The feminine in the dwelling provides the conditions for the man to go out into the world. We therefore have a conception of the feminine that situates the feminine both before the ethical and beyond the ethical. Although it may be controversial to say so, the feminine situated before the ethical appears as a transcendental figure. That is, the feminine is the condition of the possibility of ethics. The feminine provides habitation and escape. The beloved, the feminine who appears after the discussion of the ethical, in the form of eros and the possibility of fecundity, appears as both need (the present) and desire (the future). In other words, the beloved is the exterior or the beyond, and in this form we may find her transcendence. But regardless of how we situate the beloved in relation to the ethical, as either below, before, or beyond the ethical, the beloved *as* beloved remains outside the ethical. This view of the beloved, as outside the ethical, as that which draws the lover "down," is further explicated in the "Phenomenology of Eros" section of *Totality and Infinity.*

Levinas begins his phenomenology of eros by declaring, "Love aims at the other; it aims at him in his frailty [*faiblesse*]" (TI 256/TeI 233).[21] Love aims at the tenderness of the beloved. Tenderness is not something added to the beloved; rather, the beloved "is but one with her *regime* of tenderness" (TI 256/TeI 233). He continually uses language that presents the image of the beloved cast below, while the lover is raised to new heights. The beloved is described as "dark," "nocturnal," "clandestine," "deep in the subterranean dimension" (TI 257/TeI 234). The beloved oscillates between virginity[22] and profanation, between modesty and immodesty (TI 257–258/TeI 235–236).

The lover's movement before this frailty, which Levinas terms *femininity* (TI 257/TeI 234), is "absorbed in the caress" (TI 257/TeI 234). The caress, though it is like sensibility, transcends the sensible. It seeks the not-yet and aims at a "future that is never future enough, in soliciting what slips away as though it *were not yet*" (TI 257, 258/TeI 235).[23] The caress both expresses love and yet is inadequate to do so (TI 258/TeI 235). The beloved, characterized as "the virgin," is at once "violable and inviolable," the "Eternal Feminine" (TI 258/TeI 236), "the future in the present" (TI 258/TeI 236). That at which the caress aims is neither a person nor a thing (TI 259/TeI 236). The future is an intangible; it is a *not-yet.*

The relation with the beloved resembles a relation with a child, insofar as a child does not have responsibility, is carefree, coquettish, and "a bit silly" (TI 263/TeI 241). Thus, the beloved, in eros, becomes like an infant (TI 263/TeI 241). As such, she has "quit her status as a person" (TI 263/TeI 241).[24] Here Levinas reaffirms the space between the ethical and the erotic. The language of murder—or rather, the language that commands us not to murder—and the face that makes murder impossible are all alien to eros (TI 262/TeI 241–242). The feminine is without signification and thus without language, the source of all signification (TI 257, 262/TeI 234, 241). In love, the feminine acts like a child who lacks responsibility.

The face of the feminine goes beyond the face that we find in the ethical relation. The face of the feminine exists in both its purity and its profanation. The feminine, the beloved, is ambiguity itself. Here, in the childlike quality of the beloved, the face fades into the impersonal. Levinas uses this word not to connote a lack of intimacy, but to express that which is not characterized by personhood. Playing with the Other in eros resembles how one plays with a young animal (TI 263/TeI 241). In this erotic relation, he casts the woman, the beloved, as somehow not human, or at least, not an adult person engaged in the important task of ethical responsibility. She profanes because the ethical is concealed or covered over, behind the face of the beloved. Yet, it is because of her that he, the lover, can transcend. It is the beloved who makes such transcendence possible.

In the name of sexual difference and the preservation of alterity, Levinas has cast each player in this love scene in a different role. Thus, unlike the man, the woman is cast down into the abyss, into the darkness, into that which suggests a void of God and religion. The descriptions of the feminine, of the beloved, of the voluptuosity in love, serve to indicate the ways in which the face in eros distinguishes itself from the face in the ethical relation. Eros, like all other enjoyments, is to be relished in itself. But eros differs from all other enjoyments in that other enjoyments, such as eating and drinking, can be solitary.[25] Eros affirms for Levinas the exceptional place of the "feminine."[26]

Love excludes the third party. The couple is sealed as a society of two. It remains outside the political, secluded in its intimacy, its dual solitude. It is closed and non-public (TI 265/TeI 242–243). Again restating Sartre's formulation, Levinas observes that "if to love is to love the love the Beloved bears me, to love is also to love oneself in love, and thus to return to oneself" (TI 266/TeI 244). The voluptuosity in love does not transcend itself.[27] In this description we see what he means by a return to the self.

The love relationship described in *Totality and Infinity* is directed toward a future—the "*not yet.*" Levinas borrows this term from Rosenzweig,[28] and he makes this point repeatedly. As such, we find a description similar to the one we saw in *Time and the Other:* the love relation is the juncture of present and future. It is being that is also a "being not yet" (TI 257/TeI 234). "It manifests itself at the limit of being and non-being . . ." (TI 256/TeI 233). Hence, love itself provides the means by which love is a return to the self, but also that which moves away from itself. This movement away from itself is part of the future secured by the relation of love. In Levinas's analysis, the future is the child (TI 266/TeI 244). The child, the future, the transcendence of love, redeems the voluptuosity or the concern with itself. It opens up the sealed society that the lovers construct (EE 89–93/DEE 153–159). According to Levinas, love escapes itself, escapes a return to the same, when it is directed toward the future, when it engenders the child.

Craig Vasey claims that while Levinas's radical ethics gives a new vision of the world, which could be interpreted as compatible with a feminist vision, he is nonetheless blind to the misogyny at work in his philosophy.[29] Vasey directs his criticisms at the conception of the feminine in *Totality and Infinity.* He is correct to say that Levinas's view of women may have dangerous implications. But Levinas's conception of the feminine is far more complicated than Vasey suggests. The figures of the feminine in Levinas's philosophy are not simply the result of a misogynist, patriarchal perspective. They are informed by the religious tradition that influences his project.

The concerns raised in response to Levinas's account of the feminine and of love are not insignificant. His apparent separation of eros from the ethical leads us to ask what ethical responsibility we have toward our spouses and partners. If we remember that he tells us that the ethical is veiled, we can see what he means by this separation. For Levinas, it is not the case that we have no obligations to our beloved. Rather, his phenomenological description is intended to demonstrate how complex love is. In eros, we are not concerned with the other as an ethical other. If we recall his description of the ethical, this point makes perfect sense. Our relations with others in eros are distinct from our ethical relations to others. This point will be addressed in more detail in the next two chapters.

FIVE

Eros, Sexual Difference, and the Question of Ethics

The feminine is the absolute contrariety contrary.
—Levinas, *Time and the Other*

In "Choreographies," Jacques Derrida asks, "What kind of an ethics would there be if belonging to one sex or another became its law or privilege? What if the universality of moral laws were modeled on or limited according to the sexes? What if their universality were not unconditional, without sexual condition in particular?"[1] What kind of ethics indeed? Derrida's questions are directed at Levinas's philosophical project, and they illuminate what would be disturbing about an ethics that discriminates in the manner he suggests. Moreover, there is a sense in which Levinas's account comes dangerously close to such an ethics. Derrida's questions arise out of a discussion of "woman's place," particularly as described in the biblical books of Genesis and Job. What is woman's place? Responses to this question often take the form of familiar clichés such as "in the home" and "in the kitchen." Metaphorically, the Bible indicates woman's place as wife ("rib") or mother ("womb").[2] Derrida takes up these responses in light of Levinas's talmudic readings in order to explain the relation between sexual difference and woman's place within Levinas's thought.[3]

The question of sexual difference also motivates Luce Irigaray to ask Levinas, "What of sexual difference?"[4] although, ironically, Irigaray's question is motivated by her concern that Levinas neglects sexual difference. More specifically, she wonders why the feminine cannot be an other, like the son, who renders incomplete the return to self. In Irigaray's view, Levinas has never experienced "the transcendence of the other which becomes im-mediate ecstasy (*extase instante*) in me and with him—or her. . . . Pleasure between the same sex does not result in that im-mediate ecstasy between other and myself. . . . [I]t does not produce in us that ecstasy which is our child, prior to any child (*enfant avant tout enfant*). . . . Is it the fact that Levinas is a man that makes him unaware of this creation of pleasure prior to any son?"[5] This chapter will focus on the criticisms of Levinas's project, specifically with regard to the issue of sexual difference, offered by Luce Irigaray and Jacques Derrida.

IRIGARAY ON LOVE

The focus on the future, on fecundity, motivates "The Fecundity of the Caress,"[6] Irigaray's remarkable essay on Levinas's conception of love. Although indebted to Levinas, Irigaray still takes issue with the way in which his ethics, radical as it might be, nonetheless remains blind to its own limitations.[7] In particular, she takes him to task for his conception of the erotic, on the grounds that he values voluptuosity only for its utility—namely, that it potentially engenders a child. Irigaray takes issue with this view of love on two counts: first, in questioning the necessity of procreation as the end of voluptuosity, she attempts to establish that eros exceeds the merely physical; second, she calls into question the heterosexual framework that Levinas presupposes.[8] She plays on words such as "nuptials," "weds," and "threshold" to indicate what she suspects to be his unintended "purification" of eros within the context of marriage. Her style of writing, especially her repetitive use of key phrases, serves to underscore the way in which these themes, which play a significant role in Levinas's description of the erotic relation, are inverted for her own use. In Irigaray's view, Levinas characterizes voluptuosity such that it can be redeemed only in the marriage-bed, and with the intent to produce a child. And yet, Irigaray also calls into question this assumed relation, or unification, by recalling that when the erotic relation comes to an end, or rather, is fulfilled temporarily,[9] the lover is "left to his solitary call to his God,"[10] while "the beloved woman is relegated to an inwardness that is not one because it is abyssal, animal, infantile, pre-nuptial."[11] In Irigaray's description, the lovers are "withdrawn to opposite poles of life, they do not marry."[12] Thus, in spite of what they seek, lover and beloved are not unified in life. Each plays a different part in the erotic drama. He, as lover, is the subject who acts on the beloved, the passive woman who waits and receives him. And while the woman gives the man a son, it is he, the lover, who achieves transcendence. The son blocks the return to the self, the return to the same. The birth of the son causes this return to be incomplete, but only for the man. The beloved woman, through eros, maternity, and birth, makes the son possible, but it is the man who reaps this benefit, as "the seduction of the beloved woman serves as a bridge between Father and son."[13] Through her, "the beloved, who is only an aspect of himself, the male lover goes beyond love and pleasure toward the ethical."[14] Thus, here again, the woman provides the conditions that enable the man's entry into the ethical world. According to Irigaray, moreover, the entry is purchased at the expense of the woman. She is left without subjectivity, without access to the ethical, and outside any relation to God.[15] For the man to engage in voluptuosity and bring about the birth of a son, he, the lover, must tarry on the wrong side of transcendence;[16] he must risk the "loss of self in the wrong infinity."[17]

The focus of Irigaray's general project—the ethics of sexual difference—provides a clue to her approach to Levinas.[18] According to Irigaray, Levinas fails in his task. His ethics is not radical enough to take into account sexual difference and also avoid relegating women to the same secondary role generally assigned to them in the history of Western philosophy. Why is the erotic relation exempt from the ethical? It is clear that the beloved woman in Levinas's love scene plays a role that aids her lover while she is cast back down into the abyss. With the emphasis on maternity and the birth of the child as the goal of the voluptuosity, Levinas returns woman to the one place that has always been assured her.[19] According to Irigaray, Levinas makes only the woman responsible for modesty, profanation, and the secret of desire. He thus relegates her to a place and to an unfair responsibility (to which she, but not he, is held), both of which, Levinas maintains, lie outside the ethical.

The roles allotted to woman are lover, mother, and widow (probably even in that order). Thus far in Levinas's discussion, woman, as either lover or mother, is excluded from the ethical relation.[20] His descriptions of the erotic and the ethical appear to indicate that the erotic is not included in the ethical. Thus we might arrive at the disturbing conclusion that a wife is not an ethical other to her husband. Irigaray tells us that "this non-definition of the other, when the other is not considered to have anything to do with sexual difference, gives rise to an infinite series of substitutions, an operation which seems to me non-ethical."[21] From this perspective, her claim that Levinas failed to take into account sexual difference when thinking the Other appears correct. If she is correct in her claim that the Other cannot be thought other than in terms of sexual difference, then Levinas, by failing to think woman as Other, has subsumed her into the Same. But the problematic account of the feminine and its relation to the ethical arises precisely because Levinas does take account of sexual difference. By assuming the position of the 'I' and assigning the feminine the role of the beloved, he accords a place to woman—though this place is one of the traditional roles allotted to her as lover and mother.

Irigaray's criticisms of Levinas's discussion are still more complicated. To criticize Levinas's conception of love, it may not be enough to say that he simply gives priority to the erotic relation that ends in fecundity. Recalling how Levinas set up the ethical relation, that which is not a return to the same, illuminates why he describes the erotic and the ethical in different terms. The love relationship risks this return, which is rendered incomplete by the birth of a child—a son. We may question Levinas's description at three points: (1) the structure of the ethical relation itself, as that which is projected toward the infinite; (2) his claim that the love relationship is a return to the same; (3) his claim that the birth of a child is the only way to render this return incomplete. In "The Fecundity of the Caress," Irigaray does not attack Levinas on any of these three points, though she does approach these problems in her later essay "Questions to Emmanuel Levinas." The earlier essay brings to light criticisms that are more helpful if read along with the criticisms in her later attention to Levinas.

Irigaray's primary objection is that Levinas is not aware that his analysis could be written only from the standpoint of a man. She is correct that his description assumes a masculine standpoint. However, not only is Levinas well aware of this fact,[22] but his project depends on it.[23] Moreover, it is not just the sex of the ethical other which is at stake, but also the sexual identity of the subject. It is no accident that Levinas, who is male, constructs the absolute other in terms of the feminine. As we will see later, he does not overlook heterogeneity; rather, it is a fundamental part of his argument. Irigaray's questions on this point are salient and ought to be acknowledged. She asks,

> Who is the other, the Other [*l'autre, autrui*] etc.? How can the other be defined? Levinas speaks of "the Other" [*autrui*], of "respect for the Other" [*respect d'autrui*], of the "face of the Other" [*visage d'autrui*] etc. But how to define this Other which seems so self-evident to him, and which I see as a postulate, the projection or the remnant of a system, a hermeneutic locus of crystallization of meaning, etc. . . . ? Who is the other, if sexual difference is not recognized or known? Does it not mean in that case a sort of mask or lure? Or an effect of the consumption of an other [*Autre*]? . . . Furthermore, this non-definition of the other, when the other is not considered to have anything to do with sexual difference, gives rise to an infinite series of substitutions, an operation which seems to me non-ethical.[24]

Rather than criticize Levinas for simply casting voluptuosity in a pejorative light, Irigaray attacks the very structure of the erotic relation as Levinas conceives it. She criticizes his project on the grounds that, according to his account, the erotic relation cannot provide the means for transcendence. She also questions the way in which he posits the child as that which enables the erotic relationship to transcend a return to the same. Irigaray is right insofar as she conceives the erotic relationship differently. Her criticisms, furthermore, reveal the limitations of Levinas's project—namely, that it excludes other characterizations of eros. Her critique is both complex and compelling. However, her criticisms also reveal two problems with her reading of Levinas: first, she conflates the erotic and the ethical in a manner that, when followed to its conclusion, may not actually be desirable—for her as well as for others; second, her reading reveals her own biased perspective, which neglects to acknowledge the Jewish dimension of Levinas's project.

Before moving forward, let us recall a few key points. First, the feminine serves as the interruption of the ethical, and the erotic, as Levinas conceives it, is outside the ethical relation. So, implicit in Irigaray's claim that the feminine in the erotic relationship can serve the function of the interruption is the possible equation of the ethical with the erotic. Second, the ethical relation is not named in Levinas's early book *Time and the Other*. Because several of Irigaray's comments are directed at *Time and the Other*, we need to take note of this possible confusion on her part.

In response to Levinas's discussion of fecundity, Irigaray questions why the child is necessary. Why can there not be a transcendent relationship between lovers, such that the feminine serves as the interruption? By raising this question, she has in essence asked, "Why is it not the case that the erotic relation can be the ethical relation?" In *Time and the Other*, we see the development of the subject, the move from the hypostasis, the relationship with the feminine, and the introduction of fecundity. As we later see in *Totality and Infinity*, the relationship to the child is the ethical relationship par excellence. Although the discussion of the relationship to the child appears in the last major section of this book, this relationship is what inaugurates, or makes possible, the ethical relation as such. The feminine serves a similar purpose in *Time and the Other* to that of the son in *Totality and Infinity*. As the originary experience of alterity, the feminine introduces radical alterity into the relation.

We can now return to the concerns that I mentioned earlier. First, Irigaray's proposed conflation of the erotic and the ethical requires her to configure the erotic in a way that would be undesirable. The ethical relation, at least as Levinas presents it in *Totality and Infinity*, is asymmetrical. 'I' am wholly obligated to the other without any expectation of obligation in return. In contradistinction to the idealized, or even Pauline, version of love that is characterized as not jealous, erotic love is in fact jealous. Additionally, lovers fully expect their partners to reciprocate. Not only is the expectation of reciprocity absent from Levinas's version of the ethical relation, but reciprocity would undermine his very conception of the ethical. Thus any suggestion that the erotic ought to be included in the ethical violates how

Levinas defines the ethical. Even if an erotic relationship is asymmetrical, in which one gives more than the other, this is not the asymmetry that Levinas assigns to the ethical relation, in which the 'I' gives over to the other while expecting nothing in return. I doubt that lovers would (or should) be satisfied with the asymmetry that he ascribes to the ethical relationship.

Once we acknowledge that the erotic relationship is not asymmetrical, at least not to the same degree as the ethical relation, we can look at the erotic on its own terms. If we recall even our own experiences of erotic love, we might remember how consumed we are with the beloved. And our consumption is a return to the self. We wish to draw the beloved into our lives and hold on tightly to him or her. It is not uncommon for lovers, quite literally, to lock themselves away and close themselves off from the world outside them. Levinas's description of love is not intended to denigrate sexual pleasure. His concern is that the erotic relationship has a natural tendency to seal the lovers into their own world. The child is a necessity because the child is the creation of time, necessary to escape the *il y a* (EE 89–96/DEE 153–165). The child interrupts the couple. The lover and the beloved can no longer direct their attention only to each other. The couple is turned outward, away from themselves and toward the future. We will return to this discussion in more detail in the next chapter.

My second concern is that Irigaray's reading discounts an important influence on Levinas's thought. It is possible that she is correct in claiming that the erotic does not need the child. But then, as discussed above, she runs the risk of conflating the erotic and the ethical. This conflation would be problematic for Levinas, and not simply because he is writing from the position of a male. Rather, Irigaray overlooks that Levinas writes from another "bias" as well; he writes from the position of a Jew—specifically, a Jewish man. Because Levinas is aware of the complicated relationship of his philosophy to his confessional writings, he may be motivated to assume an apparently neutral stance with regard to his Judaism. As a result, he does not acknowledge how profoundly Judaic perspectives influence his project; nor does he defend their role in his argument, since he is both hoping and presuming that Judaism is not the defining feature in his philosophy.[25] To be sure, Judaism is not a monolithic tradition. It is a complex tapestry with multiple traditions in its weave. As a result, Judaism also has a complex relationship to eros, and numerous opinions about it.[26]

JUDAISM ON LOVE

In general, the rabbis held that the primary purpose of sexual relations is to fulfill the commandment to procreate: "Be fruitful and multiply" (Genesis 1:28). However, as biblical scholar David Biale notes, the rabbis also recognized a separate, legitimate realm of sexual pleasure. These laws, called *onah,* guarantee every married woman the right to regular sexual relations, though the frequency depends in part on the husband's occupation. For example . . . sex on the Sabbath [the holiest day of the week] was not only permitted, but, in fact, required of scholars. The laws of *onah,* moreover, pertain regardless of procreation: the woman has the right to sexual satisfaction even if she is pregnant or menopausal, that is, incapable of conceiving. Not only is there a *commandment* to engage in sexual relations independent of procreation, but the purpose of such relations is explicitly to give pleasure.[27]

The commandment to engage in sexual relations and to give sexual satisfaction to one's wife is written into the *ketubah,* the Jewish marriage contract, which is read aloud at its signing—even to this day. Both parties are well aware of what each owes the other. Moreover, the laws of *onah* apply only to women. Men do not have the same claim on their wives for sexual satisfaction that wives have on their husbands. And finally, although it was thought that women were generally less inclined to ask for their sexual satisfaction, it was thought that those women who "do solicit their husbands to perform the marital obligation, will 'have children the like of whom did not exist even in the generation of Moses!'"[28] According to Biale, this comment reflects a positive attitude toward those women who take the sexual initiative.

Rabbinic commentaries that influence Judaism's view of sexuality are multifarious and run the gamut from the extreme, even shockingly, positive to the extreme, and not surprisingly, negative view of the body and of women. For example, Maimonides, writing in the twelfth and thirteenth centuries, was largely influenced by Aristotle. This meant, on the one hand, that Maimonides was hoping to accommodate the claims of religion and reason. On the other hand, it also meant that "he recoiled from the sense of touch in particular, even though he was prepared to allow some pleasure from the other, less material senses."[29] According to Maimonides, marriage, or being confined to one sexual partner, accomplished the goal of ultimately dulling sexual desire. In Maimonides's view, this goal is precisely what the (Jewish) law seeks to achieve.[30] In contrast, Rabad, a strident opponent of Maimonides, "restored the commandment of *onah* as equally legitimate."[31] He could be considered one of the earliest champions of a woman's sexual pleasure and her "right" to that pleasure. In his treatise on marriage he outlines in great detail how these laws fit into marriage: "With regard to *onah,* Rabad advances two views at once: the man owes his wife not only the *minimum* that is required by law but as much as she desires. . . . But if women are allowed as much sexual activity as they wish, the opposite is true for men. . . . If a man [engages in sexual activity] for his own desire for pleasure, not only is there no reward but he is close to sin."[32] Although the statements presented above indicate Rabad's positive and permissive attitude toward sexuality, and in particular toward women's sexuality, some elements of his treatise are not altogether charitable about the role of women within the marital relationship.

It is likely that Judaism's attitudes toward women and sexuality, and, most of all, its attitude toward the commandment to procreate, inform Levinas's thinking. His view of sexuality demonstrates Judaism's own ambivalence toward sexual pleasure and the commandment to procreate, which was issued directly from God.[33] In fact, one rabbinic text seems to indicate that it is precisely God's intervention "that can turn the purely hedonistic act to the holy purpose of reproduction."[34] The offspring alluded to here may be an actual child, and it may also be a metaphor for Israel—that is, the continuation of the Jewish people.[35]

Philo, an ancient Greek-Jewish philosopher influenced by Plato, makes a similar point in his reading of creation. Although Philo also sees the separation of the creature in the Genesis story into two beings as necessary for a relationship, he maintains that the two are subsequently drawn back to each other. Adam solicits Eve, and Eve responds by approaching him. In Philo's words,

> seeing no living thing more like herself than he, she is filled with glee and shamefastly returns his greeting. Love supervenes, brings together and fits into one the divided halves, as it were, of a single living creature, and sets up in each of them a desire for fellowship with the other with a view to the production of their like.[36]

Eros, for Philo, strikes a delicate balance between the desire for the other and the need to procreate. He thus identifies exactly what Levinas sees in the relation of love. Sexual difference motivates alterity and allows for a relationship, but the erotic relationship draws the two back into one; it is the birth of the child that interrupts the closed existence of the couple.

THE ETHICS OF SEXUAL DIFFERENCE

Irigaray calls attention to Levinas's depiction of the woman in the erotic relationship as "the beloved," which she interprets along the lines of the sexual act. With regard to the radical alterity of the feminine, and the role that the feminine plays in the movement of the discussion, no substitution can be made for the feminine—only it can play these roles. This point reveals Levinas's presumption that radical alterity must be feminine. His dependence on the construction of sexual difference for his project is evident in both *Time and the Other* and *Totality and Infinity*. Irigaray's claim that the ethical relation is constructed from a masculine perspective is correct. Unfortunately, although Levinas describes an ethical relation that arises prior to the attribution of sexual difference, the ethical relation, as he characterizes it, is nonetheless marked by sexual difference. His remarks about his own analysis, and Heidegger's, indicate that he realizes the significance of gender and of heterosexuality for his project.[37]

Derrida raises similar questions in "Choreographies," which begins with the general question about the relationship between sexual difference and general ontology, especially with respect to Heidegger's reading of Nietzsche. McDonald asks Derrida, "[I]f the question of sexual difference is not a regional one (in the sense of subsidiary), if indeed 'it may no longer even be a question,' as you suggest, how would you describe 'woman's place'?"[38] Derrida responds to this question with a discussion of the relationship between sexual difference and the gift. At the heart of this discussion lies the question about the primacy of sexual difference. Derrida wonders if sexual difference "does not remain derived from and subordinated to either the question of destination or the thought of the gift."[39] Derrida further wonders about the primacy of thinking "difference" before sexual difference.[40]

Derrida clarifies how Levinas sees the secondariness of woman. The secondariness of woman is not that she is second in relation to man. Rather, he sees sexual difference as secondary in relationship to humanity. That is, humanity is marked first, and only then does sexual difference emerge. The significance of this distinction can be understood in light of the role that alterity plays in *Time and the Other*. By making the claim that sexual difference emerges only after the ethical relation, only after the responsibility that one has to the other, he implies that ethics marks the relationship of same to other prior to the assignment of sexual characteristics. Derrida's point with regard to the relationship of sexual difference to humanity, a paraphrase of Levinas's own position, may initially allow Levinas's ethics to escape the charges against it. Derrida then claims that by assuming such a position Levinas presupposes male neutrality and male privilege in the realm of the human. What looks like neutrality is really male privilege masquerading as neutrality. And, as we saw previously, Levinas's claim that sexual difference is derived from humanity does not hold true.

We find a similar criticism of Levinas's philosophical project in Derrida's essay "At This Very Moment in This Work Here I Am." Although this essay is devoted primarily to a discussion of *Otherwise Than Being*, Derrida briefly comments on the problem of sexual difference in *Totality and Infinity*. In Derrida's view, the assignment of sexual difference apparent in Levinas's book is striking. Derrida asks, with regard to fecundity and the birth of a son, in particular, "Why should a 'son' better represent, in advance, this indifference? This unmarked difference?"[41] Essentially, Derrida is asking, Why can the future not be a daughter?[42] By organizing the discussion as he has, Levinas has assumed the structure of sexual difference. The future cannot be a daughter because the author writing the descriptions is a man.[43] In his response, Derrida notes parenthetically a comment cited in a footnote to "Violence and Metaphysics," his essay on *Totality and Infinity:* "Let us observe in passing that *Totality and Infinity* pushes the respect for dissymmetry to the point where it seems to us impossible, essentially impossible, that it could have been written by a woman. The philosophical subject of it is man."[44] Stating the views of sexual difference similar to those that he expressed in "Choreographies," Derrida, here, asserts that Levinas assumes the stance of the male subject without fully acknowledging this position. That Levinas subordinates an alterity marked by sexual difference furthermore indicates that he thinks of himself as presenting a neutral Other, one not marked by sexual difference. As we discussed in the previous chapter, Levinas claims that he subordinates sexual difference, and not woman, to alterity. But, Derrida argues, in light of the stance that Levinas takes as author, the other is marked by sexual difference and then disguised as a neutral other. The wholly other, who is not supposed to be marked by sexual difference, is found already to be marked by masculinity.[45]

The question of sexual difference remains unresolved in Levinas's project, especially in light of his subordination of ontology to ethics. Even if the question of sexual difference were not subsumed under the domain of general ontology, in Levinas's discussion sexual difference would appear to be subordinated to the ethical, to the nudity of the face. Moreover, as Derrida points out, Levinas appears caught between two options, neither of which is attractive: either he assumes sexual difference with a priority of one sex to the other, or he assumes masculine neutrality, which is, in fact, nonneutrality.[46]

In spite of Irigaray's and Derrida's concerns, and in spite of Levinas's claims to the contrary, sexual difference plays a fundamental role in the establishment of the ethical in Levinas's project. Although Levinas would like to subordinate sexual difference to the ethical, such that the ethical is not contingent on sexual difference, he nonetheless acknowledges the significance of sexual difference in his ethics, so much so that he criticizes Heidegger for his neutered description of *Dasein.* Does this criticism imply that by Levinas's own account we are not to think of the 'I,' the subject, as neutral, but rather as sexed? As noted in chapter 3 of this book, Simone de Beauvoir pointed out, in a footnote cited in her introduction to *The Second*

Sex, that when Levinas says that woman is a mystery, the implication is that woman is a mystery *for man.* Thus, the sex of the author has a direct bearing on the construction of the philosophy.

Derrida's worry that sexual difference may mark Levinas's ethics is not to be taken lightly. And, in fact, Derrida's concern motivates us to examine further Levinas's project. Doing so will help to reveal exactly what Levinas's ethics entails, what role woman plays, and why Levinas is not troubled by the description that he does provide. Our investigation will help us decide if his ethics, in spite of his claims to the contrary, is marked by sexual difference. Examining both the philosophical and rabbinic influences on Levinas's philosophy will provide us with a distinctive path into his project and offer us an opportunity to see the conception of the feminine in a different light.

Levinas's discussion in *Time and the Other* mirrors the biblical story of creation. It thus demonstrates one way in which Jewish sources influenced his philosophical writings. This discussion illuminates the leitmotif of separation and individuation. In particular, Levinas tells us that the "silence before creation" is the inspiration for his conception of the *il y a.* He also uses the biblical story of the creation of woman as the inspiration for the originary experience of alterity. The feminine thus appears as an enigma: Levinas's ethics, while marked by sexual difference, also gives a fundamental role to the feminine. The alterity provided by the face of the feminine sets the rest of the project in motion. The feminine also serves as the interruption of virility. In *Time and the Other,* the feminine shifts the emphasis from autonomy and power to the necessity of relationships and the creation of life. Let us recall that although *Isha* means woman, in the story of Adam and Eve, woman is named "Eve," and the Hebrew for Eve is *Chava*—life. It is woman who both means and creates life.

In *Totality and Infinity,* we see the relationship that the feminine has to the rest of the project. As we saw in *Time and the Other,* we cannot remove the feminine or change its status without penalty to the whole project. In other words, if it is the feminine that motivates the experience with alterity, and thus provides the mechanism for the ethical relation to occur at all, then the feminine can be "removed" only at the risk of unraveling the whole argument. Insofar as it provides the means by which the subject first contracts its existence, the feminine, conceived as radical alterity and as the first experience with alterity itself, cannot be removed. Thus, the feminine is disparaged by its exclusion from the face-to-face relation of the ethical and it seems to play a subservient role to the male. In spite of this appearance, the feminine actually plays such a central role that the argument cannot succeed without it. The feminine is so radically other that it cannot participate in the ethical relation; it can only make the ethical relation possible. By introducing alterity into the analysis, the feminine serves as a transcendental condition, that is, a condition of the possibility of the face-to-face relation. In the form of eros, the feminine helps to accomplish fecundity, and, so, makes possible the means by which asymmetrical intersubjectivity achieves transcendence without returning to itself. The ambiguous place of the feminine—that it is outside, and yet indispensable to, the ethical relation—may be why Levinas does not see its potentially pejorative place.

SIX

Ruth; or, Love and the Ethics of Fecundity

Set me as a seal upon your heart . . .
For love is as fierce as death
—*Shir Hashirim* [*Song of Songs*]

With the birth of each child, the world begins anew.
—The Talmud

Although the criticisms of Levinas's philosophy are well taken, we should acknowledge the dilemma in which he finds himself. He must write from his own point of view, that of a man, lest he be accused of trying to presume to know what love would be for a woman. In this respect, his discussion of love will clearly be lacking. On the one hand, philosophical discussions of women typically depict them (if at all) as vessels for the man's progeny. On the other hand, if women are not depicted at all, we are led to believe that they are entirely unnecessary for producing children. Such a view is illustrated in Hobbes's comment that "men spring up from the ground like mushrooms,"[1] a view that characterizes the "development" of subjectivity in Western philosophy. In spite of the possible shortcomings of his discussion, might we not commend Levinas for recognizing the significant role that women play in the birth of a child, and for attaching that role to a concrete, intimate relationship with another human? After all, he neither describes women in terms of mere utility nor advances a view of fecundity that neglects the mother. In other words, his view of love is importantly different from the standard story that we find in the history of Western philosophy. Let us turn to the development of this view.

BUBER'S SYMMETRY IN *I AND THOU*

In *I and Thou*, Martin Buber attempts to ground intersubjective relations in communication. He explains the two ways in which humans approach existence: in either an I–It or an I–Thou relation.[2] He maintains that the difference between these two approaches does not depend on the object of the relation, for the object of both relations is the same. Rather, the difference lies in the relation itself. The I–Thou relationship is predicated on openness, directness, mutuality, and presence. According to Buber, there are three possible spheres in which to encounter the I–Thou: (1) in our life with nature, such as with trees, animals, and so on; (2) in our life with humanity, such as with men and women; and (3) in our life with spiritual beings (namely, God).[3]

Buber's point is that the object within the I–Thou relation is not a Thou before I encounter it. It is the way in which I encounter it that makes the object a Thou for me. If I encounter a tree in its uniqueness as a tree, not as something to be used for firewood, and not in comparison to other trees, I may be said to have entered into an I–Thou relationship with it.[4] The same applies to an individual person. Although we may say that, by definition, a person is a 'person' by virtue of language, before I encounter her, it is the way in which I encounter her that makes her a 'Thou' for me. For this relationship to occur, I must see her, as in the example of the tree, as unique; I must be willing to respond with my whole being, and she must approach me willingly. In addition, I cannot will such a relationship to occur since, for Buber, the relationship must be mutual. I can only desire, relentlessly, that we encounter each other as Thou, that the other encounter me as I encounter her. Buber's view can be contrasted with Sartre's.[5]

According to Sartre, love is the desire to possess the other. More specifically, I recognize the freedom of the other only as a freedom that I wish to possess and dominate. In contrast to this view, Buber describes love in terms of the recognition of the other's freedom. His discussion reveals how limited Sartre's view of intersubjectivity is. Sartre maintains a view of human relations that keeps us enclosed in an I–It, without much possibility of becoming an I–Thou. For Buber, dialogue is not a dimension of the self; rather, it is part of the fundamental reality by which the self becomes a self, an authentic self. Finally, according to Buber, the intersubjective relationship is precisely that, *inter*subjective. It emphasizes mutuality. The relation does not give priority to either the subject or the other. Rather, the I–Thou relation is a relation that is found in the between.

It is with regard to this last point, viz. Buber's emphasis on mutuality and reciprocity, that Levinas diverges from Buber.[6] Levinas agrees with Buber—insofar as Buber focuses not only on the intersubjective relationship, but on the notion of communication with another as constitutive to the formation of the self. But Levinas takes issue with the mutuality of Buber's I–Thou, which, in Levinas's terms, leads to an economics rather than an ethics. In Levinas's view, mutuality leads to exchange, rather than ethical obligation. Additionally, Levinas sees a failure of Buber's ethics, since it does not begin with the other. Does the ethical not begin precisely when the I perceives the Thou as higher than it?[7] If Buber is going to insist on the reciprocity of the I–Thou relation, the question of the strictly ethical meaning of responsibility will remain problematic within Buber's framework. In Levinas's account, ethics entails an asymmetrical relation. For him, the I–Thou relation amounts to not much more than a spiritual relation, a friendship; it is not an ethical relation. Levinas does not think that Buber's I–Thou relation is wrongheaded as much as he thinks that it does not accomplish what Buber claims for it. In fact, the I–Thou relation described by Buber resembles the erotic relation that we find in Levinas's discussion of love (of course, we should bear in mind that in Levinas's analysis the erotic relation is outside the ethical relation). In his view, Buber's symmetrical relation is not sufficiently radical. According to Levinas, the ethical cannot be conceived as symmetry or one risks conceiving the relationship in terms of "I do for you and you do for me." The asymmetry of the ethical relation means that I can speak only of my responsibility for the other. We find a more direct influence on Levinas in Franz Rosenzweig's work.

THE INFLUENCE OF
ROSENZWEIG ON LEVINAS

Levinas tells us in the preface to *Totality and Infinity* that he was "struck by the opposition to the idea of totality in *The Star of Redemption* by Franz Rosenzweig, which is too often present in this book to be cited" (TI 28/TeI xvi). Levinas is indebted to Rosenzweig for his critique of totality, which is fundamental to Levinas's project.[8] As we saw in our discussion of *Time and the Other,* it is the shattering of totality—that is, the possibility of plurality—that opens up the possibility of the ethical relation. In addition to "the idea of totality," there are several other themes in Rosenzweig's philosophy that Levinas found useful.[9] First, Rosenzweig's insight into the interruption of totality provides Levinas with the grounds to claim that each individual is a unique and infinite end.

Second, Levinas sees in Rosenzweig's philosophy a reconception of the notion of the religious as non-sectarian and non-confessional. Levinas repeats Rosenzweig's statement that "the good Lord did not create religion, he created the world" (BTW 186/EDM 260). In some of his later writings, Levinas equates religion with ethics. That is, he tells us that what he means by religion is in fact ethics. And for Levinas, religion means Judaism. Thus, for Levinas, Judaism is not a religion that just happens to be concerned with morality: it is a religion whose practice is synonymous with the ethical, that is, with concern for the other person.

Third, Rosenzweig sees love as a commandment. As such, he treats love as a theme found explicitly within the Jewish tradition. Love calls me to responsibility, rather than being my release from responsibility. Moreover, it is only in love that one can be redeemed. Levinas takes up the theme that we find in Rosenzweig's *Star,* that it is in love and through marriage that the husband (i.e., the man) is able to do good works.[10] The father's responsibilities to lead the son to the marriage canopy and to good works can be seen as one continuous responsibility to enable the son to redeem himself. For Rosenzweig, love is one way in which a man realizes that he is not completely autonomous. It is in love that a man realizes his dependence and vulnerability—or, to put it simply, his humanness. However, it is also in love that we try to defy time by attempting to make ourselves eternal. This attempt arrives in the form of children. We find the themes of love and fecundity again in Levinas's analyses, in particular in *Totality and Infinity,* where the dwelling provides the condition for the interruption by the ethical—that is, makes the ethical possible.

Levinas not only affirms but also appropriates Rosenzweig's view that the Jewish people are outside history. By situating themselves in such a position, the Jews reject history as the story told by the "winners." By occupying such a place, they are better able to recognize the suffering of other "losers" and thus share the belief "that world history is not just."[11] It is the suspension of world history, of time, of deliberation, and so on, that makes ethics possible.[12]

And finally, Rosenzweig, like Levinas, and contra Buber, emphasizes the asymmetry of the interpersonal relationship, which describes Levinas's account of the ethical relation. According to Levinas, in fact, this asymmetry is the distinguishing feature of the ethical relation, as it is a relation that begins with the other, to whom I am wholly obligated and from whom I cannot claim anything.[13] As mentioned previously, this obligation to the other is an essential feature of Levinas's reconception of subjectivity. Accounts of subjectivity as developed in the modern period focused on the freedom and autonomy of the individual. Ethics was then seen as an outgrowth of one's ability to deliberate and choose for oneself. According to Levinas, ethics is that which defines subjectivity. It is obligation to the other, not one's individual freedom, that defines the subject. By reconceiving this view of subjectivity, Levinas also reconceives the notion of the other, transforming it into something positive. The other is privileged.

"FOR LOVE IS AS STRONG AS DEATH": ROSENZWEIG ON LOVE

One of Irigaray's central criticisms of Levinas's phenomenology of eros is her claim that his beloved is always the woman.[14] Levinas often refers to the beloved with a masculine pronoun. One might at first assume carelessness in his writing. But another look might suggest otherwise. Levinas's account of love is remarkably similar not only to the Song of Songs, but to Rosenzweig's discussion of this poem in *The Star of Redemption*.[15] In the Song of Songs, which is often hailed as a feminist text, the two speakers, a man and a woman, take turns expressing their love.[16] At one point, the woman says, "I am my beloved's and his desire is toward me." The beloved in the Song of Songs frequently drifts from a male to a female voice. Rosenzweig's appropriation of the Song of Songs takes note of this shift in voice, as demonstrated by his own depiction of the roles of lover and beloved. The movement of lover and beloved is significant for Rosenzweig's description of love, which identifies the role of the lover as giver and that of the beloved as receiver, regardless of sex (or gender). Another way to characterize this point would be to say that the beloved is called, or elected, while the lover is active. The logic here is less a logic of sexes than a logic of positions.[17]

For Rosenzweig, and Levinas follows his lead, the lover is significant because it is the lover who initiates the relation. The lover approaches the beloved without knowing if the beloved will return her love. In this role, the lover makes the larger sacrifice. The lover gives herself over to the beloved, and the beloved is loved unconditionally. By accepting the gift of love, the beloved gives a gift in return. The reason for giving priority to the lover over the beloved lies in the assumptions made about each. Rosenzweig assumes that the one who is the lover becomes the lover because he or she has recognized his or her own insufficiency in his or her solitude. Thus, the lover approaches the beloved. But the beloved, precisely by being the beloved, does not think of himself or herself in terms of a complacent self-sufficiency that is interrupted by the love given to him or her. The beloved, by definition, admits this lack and returns the love. However, the beloved speaks only because he or she is now being loved. It is returned with the knowledge and expectation of the original love. The love returned to the original lover is not unconditional. But, admittedly, these roles are fluid. As in most erotic relations, lover and beloved exchange positions. At different moments each says to the other "Love me!" In contrast to Kant, both Rosenzweig and Levinas claim not only that love can be commanded, but also that only love can command love.

This love is not to be confused with the Christian *agapē* or the Greek *philein*. Nor is it to be subsumed under social relations. Love, as Levinas describes it in "Phenomenology of Eros," is not the purified love of Beatrice: she is initially the object of Dante's carnal affection, but her guidance allows Dante to "overcome" this affection in exchange for something "purer."[18] Nor is it a description of love that we would find in a Freudian account, which would argue that since we are narcissists at heart, sexuality is merely a seeking of our own pleasure. For both Levinas and Rosenzweig, love is an event that begins with the other. The ambiguity of love arises because the erotic conceals the face of the Other. Levinas separates these two relationships for the purpose of description. He insists that the ethical hides behind the erotic. The movement of the lover and the beloved suggests that each can occupy the place of the other. As such, transcendence is possible for both to achieve. But this transcendence does not discount the very real, very carnal act of love.[19] As Edith Wyschogrod writes, "Sexuality, neither pleasure nor power, founds the multiplicity of human existence."[20]

According to Rosenzweig, in a claim that Levinas appropriates, love lives in the present. This point is related to Rosenzweig's belief that love is also revelation, which for Rosenzweig means the present.[21] Love sees its own urgency. For Rosenzweig, this urgency and immediacy are represented in the command cited above: "Love me!" We do not ask to be loved in the future; we want to be loved now. Love as an event is something that we desire in the present.

Yet in spite of its existence in the present, love, or rather the couple, wants to declare itself; it wants to be eternal. Although they exist in the moment of the pleasure of each other, the lovers also yearn for a love that is eternal. This eternity no longer grows in just the I and thou of the couple, but longs to be founded in the presence of the world.[22] As Rosenzweig reminds us, the beloved "pleads with her lover to descend to her so that she might set herself like an eternal seal upon his ever-beating heart." He continues, "[M]atrimony is not [merely] love. Matrimony is infinitely more than love. Matrimony is the external fulfillment which love reaches out after from her internal blissfulness in a stupor of unquenchable longing."[23] But it is precisely because of this lack of a sense of eternity that love longs for a way to make itself eternal, to live not only in this moment, but beyond this moment.[24] Love as that which exceeds the moment is the eternal victory over death. One way in which this victory is achieved is through fecundity.[25] Finally, Rosenzweig offers us another example of the relationship of marriage to the ethical. I quote him at length:

> It is significant that at a boy's birth the father prays that it may be vouchsafed [for] him to bring up his son to the Torah, to the bridal canopy, and to good works. To learn the Torah and to keep the commandments is the omnipresent basis of Jewish life. Marriage brings with it the full realization of this life, for only then do the "good works" become possible. Only the man needs to be aware that the Torah is the basis of life. When a daughter is born, the father simply prays that he may lead her to the bridal canopy and to good works. For a woman has this basis of Jewish life for her own without having to learn it deliberately over and over, as the man who is less securely rooted in the depths of nature is compelled to do.[26]

The above quotation raises two issues. The first draws attention to the relationship of marriage to "good works," and the second notes the "natural" connection that women have to the ethical. Clearly, there are dangers in stating that women are naturally "closer" to the ethical. Women in the United States were denied the right to vote because they were thought to be too clean to be "dirtied" by politics. Later, women received the right to vote for the inverse reason: it was thought that their "natural" morality would clean politics. I will return to this latter issue in the final chapters. For now, it is worth noting the similarity between Rosenzweig's view in the passage above and his general view on love. In his view, men appear to need to do the most work! They need to realize that they are not the autonomous, self-sufficient beings they are led to believe they are. And unlike women, men need to read the Torah in order to become closer to the ethical. I am less interested here in disputing Rosenzweig's claim than in examining Levinas's conception of the feminine and, in particular, eros in light of Rozenweig's claims.

THE ETHICS OF FECUNDITY

Levinas's conception of love has sparked some of the most contentious discussions about his project. Several commentators believe that he is presumptuous in speaking for women in the erotic experience. But what many commentators find most problematic is the link that he forges between eros and fecundity. Whatever might have been redeemed in his discussion of the erotic relationship is lost if the erotic appears as merely a stepping stone to the birth of the child. Moreover, he regards this event as ethically significant only for the man.

Although Levinas does focus on the end that erotic love may bring about, he also draws our attention to his own, and to Judaism's, appreciation of the significance of the erotic relation in and of itself.[27] Thus, we should consider his discussion of love not only within the context of *Totality and Infinity,* but also outside it. Situating his description of eros within Rosenzweig's discussion of love altered how we understood Levinas's account of the erotic relation. Rosenzweig's account of love, inspired by the Song of Songs, also reminded us of the influence of Judaism in Levinas's project.[28]

In "Judaism and the Feminine," Levinas recounts a rabbinic commentary on love and conjugal relations:

> [M]aternity is subordinate to a human destiny which exceeds the limits of "family joys": it is necessary to fulfil Israel, "to multiply the image of God" inscribed on the face of humanity. Not that conjugal love has no importance in itself, or that it is reduced to the ranks of a means of procreation, or that it merely *prefigures* its fulfillment, as in a certain theology. On the contrary the

ultimate end of the family is the actual *meaning* and the joy of this present. It is not only prefigured there, it is already fulfilled there. This participation of the present in this future takes place specifically in the feeling of love, in the grace of the betrothed, and even in the erotic. The real dynamism of love leads it beyond the present instant and even beyond the person loved. This end does not appear to a vision outside the love, which would then integrate it into the place of creation; it lies in the love itself. (JF 37/JeF 59)

This passage adds a dimension to Irigaray's discussion that is otherwise absent. There are two issues at stake here: (1) the significance of sexual relations in themselves; and (2) assuming an end to those sexual relations, it is not clear if the birth refers only to the birth of a child or if it is also a referent for something more metaphorical. Certainly, Levinas's discussion of love gives priority to the erotic relation that produces a child over the erotic relation that seeks pleasure in itself. Yet, Levinas also makes explicit his view that conjugal relations are important in and of themselves. This marked disparity in his views encourages us to investigate and reconcile these two apparently opposing positions. His remarks in both *Totality and Infinity* and "Judaism and the Feminine" indicate that he affirms the value of the erotic relation independently of the birth of the son. His intention here is not to say that love must be redeemed or "saved" by the birth of a child. Rather, following Rosenzweig, he believes that love cannot help but exceed itself. The birth of the child is not linked simply to sexual intercourse. Rather, the birth of the child represents the couple's desire to make their love eternal. It symbolizes love's transformation from its focus on the present to its projection toward the future. Again, Levinas is careful not to link these events simply to biology.

Given Levinas's own use of the word "conjugal," one can presume that he is referring to marriage; given his attention to fecundity, the concern that he focuses on a specifically heterosexual framework would appear to be confirmed. However, I wish to reexamine the erotic relation with an eye toward acknowledging three issues that, for Levinas, are implicated in each other: (1) the role of pleasure in the relationship; (2) the attention paid to the presence of a woman in the discussion of fecundity; and (3) the meaning of fecundity in this context.

It is clear that Levinas emphasizes the fecundity of the event in "Phenomenology of Love." But it is important to distinguish between the priority that Levinas gives to the erotic relationship that ends in fecundity, and the view that his analysis is blind to an erotic relationship that is its own end. For Levinas, there is no question, at least in his analysis in *Totality and Infinity*, that voluptuosity is granted a certain priority if it produces a child. Thus, we must attempt to reconcile his discussion in *Totality and Infinity* and his remarks in "Judaism and the Feminine."

As cited earlier, "[L]ove [which] becomes its own end, where it remains without any 'intentionality' that spreads beyond it, a world of voluptuousness or a world of charm and grace, one which can coexist with a religious civilization, is foreign to Judaism" (JF 36–37/JeF 60). This point need not imply that women be pregnant and confined to the home; nor need it imply that Judaism has a prudish attitude toward sexuality. Rather, Levinas maintains that this view of love reflects the belief in "the permanent opening up of the messianic perspective—of the immanence of Israel, of humanity reflecting the image of God that can carry on its face" (JF 37/JeF 60). The birth of the child becomes a metaphor for messianism.

According to Levinas, love desires the other such that the relation becomes a return to the same. This return is, in part, what distinguishes the erotic relation from the ethical. By adding the dimension of fecundity to the erotic relation, Levinas characterizes love as something that could aim at the future, which is beyond itself. Fecundity, then, transforms the love relationship into an ethical relationship: voluptuosity is completed when it aims toward the future and issues in the birth of a child, a son. If we recall the discussion of love found in Rosenzweig's *Star,* the couple's love exists in the present. The couple's desire to be permanent directs it toward the future—hence, the child. Levinas needs a discussion of the child, since the child represents the future. This need motivates his discussion of fecundity, since the child is the third that prevents a return to the same. The lovers run the risk of being caught in a closed circle—a twosome—that allows them to neglect the world around them. Certainly, one can see the merit of Levinas's description of love. New lovers often, quite literally, close themselves off to the world. The birth of a child permanently disrupts that closed society of two. Thus, fecundity has priority not because sex is "dirty" or because sexual pleasure in and of itself ought to be forbidden. Rather, the child is the interruption of the erotic.

Thus, it is not that the discussion of eros must be accompanied by fecundity. Rather, Levinas realizes that the discussion of fecundity needs the account of eros. The two are necessarily linked. That Levinas links eros and fecundity does not necessarily indicate that he thinks that every sexual act *ought* to, or even is intended to, end in pregnancy or the birth of a child. Factually, fecundity requires sexuality, but sexuality does not require fecundity. In terms of his analysis of eros, however, Levinas does give priority to sexual activity that ends in fecundity. But he also allows for sexuality that intends pleasure for its own sake.

Clearly, the role of fecundity in Levinas's project should not be taken lightly, for it suggests the oppressive image of barefoot and pregnant women. There is, then, the danger that his conception of sexuality implies a sexuality that is "dirty" unless redeemed by its attachment to procreation.

It would help us to remember that the title of the section that precedes Levinas's discussion of fecundity is the *"Phenomenology* of Eros" (emphasis added). Levinas is describing, not prescribing, the erotic relation.

We can see in Levinas, as in Rosenzweig, that the commandment to multiply is similar to the Kabbalistic conception of *tikkun olam,* to repair the world. Levinas is not a Kabbalist, and, no doubt, he would prefer that we think of fecundity the "old-fashioned" way. However, it is possible to broaden this conception of "birth" and "child," if that extension still maintains the integrity of that which brings us out of ourselves. In any event, Levinas would acknowledge that although it is not possible for us to perfect the world within our own individual lifetimes, we have a responsibility nonetheless to make every attempt to respond in accordance with the ethical *mitzvot* of the Torah. In this case, that might mean to repair the world: to feed the children, take care of our elderly, house the homeless, and clothe the naked—in short, to respond to the call of the stranger, the widow, the poor, and the orphan.[29] We are obliged to follow these *mitzvot* in order to make "messianic triumph" truly possible (TI 285/TeI 261). We can ensure the continuation of *tikkun olam* not only by having children but also by rearing them to be responsible. Thus, we see the convergence of themes from *Totality and Infinity* and *Otherwise than Being:* the father-son relationship is the ethical relation par excellence, and I am responsible for the other to the point of being responsible for the other's responsibility. We can see this point most clearly in the relationship and responsibility that a parent has to his or her child.

Levinas's emphasis on fecundity underscores the importance of asymmetrical responsibility that is characteristically unique to the parent/child relation. The movement of the discussions, which are contained in the section entitled "Beyond the Face," parallels the movement in *The Star of Redemption.* Love brings us out of ourselves through the desire that cannot be fulfilled but that longs for eternity. According to Levinas, Rosenzweig, and Judaism, the birth of the son represents this eternity. Aside from the parent's responsibility to the child, the child is her teacher. Insofar as the child is unique, the child teaches the parent, instructs her to be attentive to the child's own growth. It is the parent's responsibility to help the child become attuned to others. And so our hope that our children will be responsible to others opens onto the hope that others will be responsible for other others.[30] This movement from love to fecundity opens finally into fraternity and community. Thus, the first moment of the ethical relation is found within this familial relation. Through my child, I am able to be responsible for the other, even after my own death. In Levinas's discussion, procreation is not about self-redemption. Procreation takes me out of myself and allows me to transcend by virtue of the ethical responsibility that attaches to it.

By realizing the disjunction between sexuality and fecundity, we open up the relation in a variety of ways. Sexuality is now an expression of love, a seeking to give pleasure to another person, and a means by which we open ourselves to the world. To disjoin fecundity from sexuality in its "moral" character is to recognize that sex does not need to be purified by children and that fecundity happens in a multitude of ways. Parents adopt children, teachers teach students, and volunteers transform others by working in and on the world. To realize that it is not sex that Levinas is trying to purify through procreation is also to realize that his framework is not contingent on heterosexuality, even if he intended it to be. The child's interruption of the lovers does not have to be biological—if it were, there would be serious problems, even for heterosexual couples. And yet, the metaphor of the parent-child relationship is effective only because it derives from the original biological reality of childbearing.

We can now briefly address Irigaray's concerns, as examined in the preceding chapter. The caress, for Levinas, does not mean an unconsummated love. Nor does it require that a consummated love always intends to culminate in the birth of a child. I suggest that we understand Levinas as offering a picture of fecundity that includes an erotic relation. He does not say that physical touch does not occur, nor does he say that it should be absent. His point is that eros in some ways actually eludes and also extends beyond the physical touch. In this sense, the caress becomes an anticipation of the future, of the father's relationship to the child. Although the child is like the father, the child is more than the father. As we saw in chapter 4, the child cannot be reduced to the father's own ego or identity. Just as the beloved eludes some aspect of "being known," so, too, the child eludes that same attempt at totalization. Irigaray correctly observes that Levinas writes from the standpoint of a man. But her observation does not go far enough. He is not writing simply as a man; he is writing as a Jewish man. Irigaray's criticisms indicate that she failed to take into account this larger context. Levinas's comments are easily misinterpreted because he fails to acknowledge adequately in his philosophical project his reliance upon this perspective.

When we examine Levinas's comments about love and sexuality with this expanded perspective in mind, they raise further questions regarding the meaning of fecundity. There is a sense in which Levinas sees the birth of each child as the birth of another member of Israel. He characterizes the birth of a child as that which signifies a projection toward the future in terms of messianism—that is, Israel. It signifies fulfilling a commandment that is older than history itself. Thus, we arrive at the religio-ethical significance of fecundity. And one cannot help but wonder what happens to Levinas's project if this point is excised from it.

We see this union of messianism and the birth of the child in the narrative of the Book of Ruth, which provides the background for the lineage of King David. We also see in the character of Ruth the means by which the description of the feminine in Levinas's analysis is both confirmed and disrupted—we might say that the disruption emerges precisely because the feminine fulfills its function so effectively.

DWELLING IN THE HOUSE OF RUTH[31]

The Book of Ruth, a touching story about a relationship between two women, Ruth and Naomi, opens a space for the questions raised thus far to be explored. The narrative of this story reveals the lack in Levinas's analysis—namely, that his project does not provide a space for a relationship between women. On this point, Irigaray may be correct. But if we keep in mind the view of women in Rosenzweig's discussion, we could offer the following explanation. Levinas's account does not provide a space for a relationship between women, but not because it is "forbidden." Rather, his description of the feminine provides an instructive model for the virile. In *Totality and Infinity*, the feminine provides the means to the ethical: first in the dwelling, in which the feminine is defined as hospitality, gentleness, and welcoming, and second in the discussion of eros, in which Levinas describes love in terms of the not-yet, or the future. In *Totality and Infinity*, he offers a view of love that is distinguished from the ethical yet provides the means to the ethical. Eros leads to the birth of the child.

Levinas constructs the ethical relation such that the feminine is excluded from it. Or is it? The story of Ruth illustrates how woman, as the very figure of hospitality and welcoming, exceeds the limits that have been set for her and thus puts into question the description of the feminine in Levinas's project. Ruth's devotion to Naomi exemplifies the response to the other in the ethical relation that Levinas describes. Ruth's actions illustrate how the feminine exceeds the boundaries that typically define her. Her actions are precisely ethical, as Levinas defines it. Thus, the role of the feminine, and of women, in the ethical relationship can be questioned. Ruth's character unites Levinas's two primary moments in the definition of the feminine: the feminine that is the condition for the possibility of the ethical (dwelling and eros) and the feminine that defines the relation (maternity). Thus, Ruth's character provides a lens through which we can view the very change in the feminine in Levinas's writings—the feminine, defined by hospitality, can no longer be excluded from the ethical relation; it must be the very paradigm of that relation.

The Book of Ruth opens by telling us that it is the time of the judgment of the judges. There is a great famine in Bethlehem in Judah and a man named Elimelech, fearing that his family will starve, takes his wife, Naomi, and their two sons, Mahlon and Kilion, to Moab. After some time, Elimelech dies, leaving Naomi widowed. Later, Naomi's sons marry Moabite princesses: Orpah and Ruth. That Elimelech took his family to Moab and that his sons married Moabite princesses are significant events: Scripture tells the Jews that "an Ammonite and a Moabite may not join the congregation—or the assembly—of God."[32] The commandment stems from a previous time in history when both of these nations were inhospitable to fugitive Jews living in the desert. Living in Moab does not promise to be easy. After ten years there, Naomi's sons die, leaving their wives—Naomi's daughters-in-law—widowed as well. Some time later Naomi hears that the Lord has come to the aid of the Jewish people by providing them with food. A stranger in Moab, Naomi is uncomfortable living there alone with no blood ties to the country. So she, with her daughters-in-law, prepares to go back to Judah. A short time into their journey, Naomi turns to her daughters-in-law and tells them to return to their home in Moab, where they may be more likely to find husbands. Each refuses, though Orpah eventually yields and returns home. Ruth, however, in her stubbornness and her loyalty to Naomi, refuses to go back. In her famous proclamation, she tells Naomi, "Where you go I will go, and where you stay I will stay. Your people will be my people, and your God my God. Where you die, I will die, and there I will be buried. May the Lord deal with me, be it ever so severely, if anything but death separates you and me."[33] Ruth continues on to Judah with Naomi and takes it upon herself to glean in the fields in order to feed both herself and Naomi. Boaz sees Ruth gleaning in the field and asks the foreman who she is. The foreman describes Ruth to Boaz as someone who "worked steadily from morning till now, except for a short rest in the shelter."[34] Boaz tells Ruth that she must glean in no other field; he will take care of her and see that she drinks when she is thirsty and that none of his servants bother her. "Why," Ruth asks him, "have I found such favor in your eyes that you notice me—a foreigner?"[35] Boaz answers, "I've been told all about what you have done for your mother-in-law since the death of your husband—how you left your father and mother and your homeland and came to live with a people you did not know before."[36] Later, at Naomi's urging, Ruth approaches Boaz when he is sleeping, and they "lie" together.[37] Ruth marries Boaz and gives birth to Obed, who becomes the father of Jesse, who is the father of David.

The story of Ruth presents Levinas with several interesting questions. How do we characterize the relationship between Ruth and Naomi? Is it ethical? Is it familial? Is it a friendship? Can it be defined within Levinas's analysis? Ruth, like Naomi, is both widow and stranger, and so we can say that both Ruth and Naomi fit literally into the place of ethical other—they are women who have God to look out for them. However, if we see Ruth and Naomi only as two women who are otherwise helpless, then we fail to see the richness of the relationship between them. Is Ruth's loyalty to

Naomi to be forgotten so that all we remember is her great-grandson, David? Is her fecundity the extent to which we see the significance of Ruth's actions? Let us begin by looking at Ruth, who is both the widow and the stranger.

Repeatedly, the Jew is told in the Bible of his obligation to the poor, the stranger, the widow, and the orphan.[38] "Stranger" is translated from the Hebrew *ger* and means simply "one who resides" or "resident alien."[39] Initially in the story, Elimelech and his family are the strangers since they are living in a place that is not their original home. However, it is also a place that was inhospitable to Jews in the past. The stranger relation is reversed when Ruth, the Moabitess, marries one of Naomi's sons. Elimelech's sons are welcomed into two Moabite families. The inhospitality of the past is transformed into hospitality by Ruth's actions. The rabbis themselves comment on this point. They tell us that the law forbidding marriage to a Moabite should be understood as a reference only to Moabites, not Moabitesses. The rabbis reasoned that it was the men who were inhospitable, since it was the men who were obliged to provide the food.

The focus here is not on Ruth's family, but on Ruth's in-laws. By putting Naomi in the position she does, Ruth is elevating her in-laws—her husband's family—above her own family. She is seen as part of Naomi's family both from the narrator's perspective and from Ruth's own perspective; hence, there is no question in Ruth's mind that she should leave Moab and return with Naomi to Judah. Whether or not Ruth has converted at this point is not clear, especially in light of the biblical injunction against such conversions. Nor is it clear what this conversion would mean. In any event, Ruth is often viewed and cited as the first convert.[40]

In the land of Judah, Ruth is a stranger. But her *strange*ness is complicated by her presumed act of conversion. If we grant that Ruth's speech to Naomi constitutes a conversion, then, presumably, her alterity evaporates. Conversion can be seen as a drawing of the other into the same, as no longer seeing the other as other. But the stranger is an individual who nonetheless retains some *strange*ness, or *other*ness. Since the stranger is the one to whom the Jew is most responsible, the conflicted identification of the convert raises questions for the Jews regarding this ethical relationship. How is the born Jew to think of the convert: as Jew or as stranger?

This question is raised again by Ruth herself, who, when wondering why Boaz has treated her so kindly, refers to herself as a foreigner. We do not know if Boaz was following the biblical command to the Jews that they "refrain from molesting the stranger or oppress him, for [they, the Jews] lived as strangers in the land of Egypt," or if he was abiding by the command that widows are to be allowed to glean in the fields. We do know from Boaz's own statement that he noticed the way in which Ruth treated

Naomi after Ruth's husband (i.e., Naomi's son) died. Ruth's *strange*ness is further complicated by the midrash commentary on David. David asks God, "How long will they rage against me and say, 'Is he not of tainted descent? Is he not a descendent of Ruth the Moabitess?'"[41] The implication of David's question is that even he, King of the Jews (and presumably those who descend from him), is stained by the strangeness of Ruth. Insofar as she occupies the place of stranger and widow, Ruth is an example of the absolute other par excellence. As such, she can occupy the ethical other to Levinas's 'I'. However, we can also view Ruth from another perspective: through her relationship to Naomi. On the one hand, we can regard Ruth's response to and care for Naomi as ethical. On the other hand, the relationship between Ruth and Naomi exceeds Levinas's category of the ethical—he leaves no place for friendship, much less for friendship between women.

What, then, are we to make of Ruth's loyalty to Naomi? Is it possible to think the ethical as a familial relation outside that of father and son? If we view the relationship from Ruth's perspective, then Naomi is the widow; while still in the land of Moab, she is a stranger; as a Jew, she is a stranger to Ruth. But she is also Ruth's mother-in-law. The connection that Ruth has to Naomi would appear tenuous after the death of Naomi's son, for the marriage between Ruth and Naomi's son was childless. Thus, there is no blood relation to join Ruth to Naomi.

However, it is clear from Ruth's actions that the bond is actually quite strong. It is Ruth who goes out to find work, who gleans in the fields, and who brings home the food. Ruth and Naomi, two widows and two strangers, who live together in their own dwelling, are family to each other. Ruth's choice to leave her mother, father, and homeland in order to follow Naomi and Naomi's God is seen as an act of loyalty by Elie Wiesel, who describes Ruth as "stubborn in her loyalty and her resolve."[42] Ruth, though she is now the stranger in the land of Judah, is the one who cares for Naomi.

Julia Kristeva describes Ruth's decision to follow Naomi as "show[ing] a devotion to Yahweh, but even more so a loyalty—that one might call passionate—between the two women."[43] In fact, the verse at Ruth 1:14 says, "Orpah kissed her mother in law farewell. But Ruth clave unto her." "Clave," Mieke Bal reminds us, is the same verb used to describe the marriage bond: a man shall leave his parents and cleave to his wife (Genesis 2:24). It is "exclusively used by the male subject and it is active, demonstrating a free choice made by the subject to renounce freedom in favor of another being."[44] This loyalty is cited as Ruth's first act of kindness, or *hesed*. And Ruth's second act of kindness is cited by Boaz when Ruth approaches him at night and lies by his feet (and the Hebrew here is ambiguous, for the word used for feet can be a euphemism for the genitals). Boaz responds to Ruth's advance, "Your latest deed of loyalty is greater than the first, in that you have not turned to younger men, whether poor or rich" (Ruth 3:10). The fruits of their union begin the lineage of David wherein Ruth's *strange*ness is at issue.

In *Engendering Judaism*, Rachel Adler offers a similar reading of Ruth's generosity.[45] Adler recalls that the Hebrew word for widow, *almanah,* derives from the verb *'alam,* meaning "to be unable to speak, silent, bound," again suggesting that it is through the man, her husband, that the woman spoke, had a voice, or had a place in society. Adler recalls that *hesed,* used three times in the Book of Ruth, means "righteousness," "loving kindness," "generosity," or "piety." It is a feeling or a character trait. This story exemplifies this trait, both by Naomi's actions toward her daughters-in-law, and in theirs (but in particular, Ruth's) toward her.[46] Even Boaz's generosity plays a role, for it is in his kindness to Ruth that Ruth is able to feed herself and then also feed Naomi. Adler reminds us also that at the end of the story, when Ruth's son is born, she hands the boy over to Naomi, who, we should recall, lost her own two sons. A chorus of women exclaims, "'A child is born to Naomi!' This child will be her redeemer, they affirm, not because of patriarchal inheritance law, but because of *hesed.* 'He is born of your daughter-in-law who loves you more than seven sons.'"[47]

We can see in Ruth Levinas's image of the feminine.[48] Ruth's hospitality—to Naomi's family and later to Naomi herself—is the very image of the feminine in Levinas's description of the dwelling. However, the relationship that Ruth has to Naomi violates the sexual division of labor that Levinas appears to assume and require. Although Ruth appears to be in an ethical relation to Naomi, and although she appears to have responded to Naomi, it is not clear that we can use such terminology with regard to that relationship. Can Ruth occupy the place of the ethical subject? If so, how will that alter the role of the feminine? I suggest that the role of the feminine is altered. Ruth does indeed exemplify the hospitality that Levinas accords to the feminine. And it is precisely in her actions of welcoming Naomi's family that we see the impulse to the ethical. Ruth then follows Naomi and cares for her. Ruth's relationship to Naomi is indeed ethical. The relationship between Ruth and Naomi exceeds Levinas's description of the feminine.[49]

In her public proclamation that she will follow Naomi, Ruth gives herself over to Naomi, Naomi's people, and Naomi's God. Ruth subverts the conception of the private, silent woman by publicly promising her devotion to Naomi, God, and the Jewish people. The words of Ruth's speech that begin with "I'll go where you go," are the words that all converts to Judaism recite out loud. Ruth sees in the eyes of Naomi the other others. She recognizes that there are others who make a claim on her and to whom she is responsible. Ruth's act of conversion is ethical. But her action is not merely ethical. In the words of her own proclamation, her act of conversion reveals its political component. Ruth's response is not just to Naomi, but to God and to a nation.

One might also ask if the narrators of this story, in their efforts to return Ruth to a traditional role by marrying her off to Boaz, are not aware of this excess. And yet, the story actually reads as that of two women who defy the categories that women are traditionally assigned. And interestingly enough, the rabbinic commentary supports this view. According to Phyllis Trible, these two women work out their own salvation, and when the men threaten to subsume them, they reclaim the narrative. In one midrash it is thought that Boaz dies, leaving Naomi and Ruth to raise the son. The emphasis at the end of the story appears to be on Naomi, who is given new life by the birth of the son, rather than on the inheritance restored to the family of Elimelech. Thus the family is once again Ruth and Naomi, a couple interrupted by a child.

Ruth's character opens up both the richness and the lack in Levinas. It reveals the stranger within us, that which makes us both same and other. And it allows us to ask after the space allotted to woman outside the erotic relationship and outside the dwelling. If my concern about the violence that men do to women in the home is well founded, then are we not obliged to ask after the adequacy of Levinasian ethics? If Levinas offers an idealized version of eros, then there is a danger in his claim that the erotic veils the ethical. However, if Levinas's account of eros is phenomenologically accurate, then we might learn about the complexity of eros from this account. The erotic relation is thorny precisely because of all the layers that cover over the asymmetry of ethics: jealousy, rage, passion, and desire.

Levinas's Hebrew roots give him profound insight into the obligation toward and responsibility for the other, especially for those who are most vulnerable. And it is also the case that his description of love is accurate. Levinas is correct that the ethical hides behind the erotic. The face of the ethical is still present, even if concealed. It is significant that Judaism has a marriage contract that intends to provide for the woman in the case of the ceasing of such "cooing and laughter." In other words, Judaism recognizes, even if its method is flawed, that lovers do not think things will go wrong; they do not think that they will ever not be in love; nor do they think, upon marrying, that one partner may hurt or abuse the other. The marriage contract and the rabbinic court, again for all its flaws, appears to be an attempt to recognize that the woman has an ethical face, a face that is sometimes hidden behind the face of the beloved. It is an explicit, even if unromantic, means to protect the parties involved. Marriage, in a Jewish view, may be the very locus of the ethical and the political. Because the ethical is veiled behind eros, a third party must enter to ensure that rights are preserved.

Levinas's project is not only about the ethical. It is also about the feminine, which plays a fundamental role in this project. If that role is altered, then we are required to investigate how, or in what ways, that alteration threatens the success of his project. Levinas puts woman—both as a figure in his project and as a (potential) reader of his philosophy—in a precarious place: the feminine is essential to his argument, such that to remove or redefine it is to put his project in jeopardy. At what point do we risk dismantling the whole philosophy so that there is little left of what Levinas has said?

The dynamic structure of the feminine, in these two early philosophical texts, illustrates the transcendental role of the feminine. Initially, the feminine is the means for the ethical relation to occur, even though the feminine does not participate in the ethical relation. However, we learn from the figure of Ruth that the very structure of hospitality moves the feminine from hospitality in the dwelling to an ethical relation. The feminine, by being the feminine, challenges Levinas's categories. Ruth's actions indicate an excess that is present in the feminine. Within a Levinasian analysis, Ruth so thoroughly fulfills the definition of hospitality that she exceeds any passive definition of woman, and she transforms the dwelling into the ethical. By gleaning in the fields, she feeds Naomi. And we should remind ourselves that Ruth's hospitality differs from Abraham's to the stranger in Genesis 18. Although it was Abraham who invited the stranger into his tent, Sarah and the servant did all the work. Thus, one might say, if taken to its limit within the boundaries of the description that Levinas provides, the feminine cannot help but to become ethical, to respond to the Other ethically. While using the feminine as a condition for the possibility of the ethical relation, Levinas creates the conditions by which the feminine can and must participate in the ethical.

It is precisely because of the character that Ruth embodies, a character that makes her worthy of being the ancestor of David, that Judaism acknowledges her as the first convert. Moreover, this is the character that exemplifies the attributes that Levinas describes in "Judaism and the Feminine" and "The Dwelling." That is, one might say that Ruth's behavior, while characteristically or stereotypically "feminine," also exemplifies the ethical response to the Other. It is Ruth—active, kind, generous, and capable—who exemplifies the ethical, precisely by living the definition assigned to her. Within a Levinasian framework, Ruth so perfectly fulfills the definition of hospitality and love that she exceeds the traditional definition of a passive woman, and transforms the image of the feminine in the dwelling.[50] Just as Ruth underwent a conversion, so, too, does the feminine.

Levinas's use of the feminine is not accidental, and he finds his conception of the feminine in the Hebrew tradition. It is the feminine that is necessary for his critique of virility and counter to a philosophical tradition obsessed with death. As a result of this formulation, the feminine does, in spite of what Levinas previously said, participate in the ethical. We see this most clearly in the role of the feminine in *Otherwise than Being*, his most mature work, in which he names the feminine "maternity." However, before turning to the account of the feminine that participates in the ethical, let us take a brief detour and consider why Levinas uses the feminine in the way he does. By turning back to themes from *Time and the Other, Totality and Infinity*, and *Otherwise than Being*, we can see where virility goes wrong, why it needs to be tempered, and what it needs to learn.

SEVEN

Cain and the Responsibility of Choice

Am I my brother's keeper?
—Genesis 4:9

Thou shalt not murder.
—Deuteronomy

Rashi's reading of the creation story allows us to see how basic the idea of alterity is to Jewish thought. His interpretation highlights the strange conception of time that informs the creation story. On the one hand, the Torah is received by those who would be called Jews at the time of creation. On the other hand, Abraham, who is the first Jew, does not have access to the Torah. Judaism claims that Abraham had to have received the Torah, at least in some sense. If not, it would be possible to be a Jew without the Torah. Regardless of how one practices Judaism, the Torah is central. Time, then, plays games with us as we try to understand what it means for a people to have accepted the Torah before the events described in it have taken place. One explanation is to say that the Torah is the way to the ethical.

Although the Torah is usually read as cosmogony, as a story about the creation of the world as such, some passages in the midrash support another interpretation. The word "Torah" is often translated, or mistranslated, as "Law." For our purposes, however, a more useful translation might be the one offered by Hermann Cohen: "instruction," "path," or "ethics." In this case, Cohen means "instruction and knowledge *of morality.*" If we read Genesis as ethogony rather than cosmogony, shifting our emphasis from the world created as such to the creation of a moral universe, then our conventional understanding of the stories that follow Genesis 1 changes dramatically. According to this interpretation, by accepting the Torah, one accepts a path or an obligation to become ethical. What was given at Sinai at the time of creation was a path to ethics.

However, the acceptance of the Torah not only prompts God to close the abyss physically, it also provides the path for the way a Jew is to live his or her life. The return to the chaos and emptiness before creation could refer to a life without ethics. Thus, this time before creation describes a chaos and terror similar to the life that Hobbes describes in his view of the state of nature.[1] If the Torah is the path to the ethical, and the receiving of the Torah took place at the time of creation, then we can infer that the ethical was present prior to the reception of the Ten Commandments by Moses. It therefore makes sense to ask about the relationship of education to ethics.

THOU SHALT NOT MURDER

Near the beginning of *Otherwise than Being,* Levinas writes,

> [T]he relationship with a past that is on the higher side of every present and every re-presentable . . . is included in the extraordinary and everyday event of my responsibility for the faults or misfortune of others, in my responsibility that answers for the freedom of another, in the astonishing human fraternity in which fraternity conceived with *Cain-like sober coldness* [*sobre froideur caïnesque,* translation modified], would not by itself explain the responsibility between separated beings it calls for. The freedom of another could never begin in my freedom. . . . The responsibility for the other can not have begun in my commitment, in my decision. (OTB 10/AE 24, emphasis added)

There are two points to be noted in the above quotation. The most obvious is the relationship of freedom to responsibility. What choice do we make in being responsible? It might seem heretical to ask such a question. The answer should be obvious. We are responsible *because* we are free. We typically believe that it is only in light of recognizing our freedom and our ability to make choices that we can even speak of responsibility. Levinas's answer differs from the received view of the Enlightenment. Our responsibility begins prior to our freedom. We will return to the question of freedom later in this chapter, but let us note its relationship to the second point revealed by the above quotation.

What are we to make of Levinas's cryptic reference to Cain's "sober coldness"? The two questions are related. Once again, Levinas makes reference to a biblical figure to express what mere words often fail to convey, thus exposing his own discomfort with Cain's cold response. This reference reflects the double violence that Cain inflicted: first, when he killed Abel; and second, when he renounced any sense of human fraternity by asking,

"Am I my brother's keeper?" On the one hand, Cain's response reveals him to be an individual with no sense of a connection to humanity. And in fact, one might even ask what such a connection would have meant to someone prior to an action that necessitates such a relationship. On the other hand, however, Cain's question implies that he had a choice to be or not to be his brother's keeper. The reality of this choice is precisely what Levinas denies. He reiterates these themes of responsibility, choice, and Cain's response in "God and Philosophy,"[2] in which he insists that responsibility for the other is prior to freedom: "Biological human fraternity, considered with the sober coldness of Cain, is not a sufficient reason that I be responsible for a separated being. The sober, Cain-like coldness consists in reflecting on responsibility from the standpoint of freedom or according to a contract. Yet, responsibility for the other comes from what is prior to my freedom" (GP 71/ DP 117). Responsibility is neither something contracted, nor something remembered. And so Levinas writes, "The passivity 'more passive than any passivity' consisted in suffering an unassumable trauma—or, more precisely, in having already suffered it in an unrepresentable past that was never present" (GP 70/DPP 116). Cain's coldness, one might say, inaugurates what becomes the virile, which is a variation on the *conatus essendi*. An examplar of this *conatus essendi*, Cain is more interested in self-preservation, even vanity, than in any connection to his brother. Cain is chosen, but he does not respond.

The passivity to which Levinas refers is one's inability to assert oneself successfully against obligation. One can choose not to help someone, but one cannot decline the already existing obligation to do so. The passivity of the subject refers to the subject who is a hostage to the other with regard to obligation or responsibility. Thus, when Levinas refers to one's "proximity" to the other, he means one's obligation to the other. My obligation binds me to another. It is what keeps me close to the other: "[T]o approach is to be the guardian of one's brother; to be the guardian of one's brother is to be his hostage. This is immediacy. Responsibility does not come from fraternity; it is fraternity that gives responsibility for the other its name, prior to my freedom" (GP 72/DP 118). Proximity thus implies the absence of mediation in my responsibility for the other, and thereby a responsibility before freedom and knowledge.

Cain's "sober coldness" indicates that he thinks of responsibility in the form of a contract (GP 71/DP 117). Cain's "sober coldness" prompts the response that he gives when God asks him about his brother Abel. Cain replies, "Am I my brother's keeper?" Biological brotherhood begins with Cain and Abel. They are the first blood brothers, and it is in the rupture of this relationship that the first violation of fraternity occurs. In asking if he is his brother's keeper, as if he had a choice in the matter, Cain implies that responsibility is something he chooses. Levinas's discussion indicates that Cain is sadly mistaken.

Levinas's goal in *Totality and Infinity* is to characterize the "Same" in its relationship to the "Other." This Other cannot be reduced to the Same, cannot be subsumed under the Same, and continually eludes any attempt to grasp it without remainder. As Levinas develops the "face-to-face" relationship in *Totality and Infinity,* it is the paradigm of the ethical relationship. It characterizes the claim of the other, who disrupts the spontaneity of my enjoyment and "brings me back" to the seriousness that the ethical relationship requires of me. In Levinas's view, the face belongs to another human being—as opposed to some other type of alterity—whose presence disrupts my enjoyment of, or taking pleasure in, my existence as a human being.[3] The relation between the Same and the Other is asymmetrical; the face-to-face relation is not reversible. Although I can talk about the relation that the Other has to me, to do so is already to move away from the face-to-face relation.[4] The expression "face-to-face" refers to the singular obligation that I have to the other, the claim that the vulnerability of the other makes on me. It does refer to a symmetry that exists between the other and me.

The absolutely other, the ethical other, can be understood by Levinas's use of the biblical expression that denotes those to whom we are most obviously ethically obligated: the stranger, the widow, and the orphan.[5] One's ethical obligation to the stranger arises precisely from the fact that the stranger is the person who has no ties, specifically no family ties, to oneself. The stranger, like the widow and the orphan, has no claim on me except that he or she is human. The ethical other is the one to whom I am wholly and unconditionally obliged. My freedom is mine only because I am already obligated. It consists only in whether and how I act on that obligation, but not in having the obligation itself. The meaning of "the face," as Levinas wants to convey it, is undoubtedly mysterious. It is difficult not to envision the face as the face of *someone*—in short, a particular face. However, Levinas does not mean a face that we actually see. In the interview published under the title "Intention, Event, and the Other," he tells his interlocutor, "'Face,' as I have always described it, is nakedness, helplessness, perhaps an exposure to death."[6] For Levinas, the face thus signifies the vulnerability of the other, the exposure of the other to me. And, as Levinas also tells us, the other is someone who wants to kill me.

In addition to the difficulty involved in merely understanding what is meant by "the face," one's relation to the face of the other is ambiguous. The command "You shall not commit murder" (TI 199/TeI 173) is compelling precisely because "the Other is the sole being I can wish to kill" (TI 198/TeI 173).[7] The Other provokes me because my desire to kill arises from an inability to co-opt the other person into the same. As much as I may try, I cannot relieve him or her of alterity. We will return to this theme below when we examine Levinas's related claim that I also cannot kill the Other. These same concerns regarding the face, responsibility, and the temptation to murder can be seen quite clearly in the biblical story of Cain and Abel, where the first killing of another human occurs and where, in spite of the lack of precedent, the killer is held morally accountable.

RAISING CAIN

"And Cain said to Abel . . . "[8] What was it that Cain said to Abel? Many of the translations fill in this blank with "Let us go outside." It is outside, where there are no witnesses, is no cover or protection, that Cain kills Abel. Most of us, upon being asked, "Is Cain responsible for the killing of Abel?" would respond with an emphatic "Yes." And if we were asked why we think so, most of us would say, "He is responsible because he committed the action." The responsibility that Levinas seeks to articulate, however, is not causal, but ethical. Is there any evidence in the story to indicate that Cain is morally responsible, that he should be held accountable for the killing of his brother? The narrative reports no discussion of moral education. Until this point, no one had died. Even though the move from Eden signaled the mortality of Adam and Eve, it is not clear that either of them knew what this mortality meant, or knew it in any profound way. No death had yet been recorded. One might conjecture that Cain could not have had any sense of mortality or morality, since there is nothing to indicate he had any moral education. This view is supported by midrash commentary, in which the rabbis speculate that Cain argued with God about Cain's responsibility.

> "Where is Abel[9] your brother?" God questioned. God expected Cain to answer, "I did wrong in killing him and regret my deed." But instead Cain brazenly replied, "I was made guardian of field and vineyard. Am I my brother's keeper? Do I know where he went? You are the Guardian of all creatures, so why should You inquire of me as to his whereabouts?" Cain's reply also included a subtle reproach to [God]. His words intimated, "You are the Guardian of the universe! Why then did You allow me to kill him?"[10]

Cain continues, in this speculative dialogue, "It was You who created me with a *yetzer hara* [evil inclination]. Then You aroused my jealousy by accepting my brother's sacrifice. . . . You did not prevent me from killing him. Why do You then blame me?" But God does not accept this argument and tells Cain that he is responsible not only for his brother's blood but also for the blood of his brother's unborn offspring. The line at Genesis 4:10 reads, "What have you done? Hark, your brother's blood cries out to Me from the ground."[11] But in the Hebrew text, the word used to indicate Abel's blood is written in the plural: "bloods." So, in addition to the victim, there is the matter of progeny, those never to be born. The Mishna Sanhedrin 4:5 tells us that this passage conveys the unique nature of murder: "Whoever takes a single life destroys thereby an entire world."[12] John Llewelyn affirms this rabbinic sentiment in *The Genealogy of Ethics,* when he tells us that murder is so devastating precisely because "if the very expressing of that judgement [the judgment of God] is expressed through 'Thou shalt not kill,' that judgement owes some of its force to generations to come. For to kill the person facing me is to kill the multiple generations to which he or she might have given birth."[13] Thus, the following questions remain: Why did God allow Cain's murderous intentions to come to fruition? Why did God not protect Abel? Moreover, why does it appear that God did not condemn Cain to death, as would be the case for other murderers? The response that the rabbis give in Genesis Rabbah 22:26 emphasizes Cain's ignorance of death. The rabbis argue that Cain could have had no way of knowing that his blow would extinguish Abel's life. So, the rabbis claim, Cain is guilty of homicide, not murder.[14] According to Rashi, Cain is guilty of murder, but his punishment is delayed seven generations. The midrash claims that Lamech, a direct descendant of Cain, rises up and slays Cain. Responding to this, Rashi claims that the line that reads "Vengeance shall be taken sevenfold" should be understood to mean that God does "not wish to take vengeance on Cain now, but at the end of seven generations [God] will execute [His] punishment upon him, that Lamech, one of his descendants will arise and slay him. . . . Vengeance will be taken in the seventh generation."[15] In spite of the discrepancy between homicide and murder, the role of personal responsibility is nonetheless affirmed. That the killer is held accountable indicates that the immediacy of the face and what the face expresses are taken as given. Even if Cain could not have known the full extent of his actions, there is something that he is expected to have known. In his essay "A Religion for Adults," Levinas employs the biblical story and the rabbinic commentary on it to illustrate the depth of

> the personal responsibility of man with regard to man [which] is such that God cannot annul it. This is why in the dialogue between God and Cain— "Am I my brother's keeper?"—rabbinical commentary does not regard the question as a case of simple insolence. Instead it comes from someone who has not yet experienced human solidarity and who thinks (like many modern philosophers) that each exists for oneself and that everything is permitted. But God reveals to the murderer that his crime has disturbed the natural order, so the Bible places a word of submission into the mouth of Cain: "My punishment is greater than I can bear." The rabbis pretend to read a

new question to this response: "Is my punishment too great to bear? Is it too heavy for the Creator who supports the heavens and the earth?" (RA 20/ RdA 36–37)

But the relationship of moral education to responsibility still seems in question. If we say that the face of Abel *was present* and that Cain was able but did not respond to the "Thou shalt not kill" expressed by that face, then we must assume that Cain knew what mortality meant. We must assume that Cain could have been (but was not) attuned to the suffering of the other. On the one hand, Levinas must assert that responsibility is not cognitive. The claim that the other has on me is independent of my thinking about it. My concern is the issue of attunement. How does one become attuned to the other? Here is where the father-son relationship that Levinas discusses in *Totality and Infinity* can be of use to us. Levinas's interest in this relationship lies within the unique relationship that a child has to the parent: the child was both "him and not him." A parent has an obligation to respect the uniqueness of the child, that is, to respect that the child is not the parent. This means that no matter how much the parent may wish the child to grow up to be "just like him," the parent must keep a watchful eye to allow the child to become his or her own person. We can also see clearly the asymmetry in the parent-child relationship as Levinas describes it. It is parents who tend to their children in the middle of the night, when a child wakes up sick or scared. A parent with a healthy relationship to a child does not expect the same in return. And certainly a very young child who still sleeps in a crib would be unable to rush to a parent's side. However, in light of Judaism's emphasis on the obligation of parents to teach their children well, I suggest that the responsibility the father has to the son is to care—in the broadest sense of the term—for the child. Woven through Deuteronomy is the following command: "And make [these things] known to your children and to your children's children" (Deuteronomy 4:9). Parents are to teach their children never to forget about injustice and always to be ethical. Thus, we could say that it is the parent's responsibility to raise a child to be attuned to the other. Levinas's philosophy does not give us a mechanism for understanding how or when this attunement occurs. Why are some people attuned to the suffering of the other, while others are not? The issue of child development is significant if we are going to hold Cain responsible for his lack of attunement to Abel. Thus, we would need to consider all the questions raised by psychology, and even psychoanalysis, if we are to address this problem adequately. But in Levinas's view, the issue is not when a child becomes attuned. Rather, the issue is being able to ask after one's own responsibility. His concern is to shift the definition of subjectivity from a Kantian "I think" to "I am responsible" (GP 58–61/DP 99–102).

The story of Cain and Abel suggests that this first killing must take place before the meaning of "Thou shalt not murder" is realized. This story reveals my interminable responsibility, the responsibility that *I* have and that *I* cannot relinquish. But it also reveals the responsibility that had no beginning and that I did not choose. Moreover, this story illustrates the unique way in which responsibility takes hold of the subject. Although God can punish Cain for his actions, God cannot exonerate Cain. As Levinas says in the passage quoted above, Cain's crime disturbed the natural order; thus, it is for Cain to rectify this disruption. However, the unique nature of murder, such that the victim has been annihilated, makes this task all the more problematic. Cain cannot be exonerated, since the only person who can exonerate him, Abel, no longer exists. This story is not unlike the one told by Simon Wiesenthal in *The Sunflower*,[16] in which a young Jew is summoned from a death camp to the bedside of a dying Nazi soldier. The soldier tells the story of his participation in the burning alive of an entire village. Unable any longer to bear the burden of his guilt, and terrified of dying with it, he asks for absolution from the Jew. The Jew turns and leaves the room without speaking. This story does not present us with any clear solutions to the problems of guilt and atonement.[17] But from an explicitly Jewish perspective, the Jew would have overstepped certain boundaries had he absolved the Nazi of his crimes. Levinas recites the Jewish view of this problem when he tells us,

> Jewish wisdom teaches that He Who has created and Who supports the whole universe cannot support or pardon the crime that man commits against man. "Is it possible? Did not the Eternal efface the sin of the golden calf?" This leads the master to reply: the fault committed with regard to God falls within the province of divine pardon, whereas the fault that offends man does not concern God. The text thus announces the value and the full autonomy of the human who is offended, as it affirms the responsibility incurred by whosoever touches man. Evil is not a mystical principle that can be effaced by a ritual, it is an offence perpetrated on man by man. No one, not even God, can substitute himself for the victim. The world in which pardon is all-powerful becomes inhuman. (RA 20/RdA 37)

Herein lies the basis for Levinas's claim that murder is ethically impossible. In his view, "killing annihilates" (TI 198/TeI 172). Yet, in spite of this attempt at annihilation, the face resists. The resistance that he sees is ethical. This is not to say that he thinks that killing can never take place, for clearly it does. In "Ethics and Spirit," he anticipates his philosophical position in *Totality and Infinity*.[18] I quote Levinas at length:

> Only the vision of the face in which the "You shall not kill" is articulated does not allow itself to fall back into an ensuing complacency or become the

experience of an insuperable obstacle, offering itself up to our power. For in reality, murder is possible, but it is possible only when one has not looked the Other in the face. The impossibility of killing is not real, but moral. The fact that the vision of the face is not an *experience,* but a moving out of one-self, a contact with another being and not simply a sensation of self, is at-tested to by the "purely moral" character of this impossibility. A moral view [*regard*] measures, in the face, the uncrossable infinite in which all murder-ous intent is immersed and submerged. This is precisely why it leads us away from any experience or view [*regard*]: it is not *known,* but is in *society* with us. The commerce with beings which begins with "You shall not kill" does not conform to the scheme of our normal relations with the words, in which the subject knows or absorbs its object like a nourishment, the satisfaction of a need. It does not return to its point of departure to become self-content-ment, self-enjoyment, or self-knowledge. It inaugurates the spiritual journey of man. A religion, for us, can follow no other path. (ES 10/EeE 23)

In the biblical story of Cain and Abel, we find much of the inspiration for Levinas's account of the face-to-face relation and his focus on the moral imperative "Thou shalt not murder." We also find the inspiration for his understanding of the ethical as a response and responsibility, rather than as a set of rules for prescribing behavior. We can see here that he understands the ethical as a response occurring at the precognitive, pre-epistemic, pre-ontological level, rather than at the level of rational discourse, moral edu-cation, or abstract moral rules. Levinas observes that "[T]his temptation to murder and this impossibility of murder constitute the very vision of the face. To see a face is already to hear, 'You shall not kill,' and to hear 'You shall not kill' is to hear 'Social justice.' And everything I can hear [*entendre*] coming from God or going to God, Who is invisible, must have come to me via the one, unique voice. 'You shall not kill' is therefore not just a sim-ple rule of conduct; it appears as the principle of discourse itself and of spiritual life. . . . Speech belongs to the order of morality before belonging to that of theory. Is it not therefore the condition for conscious thought?" (ES 8–9/EeE 21).[19] Here, we encounter once again the theme of doing be-fore hearing. This relationship between theory and practice, found in the above quotation, is, again, reminiscent of the Hebraic phrase, "To do and to hear [understand]."

The emphasis on the relationship to the other and the move away from rational decision making that characterizes Levinas's conception of ethics gives rise to what looks like a similarity between his ethics and what is known as feminist ethics of care. However, this similarity is superficial, and it is worth looking at why this is the case.[20]

The classic debate in contemporary ethics revolves around the relation-ship between the universal and the particular. The history of philosophy and the ethical theories that generally emerge from this history promote ethics as a collection of universal principles by which we guide our lives, and which aid us in making ethical decisions. In response to this view, a variety of ethical positions emerged and were united under the umbrella label "ethics of care." These theories have their origins in Carol Gilligan's moral theory.[21] Gilligan was responding directly to Lawrence Kohlberg's theory of moral development. Given the influences on Kohlberg, in particular that of Immanuel Kant, one could say she was responding indirectly to certain moral traditions in the history of philosophy. Kohlberg claims that: (1) the highest moral level is the universal, and in particular the preservation of any human life; and (2) women never achieve this level of morality.

Gilligan borrows heavily from Nancy Chodorow's conclusions in psychoanalytic theory,[22] in which Chodorow develops a conception of gender identity that assumes that boys and girls are nurtured by a single parent: the mother. According to Chodorow, because girls are intended to develop a gender identity that is similar to that of their mothers, they (little girls) have difficulty developing autonomously; conversely, little boys have difficulty developing an identity that takes into account its previous relationship to other people, namely, the mother. From this model, Gilligan concludes that women's moral development is heavily influenced by an identity that is situated squarely within relationships with others. Thus, women's moral development always has as its concern the interests, pains, and sufferings of the others who are affected by the individual's actions. If one contrasts theories of justice with theories of mercy, then the contrast also holds for male and female, whereby the former are considered justice-oriented and the latter mercy- or care-oriented. Gilligan's research, and the theories that resulted from it, have been criticized for a number of reasons. One important criticism revealed that her study did not acknowledge the differences among women. These differences may indicate that not all women theorize, morally or otherwise, in the same way.[23]

It is worth noting that although Gilligan and Levinas employ different methods, each responds, either directly or indirectly, to the way that the history of philosophy has conceived the ethical. So it will come as no surprise that, in spite of their various differences, Levinas and Gilligan would have similar views of the feminine and the ethical. Thus, the criticism of Gilligan's theory that charges her with essentializing women could apply equally to Levinas with regard to his portrait of the feminine in general, and of maternity, in particular, as the ethical relation par excellence.

In spite of these apparent similarities, Levinas's conception of the ethical differs from that which feminists call ethics of care. His conception of the ethical is that which interrupts being, and which does not include decision-making. The various ethics of care operate at the level of decision-making. Although offered as an *alternative* to moral reasoning based on universal principles, ethics of care is still an alternative form of decision-making. It tells us that taking into account the particularity of the situation and the relationship that one has to others are legitimate concerns in making ethical decisions. Yet, even care ethics presupposes the same thing that principled decisions presuppose—a notion of response that already takes into account the possibility of the ethical as an interruption. Thus, what the story of Cain and Abel reveals is not the problem of familial ties and choices to be made in relationship to those ties as illuminated in the ethics of care theories. Rather, in Levinas's view, the story reveals the inability for Cain to respond at all to Abel. It is not that Cain had a choice and chose the path of justice as opposed to care; Cain's actions reveal his disconnection from humanity and his inability to respond ethically.

There are many other examples of fraternal discord in the Bible, such as the stories of Jacob and Esau, Isaac and Ishmael, and, of course, Joseph and his brothers. While many of these stories tell tales of immorality, broken promises, and betrayal, the story of Cain and Abel is unique in that it illustrates both the significance of murder and the question of responsibility. Cain kills Abel before the receiving of the Ten Commandments; he kills him before receiving any kind of moral education; and he kills him with what appears to be a will. Since our justification for moral accountability typically lies in a claim that the individual *knew* what he or she was doing, where is our warrant for holding Cain responsible? *If* we are going to hold someone responsible, it must be the case that he or she knew what he or she was doing and knew it was wrong. But "knowing," here, means rational knowledge of a moral law. Freedom means the freedom to do otherwise, the freedom not to be obligated.

EIGHT

Abraham and the Tempering of Virility

> The role of the philosopher is to prepare for death.
> —Socrates in Plato's *Phaedo*

> We must remind ourselves that the Holocaust was not six
> million. It was one, plus one, plus one.
> —Judith Miller, *One by One by One*

> Do justice. Carry out acts of righteousness.
> —Isaiah, 56:1

> Can we still be Jewish without Kierkegaard?
> —Levinas, *Difficult Freedom*

What does Judaism make of the *Akedah,* a story that is not only part of its holy book, but whose main character, Abraham, is the father of Judaism? This chapter will revisit the Jewish writings on this story, bearing in mind, of course, that this is only one reading, since Judaism comprises a plurality of views. It is in the *Akedah* that I find the most powerful intersection and most useful blending of themes from Levinas's philosophical and confessional writings. By reading these writings in light of each other we reveal an unorthodox interpretation of the binding of Isaac. Ironically, this task can be most usefully accomplished by taking seriously the interpretation advanced by Søren Kierkegaard, a nineteenth-century Protestant philosopher.

Although Levinas expresses reservations about Kierkegaard's reading, it is Kierkegaard who gives us a strong psychological reading of Abraham, before whom we fear and tremble. It is ultimately from Kierkegaard's psychological profile of Abraham that Levinas's concern derives its force. Levinas's depiction of responsibility as substitution—"Not only can no one stand in for my responsibility, but I am responsible for the other's responsibility"— can also be understood more clearly as the concern that one will kill another rather than be killed by another. That the gravity of this responsibility supersedes even a responsibility to God can be seen in both Levinas's and the rabbis' response to the story of the *Akedah*. The task of this chapter is twofold: (1) to examine the possibility of locating a genesis of the ethical; and (2) to explore Levinas's conception of responsibility by using the images that we find in the *Akedah*.

ON NOT SUSPENDING THE ETHICAL: TAKING ANOTHER LOOK AT THE *AKEDAH*

The *Akedah* is one of the more troubling narratives in the Torah, for it tells the story of God's command that Abraham willingly sacrifice his own child to God in order to prove his faith. Judah Goldin, translator of *The Last Trial*, Shalom Spiegel's elegant commentary on both the *Akedah* and the poetry arising from the story of the *Akedah*, refers to the *Akedah* as the most terrifying narrative in all of Scripture. Let us reacquaint ourselves with the story in Genesis 22:

> 1] Some time afterward God put Abraham to the test. He said to him, "Abraham," and he answered "Here I am [*hineni*]." 2] And He said, "Take your son, your favored one, Isaac, whom you love, and go to the land of Moriah, and offer him there as a burnt offering on one of the heights which I will point out to you." 3] So early next morning, Abraham saddled his ass and took with him two of his servants and his son Isaac. He split wood for the burnt offering, and he set out for the place of which God had told him. 4] On the third day Abraham looked up and saw the place from afar. 5] Then Abraham said to his servants, "You stay here with the ass. The boy and I will go up there; we will worship and we will return to you."
> 6] Abraham took the wood for the burnt offering and put it on his son Isaac. He himself took the firestone and knife; and the two walked off together. 7] Then Isaac said to his father Abraham, "Father," and he answered, "Yes, my son." And he said, "Here are the firestone and the wood; but where is the sheep for the burnt offering?" 8] And Abraham said, "God will see to the sheep for His burnt offering, my son." And the two of them walked on together.
> 9] They arrived at the place of which God had told him. Abraham built an altar there; he laid out the wood; he bound his son Isaac; he laid him on the altar, on top of the wood. 10] And Abraham picked up the knife to slay his son. 11] Then an angel of the Lord called to him from heaven: "Abraham, Abraham!" And he answered, "Here I am [*hineni*]." 12] And he said, "Do not raise your hand against the boy, or do anything to him. For now I know that you fear God, since you have not withheld your son, your favored one, from me."

The test, as Abraham understands it, is to take Isaac, his beloved son, through whom God has promised the fulfillment of the covenant, up to Mt. Moriah, where he is to be offered as a sacrifice. It is in the absurdity of the situation that Abraham's faith is tested, for God has promised that Canaan will be delivered through Isaac; but now God is asking that Isaac be sacrificed. Because of God's initial promise, Abraham must believe that Isaac will be returned to him, although this seems impossible.

The story was given new force through Kierkegaard's reading of it in *Fear and Trembling*.[1] As Kierkegaard teaches us, writing under the pen name Johannes de Silentio,[2] it is not clear that we can truly understand the anguish that Abraham must have felt at having to pass such a test. According to Kierkegaard, the kind of faith that Abraham exhibits is not the faith talked about in modern days, where faith has become too easy. De Silentio wants to take seriously Abraham's struggle, which Christianity wants to ignore by redefining faith. According to Kierkegaard's reading of contemporary Christianity, God cannot ask us to do what God asked Abraham to do; God cannot ask us to be unethical. Thus, the conventional Christian faith of modernity appears easy to attain, since it does not ask much of the "faithful." It is in reading Kierkegaard seriously that we actually find a way to refuse the conclusion at which he arrives: that we fear and tremble before Abraham because there can be a teleological suspension of the ethical. By reading the binding of Isaac and *Fear and Trembling* in light of Levinas's conception of the ethical, we can see that there is another possibility of understanding God, one which also disallows the teleological suspension of the ethical. This possibility suggests that it is not obedience to God that takes precedence; that God could willingly and knowingly deceive us; but that it is our responsibility to the other person that is primary. My claim here is that the test that Abraham had to pass was precisely a test of the ethical, but not the ethical as the universal. Rather, it was a test of his obligation to his son, to the other person. And I claim that Abraham passed that test when he was ready and willing to put down the knife.

For de Silentio/Kierkegaard, the turning point in the story—the truth of the story, so to speak—is revealed in Abraham's faith in the absurdity of the situation: that God will take Isaac *and* that Isaac will be returned to him. That is what makes the request for the sacrifice absurd. Even in the section of *Fear and Trembling* called "The Attunement," where de Silentio helps us to see with what Abraham must be struggling, the focus is on faith. In this case, the concern is that Isaac will lose faith in God. Kierkegaard's concern is with the logical possibility, or impossibility, of the situation. But we might ask if he has failed to see the real concern: the father of Judaism has just been asked by God to kill his own son for an apparent test. For now, let us leave open what this test involves.[3]

If we refocus our attention on Kierkegaard's reading of Abraham, we will find some insight into this test. If we follow Kierkegaard, we can pose to ourselves Kierkegaard's own question: Why do we tremble before Abraham? And it is here that we receive a promising answer. We fear and tremble before Abraham because we fear and tremble before God: God can ask all kinds of things of us and Abraham is presented as someone who is willing to do what God asks. Abraham has the kind of faith that Kierkegaard admires but that he believes society has forgotten; it is a faith so profound that Abraham is willing to kill his child for it.

Kierkegaard is correct in his reference to that before whom we fear and tremble. But this is also the point at which he goes astray. Kierkegaard cannot move forward in his understanding of Abraham precisely because his focus remains on Abraham. De Silentio appears to be afraid of this faith. He admires it, but he also fears it. Kierkegaard cannot understand Abraham, and his continued focus on Abraham distracts him from a larger question: Of what is God capable? Although the reason is not clear, de Silentio does not entertain the possibility that God is variable. Or, this possibility disappears behind the absurdity of the situation. Regardless, he focuses on Abraham so that neither he nor the readers look behind Abraham at God. But it is by looking at God that we come to the possibility of admiring Abraham while also giving up what Kierkegaard calls the teleological suspension of the ethical—a suspension of the ethical, understood as the universal, for something higher (in this case, Kierkegaard's conception of the religious sphere). Although de Silentio mocks Christianity, he does so by keeping the ethical structure, as he understands it, in place. Thus, his challenge to Christianity, if it is indeed a challenge, does not go far enough.

From Kierkegaard's perspective, if we are to admire Abraham as a man, we must allow for the possibility of the teleological suspension of the ethical, which he enacted when he raised the knife to Isaac. A suspension of the ethical would be any lapse of the ethical, such as a crime or sin. But the key here is Kierkegaard's use of the term "teleological." The suspension occurs in favor of a domain or realm that is considered *higher* than the ethical. It is precisely this feature of the story, and Kierkegaard's interpretation of it, that makes Levinas uncomfortable. His discomfort is shared by Judaism in general. Most of the rabbinic commentary on this story reveals, or maybe even betrays, the discomfort that the rabbis feel.[4] One rabbi's uneasiness can be seen in the following midrash, in which Rabbi Aha presents a speculative dialogue between Abraham and God, in which Abraham wonders about God's indulgence in prevarications. Abraham has problems reconciling three things: (1) God's promise to fulfill the covenant through Isaac; (2) God's command to offer Isaac as sacrifice; and (3) God's command to Abraham to abort the sacrifice. God responds by saying that he will not change any part of what he has commanded. According to the rabbi, God says the following:

> O Abraham, My covenant will I not profane. And I will establish My covenant with Isaac. When I bade thee, "Take now thy son," etc. I will not alter that which is gone out of my lips. Did I tell thee, Slaughter him? No! But, "take him up." Thou hast taken him up. Now take him down.[5]

In other words, the rabbi speculates that, for whatever reason, God merely asked Abraham "to take Isaac up," not to offer him up as a sacrifice. The root from which this word is derived is *ayin, lamed, heh*. It could be rendered as *aliyah,* which is translated literally as "to take up" and used to describe the movement of a Jew who approaches the *bimah* to read from the Torah, or to describe a religious trip that a Jew makes to Israel. But its root is also seen in *la'ola,* which means "to offer up," as in a sacrifice. So, the rabbi speculates here that Abraham misunderstood God's command; the command to sacrifice Isaac was fabricated by Abraham, not commanded by God.[6] The rabbi's attempt to "save" God, and Judaism, from the violence implied in a request for such a sacrifice reveals just how troubling this story is to the rabbis. This midrash almost appears humorous. Yet it is intended to be sincere.

In spite of its sincerity, however, the midrash does not do justice to the story itself; nor does it do justice to Abraham, who is presented as a buffoon. By means of this interpretation, the rabbi is trying to "save" God by making God appear less frightening. In this rabbi's view, God could not have asked Abraham to kill his own son. The mistake is Abraham's.

We could offer a different, but equally speculative, interpretation of the story in support of the rabbi's concern. We could suppose that God knows what Abraham is thinking and lets him continue up the mountain with Isaac, knowing that he believes he must kill Isaac. Regardless, by casting the story in terms of Abraham's "mistakes," the rabbi does not take seriously Abraham's real struggle to understand what God wants. By implication, the rabbi also does not take seriously what God might ask of us. In particular, the rabbi does not allow for the possibility that God might have intentionally deceived Abraham. If this rabbi's interpretation is correct, then what do we make of a religion in which the message of God is to be followed literally, but the person whom we think of as closest to God, chosen to carry out God's will, misunderstood it? This question leads us to wonder if God's "test" was not a test of simple obedience to God. And when we consider what the test is, the fact that Abraham picked up the knife cannot be separated from the fact that he also put down the knife.

LEVINAS'S RESPONSE TO KIERKEGAARD

In *The Star of Redemption,* Franz Rosenzweig claims that if humanity is to be truly free, God must also be truly free, and that freedom includes the freedom to deceive us.[7] In addition, God must make God's own actions difficult, if not impossible, to understand, lest we be too willing to follow God's will blindly. If it were not the case that we had to choose for ourselves, then the fearful and the timid, those most likely to follow God's will out of fear, would be the most pious. In order to be truly free, we must be free to defy God's will.[8] A God who wants us to be free will therefore deceive us. We fear and tremble before a God who can ask us to commit a murder precisely because we must choose not to do so. We fear and tremble before a God who is also free and who will not do our ethical work for us. It is, as Levinas would say, a "difficult freedom" to bear.

On this view, Abraham would not be admired for his obedience to God, especially since that obedience leads him to the brink of sacrificing his son. This view of human freedom, which is set *against* obedience even to God, supports Levinas's assertion that a suspension of the ethical that allows for the sacrifice or murder of another cannot be tolerated. However, his concern is not whether God would demand this kind of action of us, even though he assumes that God must be compassionate. He focuses instead on our responsibility and our response to the other person.

Levinas's criticism of Kierkegaard focuses on the latter's understanding of the ethical. For Kierkegaard, the ethical is defined as the universal. At the religious level, the particular is reclaimed, but in a higher form than at the level of the aesthetic. On Kierkegaard's understanding of the ethical, the singularity of the self, and of the other, is lost in a rule that is valid for everyone. Levinas's criticism rests on his claim that "the ethical is not where [Kierkegaard] sees it" (PN 76/NP 90). Although both Levinas and Kierkegaard criticize the ethical understood as the universal, Kierkegaard still understands the ethical *as* the universal. It is tempting to equate Kierkegaard's religious level with Levinas's conception of the ethical, since both are higher than the universal. Their criticisms of the ethical do not, however, bring them to the same place.

On the views of both Kierkegaard and Levinas, proponents of the conception of the ethical as the universal do not typically allow for something higher than the universal. For Kierkegaard, this means that there is no place for faith or for the religious as something higher and individuating. For Levinas, this means that the particularity of responsibility is lost. Thus, Levinas's ethical is a responsibility first to the other, while Kierkegaard's religious is a responsibility first to God. This is why Levinas claims that Kierkegaard's violence emerges precisely when he "transcends ethics" and ascends to the religious (PN 76/NP 90). Although the religious, in Kierkegaard's account, reclaims the particular, this conception of the religious cannot be seen as Levinas's account of the ethical.

The ethical that is suspended for Kierkegaard, then, is the ethical understood as the universal in Levinas's view. Thus, the religious, as Kierkegaard defines it, appears to suspend the ethical, even as Levinas understands it. In Levinas's view, an account of the religious that allows for, or even requires, the sacrifice of another person cannot be considered the ethical. A conception of the ethical that accounts for the singularity of the 'I,' that poses the 'I' as a unique individual, and that implies an infinite requirement of a responsibility toward others is missing from Kierkegaard's religious stage. In Levinas's view, Kierkegaard's religious stage not only entails a suspension of the ethical qua the universal, but also allows for a renaming of a murder so that a sacrifice can be made in the name of God. Thus, Levinas would have to say that there is not an account of ethics, such as the one that he puts forth, in Kierkegaard's account of the religious.[9]

I realize that Kierkegaard conceives of a level or sphere of existence higher than the ethical defined as the universal. But I wish to underscore Levinas's concern when the ethical is defined as such. The danger in Kierkegaard's interpretation is that in spite of the anguish that Abraham must have felt, he still felt compelled to obey God, and this obedience led to the potential sacrifice of his son. That Abraham is admired for this part of the test is, at best, curious. Abraham may have struggled, as Sartre also points out, with questions about who was asking him to commit this act.[10] But Abraham nonetheless made the choice and took a leap of faith to obey God. Levinas's concern is that this obedience to duty that we find in Kant is then essentially taken up in Kierkegaard.

Both Levinas and Kierkegaard have a concern that the ethical will be disrupted by such a suspension of the ethical. And for Kierkegaard, the possibility of a suspension must remain open. Levinas also wants to disrupt the ethical defined as the universal. But he does not think that any stage that would allow, or even require, the sacrifice of another person is higher than the universal. This is precisely the opposite of the disruption he has in mind. Thus, it is here that Levinas and Kierkegaard part company. However, if we part company with Kierkegaard, we must ask how we can retain our admiration for Abraham.

As we just discussed, in Levinas's account there cannot be a teleological suspension of the ethical. Any suspension of the ethical would entail not merely the disruption but also the annihilation of the ethical. If the ethical can be suspended and Isaac sacrificed, then the ethical is no more. We might then ask whether there is another way to engage this fear and trembling. Must it be brought on only by a suspension of the ethical? Although Levinas leaves Kierkegaard behind, it is here that we should not only not leave Kierkegaard behind, but also engage him directly. It is here that we should help him further his inquiry. He does not want to give up on Abraham. He sees him as an admirable figure. For the Jews, of course, he is an admirable figure, although not for the same reasons.[11] But Kierkegaard does not know how to proceed. Abraham is admired for his faith, but his faith is displayed in light of his willingness to sacrifice Isaac. And yet, Kierkegaard reveals his own reservations about Abraham when he confides that Abraham both awes and repulses him.

If we take seriously Kierkegaard's reading of the story, then we must imagine that it took all of Abraham's strength, emotional and otherwise, to get him to the point of raising his knife. Kierkegaard gives us an excellent psychological profile of Abraham. He reminds us of the time it took for Abraham to make the decision: that he had to lie to Sarah, travel up the mountain, cut the wood, and then bind Isaac. To read *Fear and Trembling* is, to be sure, not to take lightly what Abraham is asked and commits himself to do. In light of Kierkegaard's psychological profile, which illuminates how difficult it must have become for Abraham to raise the knife to his own son, we can ask after what must have happened that he so easily put the knife down without so much as a question to the angel. If nothing else, inertia alone might have prompted him to execute God's command.[12] Consequently, Levinas believes that the dramatic moment of the story occurs when Abraham listens to the angel of the Lord, who tells him, "Do not lay a hand on the lad" (Genesis 22:12). This moment in the story illustrates the point at which the focus shifts from Abraham to Isaac. Thus, on Levinas's view, the story is no longer about Abraham as a man of faith and his perceived duty to God; rather, it is about Abraham's responsibility to Isaac.

This shift in focus also reveals that there is a gap in the narrative. But we notice this gap only if we pursue a line of interpretation that Kierkegaard began but did not finish. In spite of Kierkegaard's brilliant commentary on this story, he misses something.[13] It is this lack on which Levinas focuses and that I wish to explore. Let us return to the story and attempt to fill in the gap. We will pay particular attention to the passage in which the angel tells Abraham, "Do not lay a hand on the lad."

REREADING ABRAHAM THROUGH LEVINAS

Kierkegaard's *Fear and Trembling* teaches us not to read the *Akedah* too quickly. Thus, we should take him at his word and follow his directions: we should read the story slowly and carefully. And we should read the story to its end. If we stop halfway through the narrative, then Kierkegaard's insightful commentary might teach us only about the profundity of faith—a faith that we cannot understand. We might never question the very command to kill Isaac that led to that faith. And we might never wonder why Abraham did not complete the task commanded of him. In fact, if we stop halfway through the narrative, we might not learn that Abraham aborted the sacrifice. But if we stop where Kierkegaard stopped, then Kierkegaard's reading seems the most plausible. So if we apply Kierkegaard's lesson to himself and read the story to its end, we may discover another message in the book.

According to Levinas, "That Abraham obeyed the first voice is astonishing: that he had sufficient distance with respect to that obedience to hear the second voice—this is essential" (PN 77/NP 90). Levinas's focus on Abraham's sensitivity in hearing the second voice is significant. He does not want us to neglect the fact that Abraham stopped when the angel of the Lord spoke to him. But his ability to hear "the second voice" indicates his receptivity to the other. And, in Levinas's view, it is more extraordinary than Abraham's initial faith.[14] Let us consider what it means that Abraham heard the second voice and put down the knife.

Levinas insists that responsibility presupposes response. And it is precisely this conception of response that we see in Abraham at the point when Abraham aborts the intended sacrifice. An angel of the Lord says, "Abraham, Abraham."[15] The repetition is potentially significant for, as one midrash tells us, this repetition implies that the first call is to Abraham himself, and the second call is to all future generations. Abraham replies to the angel, "Here I am [*hineni*]." The angel then says, "Do not lay a hand on the lad." The standard reading of this story maintains that, although it was God who initiated this sequence of events, it is an angel who brings them to an end. But this reading only leads to another "existential" problem. Sartre indicated that Abraham might have wondered—indeed, should have wondered—if it really was God who issued the initial command. Similarly, should not Abraham have wondered whether this command was really from an angel of the Lord? The reappearance of this existential problem returns us to the difficulty posed in different ways by both Rosenzweig and Levinas regarding the relationship of God to response. Do we want an ethics that requires us to wait for God to tell us what to do? And do we want an ethics that requires that our first allegiance be to God rather than to a human other?

These questions reveal the significance of the gap in this narrative, illustrated by Abraham's two actions: raising the knife and then setting it down. Like the rabbis, I claim that the angel's command not to lay a *hand* on the lad indicates that Abraham no longer holds a *knife* in his hand. The rabbis interpret the command from the angel as necessary to prevent Abraham from strangling Isaac. They believe that when Abraham raised the knife, the angels wept and the knife melted. Determined to go through with the command from God, Abraham proceeded to strangle Isaac. I, however, interpret the command not to lay a hand on Isaac as an indication that Abraham put down the knife willingly. On my reading, Abraham has turned away from obedience to God and toward the face of Isaac. Thus, his faith in God is ultimately revealed by the ethical response to the other.

The "Here I am" (*me voici*), *hineni* in Hebrew, implies a sensitivity, a total awareness, or a readiness to respond. In a sense, it implies that the response actually precedes the utterance. According to Rashi, "Here I am" is "the response of the pious," and it means, "I am ready": it is "an expression of humility and readiness."[16] Thus, to utter "Here I am" indicates that one is already ready to respond or, put more strongly, it is to have responded already—in this case, if not to the angel, then to Isaac. This view is borne out by Levinas when he cites Isaiah's claim that "before they call, I will answer."[17] The response to the other, the response in responsibility, is the same as the response that Rashi speaks of in *hineni*. Both imply an openness to the other and a willingness to respond. Thus, Levinas is right to call our attention to the second voice that Abraham hears. If Abraham was ready to kill Isaac, then it is extraordinary that he is ready to hear the second command, the command not to continue and a command given to him not by God but by a messenger of God. This point is significant even for de Silentio, since it means that Abraham is no longer in an absolute relation to the Absolute. The relationship between Abraham and God is now mediated, and the immediate relationship has shifted to Abraham and Isaac. The shift from God to Isaac is the shift to what Levinas calls the ethical, the face-to-face.

We might interpret this story in terms of Abraham having already turned back to the ethical (or maybe having turned toward it for the first time), but only if the ethical is to mean something different here from what it means for Kierkegaard. In any event, for Levinas, this turn to the ethical does not involve turning back to the universal. In other words, the Levinasian conception of the ethical would demand a fourth category for Kierkegaard. We might say that at the moment that Abraham raised the knife he saw the face of Isaac, and he did so for the first time. That is, we might say that he saw it in a way that demanded response, that commanded him—a command prior to God's—to respond to a face that signified the particularity of the Other, rather than the universal of a nation.

Levinas correctly observes that the ethical cannot be commanded by God—certainly not in the form of rules. If this were the case, then our ethical relationship to the other would be mediated by the rules that we must consider before acting. Abraham's receptiveness to the second voice implies that he had already turned toward the ethical. Thus, Abraham did not need the angel to identify himself. The source of the command did not matter. And as Levinas suggests, this receptiveness is the essential moment in the story. Abraham was responding to the fact that he was *already claimed* by Isaac, that he was *already obligated* to Isaac. And this reading supports my suggestion that Abraham had already put down the knife. He had already responded to the face of Isaac. Thus, the angel's voice is not a command to initiate a response; rather, it is a response to Abraham's response *already* in motion.[18] Thus, the angel's command is superfluous. In responding to the angel calling his name, Abraham already recognized the alterity of Isaac.

We have at least two Abrahams: the Abraham who went up the mountain prepared to sacrifice his son, and the Abraham who countermands the command of God, who listens to an angel say "Do not continue with this action." That is, we have a second Abraham who displays his genesis as an ethical agent. In that event, something happened to Abraham on Mt. Moriah, an event not recounted in the written Torah. It might even be necessary that it not be written into the narrative. This gap in the narrative could suggest that it is only through Abraham's bodily actions, through his preparations to sacrifice Isaac, that he has the epiphany of the ethical. And we might say that we would "see" what Abraham "sees" only if we had to fill in the gap ourselves. What we learn from Abraham is more meaningful to us this way than if it were told explicitly to us.[19]

If we read this part of Genesis, especially Abraham's "Here I am," as a sign of his turn toward the ethical, then an interpretation could unfold in a number of different directions. We could say that God saw the need to stop the sacrifice that was about to take place, and Abraham was ready to be stopped. We could also say that Abraham was ready to defy God even if the angel had not arrived to stop him. If we pursue this latter interpretation, then we might approach Levinas's understanding of what it means to love the Torah—that is, the ethical—more than God. Levinas illustrates what he means when he affirms Yossel ben Yossel's remark that "even if I [Yossel ben Yossel] were deceived by him [God] and became disillusioned, I should nevertheless observe the precepts of the Torah" (LT 144/AT 204). Levinas asks, "Is this blasphemy?" and he replies, "At the very least, it is a protection against the madness of a direct contact with the Sacred that is unmediated by reason. But, above all, it is a confidence that does not rely on the triumph of any institution, it is the internal evidence of morality supplied by the Torah. . . . Loving the Torah even more than God means precisely having access to a personal God against Whom one may rebel—that is to say, for Whom one may die" (LT 144, 145/AT 204).[20]

Thus, it is when Abraham sees Isaac's face that he shifts his responsibility from God to Isaac, his son. Abraham's willingness to sacrifice his child and then his receptiveness to Isaac's "face" depict the necessary moments in the genesis of the ethical. Although Levinas does not want to locate the ethical in an *arché*, for responsibility is to be an-archical, there nonetheless remains a sense in which we must still explain the ethical. We can explain his conception of the ethical in terms of attunement to the face of the other.

We could suggest that the Cain and Abel story required the murder of Abel in order for the force of the "Thou shalt not kill" to be revealed to us. But it is not only unnecessary that Isaac be sacrificed; it is also essential that he not be sacrificed. The ethical was present for Cain and Abel, but Cain failed to respond to the face of Abel. Levinas identifies Cain as unable to respond to the face of Abel. He is detached from human fraternity. If we synthesize the readings of Kierkegaard/de Silentio and Levinas, we may conclude that Abraham is a knight of faith, as Kierkegaard suggests. But we can also agree with Levinas that the essential moment in the story is the moment at which Abraham refuses to sacrifice Isaac. If Judaism is to begin with Abraham, then the moment when God commands Abraham is precisely the moment when Abraham must love the Torah more than God.

We can say, then, that Abraham needed to have faith in God so that he would be brought to the point of offering Isaac up and then see the face of the other in Isaac. That is, we could accept Kierkegaard's reading that Abraham's ascent with Isaac is a story of Abraham's faith. I maintain that Abraham needed to have this extraordinary faith in order to come to the brink of committing a horrific act so that he could see what it is that God *really* wants. Regardless of what God tells us to do, we must first and foremost respond to the other person. If Abraham were commanded to perform this act again, he would not. He has learned the lesson he needed to learn. To respond to Isaac *is* to respond to God.

This moment in the story directs our attention from the dispensers of violence to the victims, those who suffer that violence.[21] This is true even, or especially, if that violence is administered in the name of God. We can draw on the images of the *Shoah* that appear in *Otherwise than Being* to support the claim that Kierkegaard's reading of this story expresses precisely the problem that Levinas has with the history of philosophy and the moral theory that springs from it. His references to the "too-tight skin," "persecution," "being a hostage," and "feeding the hungry" summon powerful images in a book that explores in detail the ethical claim of the other.

Levinas suggests that Western philosophy's focus on rationality and universals led to the sacrifice of the individual in the name of a greater good. We can see this sacrifice enacted most clearly in the way that national policy often sustains a form of theodicy: the suffering of individuals is justified in the name of a greater good for everyone else concerned. From the events of Nazi Germany we have countless examples, including Eichmann at his trial in Jerusalem, of those who claimed "just to be doing their duty."[22]

The conflict between duty and responsibility in Kierkegaard's reading of the *Akedah* is also apparent in the activities of Nazi Germany. Levinas's concern issues precisely from this commitment to this kind of duty. *Fear and Trembling* demonstrates this conflict in de Silentio's/Kierkegaard's characterization of the tragic hero, who is contrasted with the knight of faith. But regardless of the distinction between duty to God and to the state, the loss of the ethical in the name of duty is precisely what Levinas fears. The *Shoah,* although certainly an extreme expression of this loss, nonetheless was the outcome of a view that condones the subordination of the ethical to duty.[23]

THE GIFT OF DEATH AND
THE POLITICS OF RESPONSIBILITY

The conflict between duty and responsibility is not as easily resolved as we might wish it to be. Levinas recognizes the potential conflict that may arise between one's love of God and one's responsibility to the other. Derrida also alerts us to the aporia of responsibility in *The Gift of Death:* to be responsible means also that one is irresponsible in a variety of ways. He begins his discussion with a reading of Jan Patočka's book.[24] Early on, he tells us that "[r]eligion is responsibility or it is nothing at all."[25] This necessary connection is one that he takes to its extreme and ultimately disrupts. He complicates Kierkegaard's reading of the *Akedah* and the themes that emerge from it (e.g., responsibility, religion, ethics, and sacrifice). And he indicates the ways in which sacrifice, of one's self and others, can be seen as part of one's everyday life. Thus, he asks, What does it mean to give oneself death? This question asks after the meaning of sacrificing one's life for another. Ultimately, he is interested in the relationship between putting oneself to death and dying for another.[26]

Derrida focuses his attention on the traditional conception of sacrifice—that one person would "die for" another. He intends to undermine this conception by revealing a paradox of responsibility that results from two competing conditions in our conception of responsibility as outlined by Patočka: (1) We wish to subject responsibility—that is, responsible decision-making—to knowledge of what we are doing; and (2) such knowledge would "define the condition of impossibility of this same responsibility—if decision-making is relegated to a knowledge that it is content to follow or to develop, then it is no more a responsible decision, it is the technical deployment of a theorem."[27] In other words, our competing responsibilities require us to offer a justification of choices by giving an accounting of them. But it is precisely this justification that renders our actions the result of calculation and rationalization. In Derrida's view, this paradox characterizes the "relation between the Platonic and Christian paradigms throughout the history of morality and politics."[28] Nonetheless, Patočka's view of responsibility is strikingly similar to Levinas's. Patočka maintains that there is no binding responsibility that does not issue "from a person such as an absolute being who transfixes me, takes possession of me, holds me in its hand and in its gaze."[29] Derrida weaves the genealogy of responsibility into a discussion of the gift and of death—the gift of death.

Patočka's discourse on sacrifice and dying and Levinas's conception of responsibility and sacrifice are, in part, a response to Heidegger's conception of death found in *Being and Time.* Heidegger's discussion of death generates a paradoxical view of sacrifice. On the one hand, what allows me to give up my life for another is that my death is precisely my own. On the other hand, because my death is entirely my own, no one can stand in for me. No one can substitute her life for mine, nor can mine be substituted for hers. Thus, the sacrifice that one makes by giving up one's life for me is merely to have stood in for me at a particular moment. Although it is not *this* bullet that kills me, it may be some other bullet, some other disease, or simply the stopping of my heart when I get too old. The fact that I will die, and that I could die at any moment, remains. The Heideggarian view of death reminds us of *Dasein's* anxiety in the face of one's own death. His view of death ultimately undermines the possibility of sacrifice, insofar as the other cannot take away my finitude or substitute his for mine. Thus, in his account of death, sacrifice is impossible.

Derrida's discussion in *The Gift of Death* disrupts our everyday understanding of sacrifice and responsibility. This disruption obliges us to be less complacent and less self-satisfied with who we are and what we do. His discussion urges us to realize not only that sacrifice occurs on a continual basis, but also how sacrifice has become essential to our justified way of existence. On Derrida's interpretation of the *Akedah, the ethical is the temptation.*[30] Abraham is tempted by the ethical and the consolation that it gives him in the choices that he makes. But it is also a temptation that he needs to resist, for to succumb to this moral temptation would be to lose his ultimate responsibility along with his singularity; it would "make him lose his unjustifiable, secret, and absolute responsibility before God. This is ethics as 'irresponsibilization,' as an insoluble and paradoxical contradiction between responsibility *in general* and *absolute* responsibility."[31]

Thus, Derrida observes that the story of Abraham illustrates the utterly horrific—namely, the willingness of a father to sacrifice his son. And it also illustrates another example of the aporia of responsibility: it reveals the overlapping layers of Abraham's responsibility—to Sarah, to Isaac, and to

God—and how responsibility to one necessarily entails neglecting the others. How is he to choose? As Derrida himself remarks, "I cannot respond to the call, the request, the obligation, or even the love of another without sacrificing the other other, the other others. . . . As a result, the concept of responsibility, of decision, or of duty, are condemned a priori to paradox, scandal, and aporia."[32] Thus, he recognizes that responsibility and sacrifice are more than just aporias. The relationship between the two permeates our everyday life.

We may look upon the attempted sacrifice of Isaac as an abomination, and we may maintain that, God's command notwithstanding, Abraham is still (almost) a murderer within the framework of the ethical. Were Abraham to attempt the sacrifice today, surely he would be condemned by any civilized society. In spite of our horror at Abraham's actions, Derrida's discussion reveals the way in which *we* not only live with the sacrifice of others, but also *require* that sacrifice in order for our lives to continue as we know them and want them to continue. In fact, the sacrifice of others so deeply forms the basis of our ethical lives that Derrida asks, "Is it not inscribed in the structure of our existence to the extent of no longer constituting an event?"[33] He further observes that the society that would be quick to condemn Abraham is also the society whose smooth functioning,

> monotonous complacency of its discourses on morality, politics, and the law, and the exercise of its rights (whether public, private, national, or international), are in no way impaired by the structure of the laws of the market that society has instituted and controls, because of the mechanisms of external debt and other similar inequities that same "society" *puts* to death or (but failing to help someone in distress accounts for only a minor difference) *allows* to die of hunger and disease tens of millions of children (those neighbors or fellow humans that ethics or the discourse of the rights of man refer to) without any moral or legal tribunal ever being considered competent to judge such a sacrifice, the sacrifice of others to avoid being sacrificed oneself. Not only is it true that such a society participates in this incalculable sacrifice, it actually organizes it. The smooth functioning of its economic, political, and legal affairs, the smooth functioning of its moral discourse and good conscience presupposes the permanent operation of this sacrifice.[34]

Derrida's insight into the aporias of responsibility cannot leave us unchanged with regard to how we think about ourselves and the way we regard Abraham. And yet, the observation that competing responsibilities claim us is nothing new. Derrida's point is far more severe. Even in our acts of responsibility to others we are irresponsible. There is no escape from the economy of sacrifice. Levinas's conception of responsibility includes the relationship between the political and the ethical, and he is well aware of the competing claims on our lives. For Levinas, the two cannot exist apart from each other. Levinas separates them for the purpose of his discussion. However, he acknowledges that the third party—the introduction of the political—is always present. And I cannot be indifferent to this relationship between the neighbor and the third party when I approach the other. For Levinas, "[t]here must be justice among incomparable ones" (OTB 16/ AE 33). However, this is precisely what is at issue in the relationship of the saying to the said, of ethics to ontology. According to him, we need to account for the infinite ethical responsibility to the other. But we need to account for this responsibility while not forgetting the third party, the other others who also make a claim on me, who demand things from me, and who need infinitely in a world of finite goods. We need to realize these things without reducing the saying to the said. This reduction has been the norm in philosophy, which cannot see beyond being. Levinas's purpose in emphasizing responsibility is similar to the traditional Jewish response to the *Akedah:* we are ineluctably bound to others. Our subjectivity arises in our response to the other, not in our freedom.[35] Our freedom is made possible by the constraints and the boundaries placed on our lives by our relationships with others.

BINDING ABRAHAM

If we read the *Akedah* in light of *Totality and Infinity,* we could say that the father-son relationship that Levinas describes reveals itself in the *Akedah* as it does nowhere else. Nowhere in Judaism does fecundity mean more than in Abraham's relationship to Isaac. In this relationship, the son's life—not to mention the future of Israel—is literally suspended in his father's hands. Thus, we might say, in contrast to Kierkegaard's view, that we admire Abraham not for his faith, but for his turn toward the ethical indicated by his turn toward Isaac. It is an ethical dimension defined not in terms of the universal, as Kierkegaard describes it, but in terms of a response to the other. It is an ethical dimension that emphasizes responsibility to the other, where the uniqueness of the 'I' and the 'I''s responsibility is infinite and irreplaceable.

In his "Preamble from the Heart," Kierkegaard/de Silentio implies that Abraham must give Isaac up so that he can get Isaac back and receive him properly. We might say that this is true, but not for the reasons that Kierkegaard gives. The proper way for Abraham to receive Isaac back was to realize his responsibility to him, to realize, as the Hebrew title of the story suggests, that he is bound to Isaac. Thus, contrary to Kierkegaard's claim that Abraham suspended the ethical, it might be the case that Abraham did not understand, did not yet see, the ethical—in Levinas's sense of the term—at all. And perhaps his willingness to suspend the ethical/the universal helped him to be ethical for the first time.

Rosenzweig elegantly describes the development of humanity from Adam, who did not hear God, to Abraham, who did, in terms of the recognition of responsibility. Upon being asked where he was, Adam did not reply with an 'I.' He did not say, "Here I am." Rather, he said, "She did it." According to Rosenzweig, "[M]an . . . now called by his name, twice in a supreme definiteness that could not but be heard, now he answers, all unlocked, all spread out, all ready, all-soul: 'here I am.'"[36] The "Here I am" marks the crowning moment of subjectivity. In Levinas's view, the ethical, defined as response to the other, is the religious, and therefore both are outside the ontological realm. The point at which Abraham hears that second voice is the moment when he hears the voice that leads him to the ethical. It is this moment that is not only essential, but "the highest moment in the drama" (PN 77/NP 90). As Levinas says, we rise to the level of the religious precisely when we are ethical (PN 77/NP 90). And I would maintain that Abraham's ability to "hear" the second voice indicates that he has already seen the face of Isaac.

There is a sense in which Kierkegaard's reading, although brilliant in its own right, is also deficient. What he attempts in *Fear and Trembling* the rabbis have done for centuries before him. There is no doubt that Kierkegaard gives us a different reading from the collection of midrashim in the Judaic tradition. But although he asks us to read the story slowly and carefully, his reading does not abide by even his own rule. Kierkegaard is dissatisfied with the naive understanding of faith. He thinks that we claim to understand Abraham without truly understanding what faith can ask of us, and his essay on the *Akedah* asks us to consider Abraham carefully. However, Kierkegaard does not read the story to its end. He stops precisely where the drama begins, namely, when Abraham hears the angel, when Abraham puts down the knife, when Abraham sees in the face of his son the true meaning of the religious, when he sees that to love the Torah more than God, to love the ethical more than God, is actually to see the trace of God in the Other. Kierkegaard's drama ends where the climax begins for Levinas: when Abraham realizes that to be irresponsible to God and responsible to Isaac is precisely to be responsible to God.

It is necessary that we realize that our responsibility to God is precisely to be responsible to others. And it is significant that Abraham does not kill his son. Nonetheless, there is something jarring about this story. There is something peculiar about the testing of Abraham. It is in Abraham's seeing of Isaac's face and his turn from an absolute responsibility to God to his responsibility to his son that we see virility tempered. But we can ask, nonetheless, if we are to conclude from Levinas's description of the ethical and from the stories in the Hebrew Bible that without the feminine we wind up with a man who raises a knife to his son.[37] Might the response to the ethical appear differently if it were defined in terms of the feminine? By turning to Levinas's account of maternity, we find an alternative view to Derrida's assertion that even the ethical cannot escape the *economy* of sacrifice.

NINE

Maternity, Sacrifice, and Sarah's Choice

Rakhamim [mercy] is the relation of the uterus [*rekhem*]
to the *other,* whose gestation takes place within it.
Rakhamim is maternity itself. God as merciful is
God defined by maternity. A feminine element
is stirred in the depth of this mercy.
—Levinas, *Nine Talmudic Readings*

Whatever Sarah has said to you, listen to her voice.
—God to Abraham, Genesis 21:12

It is precisely in the relationship of a mother to her child that we detect the problem that arises with the entry of a third. This is the problem to which Derrida called our attention in *The Gift of Death*. Levinas's discussion of the ethical relation and sacrifice alerts us to a potential problem within the maternal relationship. A mother may need to choose between the competing needs of her children, and one child may be sacrificed for another. Thus, the particular example of the mother-child relationship illuminates the conflict between ethics and politics on the global level: decisions need to be made, and people are often sacrificed for others. Levinas recognizes that the potential for violence remains even when it is peace that is sought, for it might be the case that in order to achieve peace, the injuries and wounds of others will be discounted.[1] In light of these problems, it is useful to turn to the maternal paradigm. The maternal bond demonstrates the strength and the fragility of the ethical. Levinas's focus on this bond shifts the philosophical discussion from a preoccupation with death to an emphasis on the creation and nurturing of life. And so sacrifice becomes the very issue on which the discussion turns.

Both Judaism and Levinas maintain that the feminine is more natural-ly attuned to the response of the other. Thus, Levinas would agree, first, that had Sarah been asked, she would not have agreed to sacrifice Isaac, and second, that this response would have earned her passing marks on the test! Levinas demonstrates this point in *Otherwise than Being*. In this book, he reconceives the feminine as maternity, which he honors as the ethical rela-tion par excellence. Thus, one's relationship to a child is still the paradigm for the ethical. However, the feminine in the role of maternity takes the place of the father as the ethical subject, found in *Totality and Infinity*.

SARAH'S CHOICE

At Genesis 21:12, God says to Abraham, "Whatever Sarah tells you, do as she says." This statement is made with reference to Sarah's wish that Hagar and Ishmael, Hagar's child by Abraham, be cast out into the wilderness. At first glance, Sarah does not appear to be particularly sympathetic to the other woman and her child. In fact, her decision to expel them from her house appears to be cold and callous. However, when we take a closer look at the events leading up to Sarah's choice, what appears to be an unsympa-thetic response turns out to be an exemplary response by a mother who sees what others cannot see, a mother who knows that sacrifice is inevitable and unavoidable. In Zornberg's judgment,

> The Sarah who could tell Abraham with such clinical decisiveness: "Cast out that slave woman and her son, for the son of that slave shall not share in my inheritance with my son Isaac," demonstrates not only inflexible will but an apparently lucid vision of reality that is hidden from the more entangled emotions of Abraham. "The matter distressed Abraham greatly, for it con-cerned a son of his" (Gen. 21:10–11). For God confirms her surgical judge-ment. He tells Abraham not merely to obey Sarah but to accept her vision of things—less confused and multifaceted than his.[2]

We may be initially sympathetic to the plight of Hagar and Ishmael. However, Zornberg illuminates what Sarah "sees" and we do not. Sarah senses that Abel's fate—the outcome of a relationship that ends in the mur-der of one by the other—will fall to Isaac. In this case, it is Isaac who is vul-nerable to the games of Ishmael. According to Zornberg, "Rashi cites the midrash that presents the game the boys are playing as a kind of William Tell game, with Ishmael shooting arrows at Isaac and then claiming, 'But I am only playing.'"[3] Ishmael's expression of injured innocence does not fool Sarah, and she foresees that there will be a struggle to the death. Regardless of Ishmael's motivations—that is, choice or non-choice in the matter of his character and actions—Sarah's responsibility is to protect her only son. She sees what Abraham cannot and what she sees does not necessarily detract from her sympathy for Ishmael. Rashi traces her ability to see this threat not simply to the fact that she is a woman, but also to the fact that she is Isaac's mother.[4]

Although Zornberg's reliance on Rashi is compelling, Sarah's choice is not unproblematic. Her decision to expel Hagar and Ishmael from the house is, to say the least, troubling. It certainly undermines any claim that women naturally treat others better than men do. Zornberg's and Rashi's need to justify Sarah's actions within the context of motherhood demonstrates their own uneasiness with Sarah's dilemma and the choice that she makes. But the problematic nature of her choice is precisely what makes it noteworthy in the context of Levinas's discussion of maternity. Her choice reveals a mother's love for her child, and it illuminates the choices she may have to make to protect that child. Sarah exemplifies Levinas's description of the relationship that ethics has to politics because her actions may actually answer questions about who counts as the Other and when—and they do so in ways that disturb us.

As does *Totality and Infinity, Otherwise than Being* presents the ethical as that which interrupts enjoyment. According to Levinas, only a being that eats can be for the other. It is only when one has something to offer the other—"the bread from my mouth"—that one can be for the other. The bread from one's mouth signifies the giving over of one's very existence. It is the openness not only of one's pocketbook, but also of the doors of one's home. It is a "sharing of the bread with the famished, a welcoming of the wretched into your house (Isaiah 58)" (OTB 74/AE 120). This responsibility for the other cannot be traced to a moment at which one remembers having contracted or chosen that responsibility, for it was not chosen.

Levinas characterizes this responsibility as vulnerability and contact; it is an exposedness to the other (OTB 75/AE 120–121). His conception of responsibility, described in *Otherwise than Being*, moves further away from a conventional understanding of responsibility. Responsibility is response to the other. Thus, the terms that he uses indicate how profound that moment of response is. To respond to the other is to be vulnerable to the other; it is not to know what might happen in that response. Levinas refers to this kind of responsibility as a "fine risk." His concern with differentiating "response" from "moralism" requires him to move away from ontological language or language that would confuse his view of responsibility with conventional ethics. Thus, he turns to "maternity," the "gestation of the other in the same" (OTB 75/AE 121) to name the responsibility that concerns him. According to Levinas, maternity "bears even responsibility for the persecuting by the persecutor" (OTB 75/AE 121), since "rather than a nature, earlier than nature, immediacy is this vulnerability, this maternity, this pre-birth or pre-nature in which the sensibility belongs" (OTB 75–76/AE 121). Prior to birth the mother's body is already in contact with an other. The mother is so responsible for this developing child that she is responsible for its responsibility. The bodily relationship between mother and child, who are connected so intimately in maternity, is the model for sensibility, the "fleshly" element of the ethical relation.

For Levinas, maternity signifies that "this proximity is narrower, more constrictive, than contiguity, older than every past present" (OTB 76/AE 121). In the state of pregnancy, a mother has no choice but to feed the fetus growing inside her.[5] Maternity is therefore the ultimate experience of giving the other the bread from one's mouth. And he reveals his recognition of this point when he observes, "[T]hat is alterity in the same . . . psyche in the form of the hand that gives even the bread taken from its own mouth. . . . Here the psyche is like [*comme*] the maternal body" (OTB 67/AE 109, translation altered).[6] Maternity, then, joins together the terms that signify the ethical: vulnerability, responsibility, proximity, contact. The maternal body is substitution par excellence. It is the example of being claimed by another. It is a responsibility that is in place prior to choice.[7]

Unlike *Totality and Infinity*, which emphasized distance and height, *Otherwise than Being* emphasizes proximity. Obsession with the neighbor indicates not only why this relationship cannot be reciprocal, but also why reciprocity is not even an issue. Levinas claims that "in this non-reciprocity, in this 'not thinking of it' is announced, on the hither side of the 'state of nature' (from which nature itself arises), the one-for-the-other, a one-way relationship, not coming back in any form to its point of departure, the *immediacy* of the other, more immediate still than immediate identity in its quietude as a nature—the immediacy of proximity" (OTB 84/AE 134). Proximity, then, could be thought of as the immediacy of the relation, rather than thinking of it in terms of physical closeness. There is no cognition, and thus no mediation. Proximity is *my* "nearness" with regard to my obligation to the other. One might say that nothing stands in my way. *My* obligation to the other demands everything from *me*, including *my* complete openness. And *my* obsession with the other indicates my "grip" on the relation.

Here again, the relationship is asymmetrical. This immediacy does not permit reciprocity. My approach to the other does not concern itself with the other's movement toward me. Thus Levinas tells us that "[my approach] consists in approaching [the other] in such a way that, over and beyond all the reciprocal relations that do not fail to get set up between me and the neighbor, I have always taken one step more toward him—which is possible only if this step is responsibility" (OTB 84/AE 134). There will always be one more step that I take toward the Other because I am responsible for his very responsibility (OTB 84/AE 134). The proximity that Levinas emphasizes indicates how my responsibility for the other is not mediated by choice or cognition. Thus, he refers to "skin," which can also be seen as a limit or a boundary. He says, "It is immediacy of a skin and a face, a skin which is always a modification of a face, a face that is weighted down with a skin" (OTB 85/AE 135).[8] And later he writes,

> It is to hold oneself while gnawing away at oneself. Responsibility in obsession is a responsibility of the ego for what the ego has not wished, that is, for the others. This anarchy in the recurrence to oneself is beyond the normal play of action and passion in which the identity of a being is maintained, in which it *is*. It is on the hither side of the limits of identity. This passivity undergone in proximity by the force of an alterity in me is the passivity of a recurrence to oneself which is not the alienation of an identity betrayed. What can it be but a substitution of me for the others? It is, however, not an alienation, because the other in the same is my substitution of me for the other through responsibility, for which I am summoned as someone irreplaceable. I exist through the other and for the other, but without this being alienation: I am inspired. This inspiration is the psyche. The psyche can signify this alterity in the same without alienation in the form of incarnation, as being-in-one's skin, having the other in one's skin. (OTB 114–115/AE 181)

One cannot help but notice Levinas's frequent references to skin. The face is that which is vulnerable, open, and denuded. Like the face, skin is also that which is exposed. One typically thinks of skin as that which protects an individual or ultimately mediates between a self and another. However, Levinas's image of skin subverts this understanding. According to him, skin serves as an image of the ethical. Responsibility for the other penetrates the skin. It is the subject who is held hostage, denuded, and is so vulnerable that he or she is exposed beyond his or her skin. Although skin can be viewed as our protection against that which is outside us, for Levinas, substitution—being so responsible that one is responsible for the other's responsibility—can be understood as "getting into" the skin of another. Thus, maternity, in which an other is quite literally inside the skin of the mother, captures most effectively the idea of "getting into the skin of another."

MATERNAL RESPONSIBILITY

In her essay "Masculine Mothers? Maternity in Levinas and Plato,"[9] Stella Sanford explores several questions regarding Levinas's conception of maternity: (1) What is the maternity of which Levinas makes use; (2) is this conception metaphorical; and (3) what are the implications of his conception of maternity, regardless of its meaning. Sandford rehearses a few of the standard perspectives on Levinas's use of the term "maternity." For example, Monique Schneider sees Levinas's use of "maternity" as a welcome reversal of the "matricidal impulses of Western thought visible already in Aeschylus's *Oresteia* and in Athena's avowal of her purely masculine parentage."[10] Although these different perspectives concern Sandford, it is John Llewelyn's reading of maternity that most interests her.

Llewelyn advances the interpretation that maternity is a corrective to the discussions of the feminine and the emphasis on paternity found in Levinas's earlier books. If Levinas is criticizing virility, then maybe the emphasis on the father at the end of *Totality and Infinity* was not helpful to his project. Maternity might be more effective for a number of reasons; for example, it can signify for both male and female. Sandford summarizes the discussion of maternity in two points: First, the maternal is not intended to designate something exclusively female. Although we have a biological understanding of maternity that excludes men, maternity can also refer to the aspect of nurturing and care involved in the biological process. This behavioral aspect of maternity need not remain exclusively female. Second, in spite of this previous point that the care aspect of maternity exceeds the biological necessity of the female body, the commentators whom she discusses share the belief that maternity does in fact refer only to the feminine.

Thus, Sandford wants to know if there can be a different genealogy that "gives birth" to a different possibility with regard to maternity. Can a conception of maternity yield something that includes men and also allows women to be something other than mothers? Because Sandford assumes that Levinas's view of eros has its roots in a Platonic conception, she compares his view of maternity to the one found in Plato's *Symposium*. But in spite of any similarity or debt that Levinas's view of eros might have to Plato, it is apparent that his conception of maternity is not indebted to Plato. Although Levinas certainly does not want to dispense with philosophy, he is nonetheless critical of what philosophy has traditionally offered in the realm of ethics. Attention to his interest in Hebrew, particularly the Hebrew word for *womb*, the physical site of maternity, may be more instructive on this point.

In a note to his essay "No Identity," Levinas confides, "We are thinking of the Biblical term 'Rakhamin,' which is translated as mercy, but contains a reference to the word 'Rekhem,' uterus; it is a mercy that is like an emotion of the maternal entrails."[11] And in the talmudic reading "Damages Due to Fire," Levinas elaborates on this discussion of mercy. He asks, "What is the meaning of the word Merciful (*Rakhmana*)?" And he answers,

It means the Torah itself or the Eternal One who is defined by Mercy. But this translation is altogether inadequate. *Rakhamim* (Mercy), which the Aramaic term Rakhmana evokes, goes back to the word *Rekhem,* which means uterus. *Rakhamim* is the relation of the uterus to the *other,* whose gestation takes place within it. *Rakhamim* is maternity itself. God as merciful is God defined by maternity. A feminine element is stirred in the depth of this mercy. This maternal element in divine paternity is very remarkable, as is in Judaism the notion of a "virility" to which limits must be set and whose partial renouncement may be symbolized by circumcision, the exaltation of a certain *weakness* which would be devoid of cowardice. Perhaps maternity is sensitivity itself, of which so much ill is said among the Nietzscheans. (DDF 183/DPF 158)

In Levinas's discussion, maternity does not function simply as a metaphor derived from the physical proximity between mother and child, although certainly he does not overlook the immediacy of the relationship. Levinas equates maternity with mercy (*rakhamim,* derived from the Hebrew word for uterus, *rekhem*), and mercy is the ethical response to the other. His references to the Hebrew show the similarity between this derivation and the central themes of *Otherwise than Being*—for example, the gestation of the other in the same. And it exposes an implied contrast with the Greek word for uterus—*hyster*—from which we (Anglophone readers) derive our word "hysterectomy." By the Greeks, and similarly by us until very recently, the uterus was thought to be the site of the emotions. Thus, if a woman was thought to be crazy (excessively emotional), the solution was to remove her uterus. As Levinas indicates in the above passage, however, he not only believes that mercy in the form of the womb—the feminine—is good, but also suggests by his comments that men should temper their own virile inclinations. And in the conclusion to the passage above, he suggests the tempering of virility—both literally and metaphorically—is symbolized through circumcision.

Although Sandford also reminds us of the biblical use of "beget"— namely, to father, Levinas is not speaking simply of "begetting." His focus on the womb leaves little doubt that he means maternity as it applies to women—gestation and birth.[12] Even if maternity were simply a metaphor, the image that Levinas has in mind is not Greek. In fact, his own references to Isaiah indicate that he draws the image of maternity from the Hebrew Bible. Throughout Isaiah, the prophet refers to the image of the womb, of the experience of birth, of the most intimate bond between mother and child. In Isaiah 49:15, for example, the prophet asks, "Can a woman forget her baby, forget to have compassion [*merachem*] on the child of her womb? Can a woman forget her sucking child?" Isaiah answers his own question: "Though she might forget, I never could forget you." Isaiah's answer indicates that there is a bond stronger than the mother-child bond: the bond between God and God's people. However, the strength of the bond between God and God's people is described in comparison to the bond between a mother and her child. Isaiah's question and answer derive their force precisely from the image of the mother-child relation. His question is intended to present this bond as the strongest possible between two humans. And this bond is surpassed in its strength only by a relationship with God.

Levinas thus develops his notion of maternity as the ethical relation par excellence in light of this image of the mother-child bond. A woman could conceivably abandon her child, and certainly this happens. But when it does happen, it nonetheless jars our sensibility, precisely because we understand the bond as Isaiah does. Levinas describes the ethical relation in terms of proximity, which he defines as an absence of space between the two, such that the vulnerability of one to the other is plainly clear.[13] One turns one's cheek to the smiter, as he tells us when he quotes from Lamentations, not after having already been injured, but rather prior to injury, as when meeting for the first time. By focusing on this interpretation of the passage, he observes something far more suggestive. To turn one's cheek toward the smiter is to display one's openness to the other.[14] To turn one's cheek for the first time is to be always already vulnerable; it is to be always already exposed to the other.

In order to illustrate the ethical relationship that he has in mind, Levinas turns to the maternal figure. In his view, the maternal exemplifies that which is held hostage ethically by the other and which gives itself over to the other completely. Once pregnant, the maternal body is transformed and immediately begins to nurture the growing fetus inside her. In the state of pregnancy, the mother cannot help but feed her child. The mother has no sooner taken in food than her body distributes that food to the fetus inside her. She does not choose to feed the child, but her body does so nonetheless.[15]

Concerned about the relationship between the figure of the feminine and ethics in Levinas's work, Catherine Chalier argues that "maternity is the very pattern of substitution." According to Chalier, substitution fulfills responsibility if we understand responsibility as that which is not chosen.[16] For her, it is the maternal body that best exemplifies substitution:

Levinas describes the maternal body as "a pre-original not resting on oneself" (OTB 75/AE 95), as a body of goodness that is devoted to the Other before being devoted to itself. In this unselfish and maternal body, subjectivity loses the substantiality and identity that would already be acquired. As a subjectivity without substitute, the maternal body has to answer for the Other and is irreplaceable in this task. The maternal body suffers for the Other, it is "the body as passivity and renunciation, a pure undergoing." It is the very contrary of the *conatus*. It is "signification for the other and not for itself." In spite of me, for the other. . . . The maternal body is ruled by the Good beyond being; it has not chosen the Good but the Good has elected it. . . . Thus it seems that maternity is the ultimate meaning of the feminine, the very metaphor of subjectivity, and of course, not only a metaphor. . . . We have to encounter this failure in the virility of being in order to understand the meaning of the Other. The maternal body knows in its flesh and blood what subjectivity means.[17]

Levinas's passage on *rakhamim* also emphasizes the need for a feminization of the virile. Thus, recalling the description of Abraham's actions in the previous chapter, one might say, following Chalier and Levinas, that Abraham needed to be feminized.[18]

According to Sandford, however useful maternity may be as an ethical paradigm, its position of priority is finally usurped by the discussion of filiality and community that concludes *Otherwise than Being*.[19] Thus, what appeared to be a corrective, in Llewelyn's view, may be undone by the conspicuous absence of maternity from these final discussions at the end of the book. Sandford's point is important, for it raises the question of priority with regard to these various relationships.

This problem first emerges in *Totality and Infinity*. Levinas describes the community as the site where the political reemerges. Thus, when the discussion of the political enters the discussion, the relationship that the father has to the child is not mentioned again. The discussion of the political usurped the discussion of paternity in *Totality and Infinity*. It is not because the maternal is feminine that Levinas drops it from the discussion in *Otherwise than Being*, since we saw the same pattern in *Totality and Infinity* with regard to paternity. Rather, his shift to a discussion of the political emphasizes his claim that the political is always present.

But I suggest that Levinas turns to the maternal precisely because it provides a more promising example of the relationship between ethics and politics. The image of maternity not only turns our attention to mercy; it also most closely resembles the first experience with the Other that he described in the father-child relation at the end of *Totality and Infinity*. He describes the child as the one who is me-but-not-me. The child joins the lovers and also interrupts their closed society. The child emerges from the love relationship, but he or she is also distinct from either of the lovers. Levinas's description of the relationship that the child has to the couple is effective. But the ethical relation that he has in mind is more effectively conveyed by the maternal relationship, in which the child lives in, is attached to, and is nurtured by the mother's body.[20] So it follows that a discussion of maternity would be incomplete if it did not address the very real violence that women commit against others, and in particular against their own children.

MEDEA ET AL.

Laurie Zoloth, a scholar of Jewish social ethics, maintains that feminism cannot move forward until it reconciles female violence, particularly the violence that women do to their children, with its view of women.[21] Children have been maimed and killed by family members since ancient times. Abel, the first murder victim, was killed by his own brother, and Joseph's brothers sold him into slavery. In the Greek tragedy *Medea*, Medea kills her own children in order to avenge her husband's infidelity. With these examples in mind, Zoloth rehearses the numerous reasons given for the violence that women commit against their children: they are poor, overworked, abused, or "sick." We frequently hear mothers say that the death of their children was a better alternative to the greater violence in store for them.[22] These arguments lead one to ask whether women's violence can ever be called genuinely "evil."[23] The reasons given for why women commit violence, especially when the violence is perpetrated against their own children, serve to divide women into two basic categories: (1) either they are "sick," in which case the violence is not "evil"; or (2) they had a "reason" that explains why they "snapped," in which case, again, the violence is not "evil." In Zoloth's view, any act of violence against children, who are always innocent victims, is always evil. In fact, violence against our own children is the greatest evil, and it happens far more often than is reported in the news.

Zoloth's concern is central both to ethics and to feminist theory. But I would add that the violence that mothers do to their children is the exception that proves the rule. On the one hand, far too many children die at the hands of their mothers. On the other hand, we might reasonably ask why more are not injured or killed. What makes maternity so interesting is precisely the range of opportunities it presents for women to harm or kill their children. Women are often alone with their children for hours on end. They are bigger and stronger than their children. They have the means, the opportunity, and the ability to carry out such an act whenever they wish. Since our society does not typically consider the job of maternity important, we do not take the necessary measures to ensure that women are not driven to these extreme acts.

Although I agree with Zoloth that violence done to children is evil, I would also suggest that her concern is for society, not for the conception of maternity that Levinas has in mind. Levinas describes the conditions for the possibility of the maternal relationship. His concern is for the conditions that need to be present in order for a mother to care for her child or for her child to thrive. I would add that our fascination with women who do kill their children might be less about the voyeurism that is normally associated with violence and more about the fact that this particular kind of violence, no matter how frequently it happens, jars us. Even with the potential violence that accompanies maternity, this relationship nonetheless effectively conveys what Levinas has in mind. The mother's relationship to the child is always one that she is free to reject. We cannot reject the obligation, but we can reject the actual practice of that obligation.

To make maternity the paradigm does not require that no one ever kill her children. That not only would be absurd, but it would also render ethics meaningless. The ethical is such *because* the Other is the sole being I wish to kill and because most of us go about our lives without yielding to the temptation. Maternity is exceptional precisely because the mother's body has no choice but to feed the child while it lives inside her; and yet, she can nonetheless choose to harm the child, even while the child is in utero. Once that child is born, she can choose not to feed it. The mother can leave her child to die. That she does not do so is simultaneously extraordinary and routine. It is because we undervalue, underestimate, and take for granted the lives of mothers and their obligations to their children that we are so shocked when one steps out of the nurturing role and, for whatever reason, intentionally kills or harms her child.[24] Thus, the bond that Isaiah so eloquently describes, a union that appears immune to the disruption of the third, is nonetheless subject to that violence. The maternal bond is cast in terms of the sacrifice that the mother must make or the violence that she commits in the face of making those sacrifices.

Contrary to Heidegger's claim that death is what separates us, for Levinas it is precisely death, and my concern for the other's death, that connects us (DFo 215/MP 262). For Heidegger, sacrifice is impossible because the other's mortality will always remain. It might not be *this* bullet that kills me, but I cannot avoid dying altogether. Thus my death is always mine. Even if my death can be put off to a later time, no one can completely take my death away from me. But Levinas criticizes the "mineness of death," which he thinks creates a paradox in the logic of sacrifice. Levinas's concern is not whether we actually die. He concedes that we are all ultimately mortal. And, for Levinas, it is precisely this mortality that makes sacrifice so significant. He believes that Heidegger's way of thinking about death leads to a failure in the possibility of sacrifice. Instead, he implores us to think of the possibility of sacrifice as an ethical structure, in which sacrifice is understood as *mourir pour*—dying for. Rather than thinking of sacrifice in its most mechanistic terms—one person dies and another lives—we should emphasize the "dying for . . . " aspect of sacrifice. One person dies-for another. This understanding of sacrifice highlights the connection that one has to another not only in the act of sacrifice, but also in our everyday lives.

Levinas's conversation with Bracha Lichtenberg-Ettinger, also cited in chapter 3, brings together the troubling connection among sacrifice, women, and childbirth. Levinas says,

> The feminine is the future. The feminine in its feminine phase, in its feminine form certainly may die bringing life into the world, but—how can I say to you?—it is not the 'dying'; for me, the 'dying' of a woman is certainly unacceptable. I am speaking about the possibility of conceiving that there is meaning without me. I think the heart of the heart, the deepest of the feminine, is dying in giving life, in bringing life into the world. I am not emphasizing dying but, on the contrary, *future.* . . . Woman is the category of future, the ecstasy of future. It is that human possibility which consists in saying that the life of another human being is more important than my own, that the death of the other is more important to me than my own death, that the Other comes before me, that the Other counts before I do, that the value of the Other is imposed before mine is.[25]

This passage certainly appears disturbing. And it would be even more disturbing if it were clear that Levinas was advocating that women die in order to give life. I prefer to take him at his word that he believes the "dying of a woman is certainly unacceptable." I suggest that this passage is disturbing because Levinas raises an issue that so few of us wish to acknowledge—women, in fact, die in childbirth. They die while giving life to another. Nature could not be more ironic. And this is especially so, since it is only with recent technology—incubators, formula, and so on—that the baby, for whom the mother gave her life, can live. Regardless, the emphasis for Levinas is not whether the child lives. Rather, he focuses on the meaning of the woman's action. Her willingness to die for her child reveals a shift in emphasis from the ego to the other, from the present to the future—and his characterization fits especially when we consider Judaism's view that children are in fact the future.

Levinas contributes to the discussion of sacrifice by shifting the emphasis from the ontology of death and sacrifice (the fact that we die) to ethics (our response to the other). In death, relations with others are not dissolved. Levinas cites the biblical story of King Saul and his son Jonathan to illustrate his claim. Rather than referring to a life "after death," Levinas emphasizes the love that exists between the two: it is a love that is stronger than death and lives on after death. Sacrifice, then, is not a losing of oneself; rather, it is a giving of oneself in the other.

This aporia of responsibility that Derrida explores in *The Gift of Death* offers insight into Levinas's turn to the maternal. The maternal figure not only exemplifies the ethical relation, but also illustrates the conflict that Levinas sees between the ethical and the political. A mother and child form a couplet, a relation of two. Thus, we can see in the mother-child relation what Levinas means by proximity, an unmediated relation. We see in the mother-child relationship an example of the ethical relation such that one gives over to the other so completely that she might give her life for the other. Maternity exemplifies a conception of sacrifice—the giving of oneself in another—that Levinas thinks exemplifies a love which, in Rosenzweig's terms, is "stronger than death."[26]

TEN

The Silent Footsteps of Rebecca

And Abraham proceeded to mourn for Sarah
and to bewail her.
—Genesis 23:2

We can now see the shift in emphasis from the masculine to the feminine, from death to life, and the role that maternity plays in that move. Levinas turns to the figure of maternity because of the image that Isaiah sees and the risk involved in it. However, Isaiah's image of maternity is not unique to him. Levinas thinks that we share this image. The image of maternity is rich precisely because it appeals to us. It offers intuitive evidence to short-circuit a reliance on the will. If, for Levinas, the problem with describing the ethical is the risk that one will lapse into the ontological, then he needs to circle around the ethical so that we can glimpse its significance without actually naming it as such.[1]

The previous chapter investigated Levinas's conception of maternity as the ethical relation par excellence. For Levinas, sacrifice is a necessary part of the ethical, and thus it is a necessary aspect of maternity. Sacrificing one's life for another ultimately expresses the interruption of the *conatus essendi*. And we see most clearly the possibility of this sacrifice in maternity. There are, of course, problems with a conception of the ethical that is characterized by sacrifice, especially when the paradigm of the ethical is the figure of maternity.

This chapter examines two competing yet complementary themes: (1) maternity demonstrates the genuine possibility of one dying for another; and (2) the feminine in the role of maternity may lose the playfulness that earlier was said to characterize it, particularly in the erotic relationship. Thus, the feminine appears to be caught between two opposing positions: on the one hand, the earlier role of the feminine included a playfulness. But the feminine remained outside the ethical, and thus appeared unimportant.

On the other hand, in Levinas's later writings, the feminine in the role of maternity is squarely situated in the ethical relation. But this description of the feminine appears to lack the playfulness of eros. It is certainly possible that Levinas separates these categories for descriptive purposes. Thus, he might not intend them to be discrete characteristics—the early role of the feminine is playful while the later role is somber and responsible. I suggest that Levinas's move to the maternal image does not require us to sacrifice the enjoyment of life, nor does it indicate that the feminine has lost its playfulness. Although responsibility is an aspect of maternity, it is not the only aspect of it. This chapter examines Sarah's relationship to both Abraham and their son Isaac, whom she conceived at the age of ninety. By considering Sarah and then Rebecca, Isaac's wife, we arrive at a conception of the feminine that is revealed through the lives of these two biblical women. These are mothers who embody both responsibility and *jouissance*.

SACRIFICING MATERNITY

The rabbis recognized the risks involved in pregnancy and childbirth and thus concluded that the first commandment, to "be fruitful and multiply," obligates only men.[2] They acknowledged that along with incurring pain, pregnancy and childbirth can endanger a woman's health and life. In recognizing the risk of pregnancy for a woman, the rabbis thought that it would be immoral to legally obligate a person to do something that causes enormous hardship and endangers life.[3] A woman risks her life in childbirth. It is not uncommon, even today, for her to die as a result of complications from the pregnancy or the labor and delivery.[4] Clearly, this is the ultimate sacrifice, which is most often not chosen. But responsibility in the maternal relation refers not only to the sacrifice that a woman might make in childbirth; it also refers to the mother's very act of nurturing the child growing inside her body. Levinas sees in maternity a love that is stronger than death; it is the excessive love of maternity that may result in the extreme act of sacrifice. Thus, he sees maternity as the ethical relation par excellence. This model, then, requires us to consider a few of its implications: (1) maternity as an ethical paradigm may lead to an essentialist view of women;[5] and (2) the ethical understood as sacrifice may be a dangerous model for women.

In her essay "The Hungry Jewish Mother," Erika Duncan relates the story of a woman who "in her dying turns away from all those she was forced to nurture in her life."[6] This figure of the Jewish woman, "the all-engulfing nurturer who devours the very soul with every spoonful of hot chicken soup she gives," is all too commonly invoked by male Jewish writers. Duncan contrasts this figure with another conception of woman that is usually forgotten, the woman who gives because doing so is her only access to love:

> In Jewish literature by women, mothers are the "bread givers" who try to make feeding into a replenishing, ecstatic act. But the mothers are themselves starved in every way, sucked dry and withered from being asked almost from birth to give a nurturing they never receive. They are starved not only for the actual food they are forced to turn over to others, but for the stuff of self and soul, for love and song. The oldest daughter in *Tell Me a Riddle* cries, "Pay me back, Mother, pay me back for all you took from me. Those others you crowded into your heart. The hands I needed to be for you, the heaviness, the responsibility." But the dying grandmother, her mother, can only chant:
> "One pound soup meant . . . one soup bone . . . Bread, day-old . . . Plea in a wood box . . . for kindling.
> I ask for stone; she gives me bread-day-old . . .
> How can I give it, Clara, how can I give it if I don't have?"[7]

Duncan concludes, "The mother's starvation is, needless to say, scary for the child, who has no choice but to take."[8]

Duncan's essay illuminates the two effects of sacrifice: (1) our exploitation of the mother who toils because she believes that is her only access to love; and (2) the child's fear when she realizes how the satisfaction of her need comes at the mother's expense. Dying in childbirth is certainly the extreme with regard to the sacrifices that mothers make. Metaphorically, women sacrifice a great deal in order to raise healthy, happy children. And we can only imagine the life riddled with guilt for the child who realizes the sacrifices that his or her mother made for him or her—either in dying or in simply forfeiting opportunities and experiences in order to care for him or her. Tina Chanter rightly points out that Levinas's ethics cannot ignore the very real historical events that have demanded and then exploited the sacrifices that women make for men;[9] nor can Levinas ignore the very real risk that women take in pregnancy and childbirth.[10]

But Levinas is not advancing a normative ethics of maternity or of sacrifice, certainly not in the conventional sense of "normative." He is neither proposing or demanding that women *become* mothers or sacrifice their lives, nor is he saying that maternity is the only ethical relationship. Men would have a difficult time achieving this end, and we know from *Totality and Infinity* that Levinas clearly includes men in the ethical relation. It is significant that Levinas uses *comme* ("as" or "like") when referencing responsibility and the maternal body. The psyche, which gives the bread from its mouth, is *like* the maternal body. A similar formulation can be found in

Richard Cohen's claim that *maternal psyche* is equivalent to *maternal body,* and in his claim that "psyche" needs to be understood as bodily, rather than as something ethereal.[11] His claims do not controvert my reminder above that the ethical is *like* the maternal body rather than only *being* the maternal body. The psyche is passive like the maternal body. The maternal body reveals this passive relationship, but it is a relationship used instructively.

Maternity, then, works as a powerful example of the ethical relation because it reveals what Levinas's philosophical language—the Greek—cannot describe. The mother's responsibility begins before she even knows of the fetus growing inside her; her body has already begun to feed and nurture the fetus before she is "aware" of its existence. Through no choice of her own, in pregnancy her life is immediately tied to the life of another. The fetus gestating in a woman cannot survive unless she participates in certain activities and refrains from certain other activities. It may not even make sense to speak of sacrifice as a normative aspect of maternity; it is encoded into the very term itself. Maternity eventually, and in different ways, involves choice and agency, but not initially. Becoming pregnant may have been a choice, and later on, the continuation of the pregnancy *is* chosen. Thus, in Levinas's view maternity exemplifies passivity in the sense that it does not will that the fetus be nourished. The maternal body is transformed without the will of the mother: a placenta forms, milk production begins, and the fetus is nourished.

What Levinas's image uncovers, however, is precisely why pregnancy and abortion are such contested issues in a hotbed of politics. The abortion debate frequently centers on who has more pressing rights—the woman/mother or the fetus. Once the argument reaches this point, neither side recognizes that the two lives are bound together. On one side, the woman is treated merely as a vessel—an incubator. On the other, the fetus is typically viewed as a disposable lump of tissue. Yet it is the joining of these two bodies that makes the issue of abortion and a woman's political right to choose so compelling. The woman's life is at risk and her life is at issue *precisely because* the fetus's life depends on hers.[12] It is precisely because of this risk that the role of maternity needs to be recognized for what it is. Levinas's discussion of maternity reveals the intimate relationship between *two* beings, a woman and the child within her body, where the mother's life is at risk simply by being pregnant. Maternity involves the giving to another that even the woman may not notice. It is a giving of herself that nourishes a growing child and that demands everything her body can offer. This is why maternity is so profound and so extraordinary, in spite of the fact that we typically view it as "natural" and mundane.

As we saw in his conversation with Bracha Lichtenberg-Ettinger, Levinas recognizes this threat to the woman's life, and he recognizes it without also prescribing it. His focus on maternity as passivity reveals the fact that the maternal body has no choice but to nourish the other within her. This exemplifies his ethical relation. But, as Levinas tells us, the political always accompanies the ethical. The *choice,* then, to *carry* a pregnancy to term and continue the risk of life is not an ethical question; it is a political question.[13] Levinas's discussion of maternity as the ethical paradigm does not undermine the possibility that the political choice to continue or end a pregnancy always remains solely the choice of the woman whose life is at stake.[14]

Questions about what is prescriptive or simply descriptive permeate discussions about Levinas's writings. So it should come as no surprise that Levinas's turn to maternity as the expression of the ethical relation raises these same questions. We should be able to take his comments about his project as a clue that his use of "maternity" is not prescriptive or normative. In *Ethics and Infinity,* Phillipe Nemo poses the following question to Levinas: "Is it starting from this ethical experience that you construct an 'ethics'? For it follows, ethics is made up of rules; it is necessary to establish these rules?" Levinas replies, "My task does not consist in constructing ethics; I only try to find its meaning" (EI 90/EeI 95). I suggest that Levinas's use of maternity is not prescriptive, but descriptive—I will return later to this problematic distinction. He is neither telling women to get pregnant nor telling them to sacrifice their lives. This view of maternity and of ethics is not a "pro-life" position, in the current sense of the term.[15] Levinas's ethics is not intended to tell us what to do, but, rather, to provide the argument for understanding the possibility of the ethical in the shadow of a world that seems to make ethics impossible. Thus, sacrifice in the form of nurturing and feeding the other becomes a substantial part of his ethics. The possibility of sacrifice demonstrates that the *conatus essendi* can be interrupted. More importantly, Levinas's application of the maternal body in *Otherwise than Being* is not concerned with the act of conception, nor is it concerned with whether a woman decides to remain pregnant. These two ends of the pregnancy spectrum are not his focus. His description of responsibility rests on the maternal body—the care of a mother for a child is the paradigmatic example of the kind of sacrifice that he has in mind.[16] Thus the maternal body demonstrates how responsibility works in all of us. We all already resemble the maternal body insofar as *we have all* been assigned, we have all been chosen.

Still, even if Levinas's descriptions are not intended normatively, the concerns that Chanter raises cannot be taken lightly. Descriptive or not, Levinas's references to maternity and his description of the feminine reinforce historical, cultural, and philosophical views of women that have shaped their lives and often confined them to oppressive and abusive conditions. Levinas's description of women as gentle, hospitable, and maternal could very easily be read not only as reinscribing the stereotypes that women have fought so hard to overcome, but also as prescribing them. And in one sense, Levinas *is* prescribing these images. But the prescription that he has in mind is not so literal as to prescribe women to become pregnant. Rather, the prescription is for *all* of us (men and women) to become *like* the maternal body.

It seems that the only way to escape the dangers of what maternity signifies is to abandon the use of the maternal as the example of the ethical relation par excellence. Yet the maternal is in fact effective for his purposes. This is precisely why it is also problematic. Chanter is correct that there is a danger in Levinas's descriptions. Her concern is that an ethics that emphasizes the feminine as the paradigm of responsibility and, ultimately, sacrifice will lead to a prescription for women's behavior. But Chanter also consciously resists reducing Levinas to simply a male chauvinist who intends to put women back into positions of domestic seclusion. Thus, if we grant Levinas the benefit of the doubt that this was not his intention, what do we make of his description and use of maternity? If we make the mistake that maternity signifies only for women, we distort not only what Levinas means by responsibility, but also who is to be responsible. Unlike the philosophers who precede him, Levinas does not mean that women are naturally more moral and that therefore it is their job to keep everyone else in line. In fact, quite the contrary: Levinas sees very clearly that virility needs to be tempered, and it is the maternal *body*—one very specific dimension, and clearly not the only dimension, of women—that is the model for teaching this lesson. And men still need to do their part in their ethical development.

In the *Feminine and the Sacred*,[17] Kristeva refers to the experience of the "face-to-face with [the] emergence of the other" as alchemy.[18] She claims that outside motherhood, no situations exist in human experience that so radically and so simply bring us to that experience. She adds that "the father, in his own, less immediate way, is led to the same alchemy; but to get there he must identify with the process of delivery and birth, hence with the maternal experience, that is, the father must himself become maternal and feminine, before adding his own role as indispensable and radical distance."[19] Because the psychoanalytic tradition influences Kristeva's thought, she concludes that the father is the third who brings the mother and child into the phallic world. This is how the call of language is generated.

Much can be made of her latter claim, and certainly one would have to accept the assumptions of psychoanalysis in order to accept her final conclusion. For example, if we view Levinas's analysis through Kristeva's lens, it is the father who moves the child *away* from the ethical and toward the political. The maternal, then, is the exemplary paradigm of the ethical. However, I am less interested in disputing Kristeva and/or psychoanalysis than in highlighting Kristeva's sensitivity to the simultaneously singular and peculiar nature of the maternal. Her insight helps to disclose an important shift in Levinas's own thinking in both the description of the feminine and the conception of the ethical. Levinas's description of the child in *Totality and Infinity* as both "me and not me" was spoken from the standpoint of Levinas as the father. The child was the ethical other par excellence. In *Otherwise than Being,* the feminine *and* the ethical are transformed into the figure of maternity, the "gestation of the other in the same." The "me, not me" formulation is now understood in terms of the mother and the child. Thus, if we remember Levinas's claim that the feminine is the interruption of the virile, we can also see Kristeva's point: the father—the masculine—can get to the experience of the other, but only by first becoming feminine.

SARAH'S LAUGHTER;
OR, MATERNITY REVISITED

Maternity does include sacrifice, but this is not all that it is. For example, we can look to Levinas's reference to maternity and see the shift in the focus of the discussion. Levinas does realize the role that death plays in ethics. Death signifies mortality and thus signifies the need for both fecundity and concern for the other. Ethics, on Levinas's account, is precisely about concern for the other's death—and hence, a concern for the other's life. Thus, his use of maternity may indicate that he wants the ethical relation, and thus his philosophical project, to signify an emphasis on life—even a love of life—rather than an emphasis on death. This does not have to mean that the maternal is the only way to express this love, nor that it succeeds in expressing this love. But it does mean that the maternal expresses it most evidently—maternity is nothing if it is not, at its most fundamental level, about the creation and nurturance of life. To recognize this fundamental aspect of maternity is also to recognize the way in which we are implicated in each other's lives from the start.

Levinas emphasizes the dual function of maternity: (1) as the image that expresses the profound role that responsibility plays in the relationship between mother and child; and (2) as an indisputable feature related to women—even if not all women, only women—that serves as the model for men. In either case, Levinas's later work primarily emphasizes the relationship of maternity to the ethical. And from his conception of maternity as the ethical relation par excellence several concerns emerge.

In addition to her concern about the image of maternity, Chanter also raises the concern that the discussion of maternity takes place in the absence of any related discussion of eros.[20] The conception of eros that preceded the discussion of paternity in *Totality and Infinity* drops out of Levinas's discussion, as it is exchanged for the discussion of maternity. Thus, we are left with an image of maternity that appears cleansed of erotic pleasure.[21] Maternity, sanitized of eros, begins to look like the Madonna often desired: not only would childbirth be necessary to redeem any act of sex, but the real desire would be for children to be born without *women* having to have sex at all. In light of Chanter's concerns, I would suggest that the eros of *Totality and Infinity* is not separate from the responsibility of maternity.

Like Chanter, I would worry if Levinas promoted such a position. However, I do not think that he is suggesting that eros be absent from maternity. Rather, his discussion of maternity in *Otherwise than Being* centers on its efficacy at expressing the ethical relation. In *Totality and Infinity*, he wished to separate the experience of the erotic from the ethical. This does not mean that the ethical and the erotic never intersect. In fact, we know that the ethical is an interruption of eros. If we read *Totality and Infinity* and *Otherwise than Being* together, we can see that Levinas has not abandoned eros. In *Totality and Infinity*, the erotic—the play between the lovers—is prior to the ethical—the birth of the child. In *Otherwise than Being*, the discussion of maternity is not a discussion of what led to the maternal body. The discussion focuses on the maternal body as such. So what if responsibility was not the only aspect of maternity? I suggest that in its most profound form maternity also displays a *jouissance* or a *joie de vivre*. And we see this other dimension of maternity in the biblical figure of Sarah.

Rachel Adler calls attention to Sarah's laughter and tells us that in order to construct a "feminist theology/ethics of sexuality, we should first retrieve the meaning of Sarah's laughter."[22] I would suggest that in order to address the charge that Levinas's account yields a "sexless mother" and a joyless maternity, we also should turn to laughter.[23] What is particularly striking about Sarah's laughter is the context in which we find it. Sarah has just been told that she will give birth to a child, and that this child will yield many nations. Upon hearing this news, Sarah laughs. And she laughs not simply because she is told that she will give birth at the age of ninety. She laughs because she also understands what it will mean to give birth to the child: she must first conceive the child, and to do that, she, at the age of ninety, as Adler observes, realizes that "'the old man and I are going to do it again!' The picture of their fragile bodies shaken by fierce young pleasures evokes from her a bawdy and delighted guffaw."[24] Sarah's thought moves from having the child to the pleasures, and the absurdity, involved in conceiving the child. So Sarah laughs, and the angel asks her why she laughs. Sarah's laughter *is* and is about eros. The angel understands only the destiny that must be realized; the angel cannot relate to the human mechanics by which this destiny is to be accomplished. Adler then reminds us that

[L]aughter, from the Hebrew root *tzahak,* is sometimes associated with biblical sex. The king of the Philistines sees Isaac *mitzahek,* "playing" with his wife (Gen. 8). Potiphar's wife accuses, "That Hebrew slave, whom you brought into our house came to me *l'tzahek bi* [to dally with me]" (Gen. 39:17). Its use in Exodus 32:6 in connection with the feast for the Golden Calf where the people "sat down to eat and drink and then rose *l'tzahek,* to make merry," leads the classical commentators to envision an orgy. Laughter is erotic, spontaneous, and anarchic, a powerful disturber of plans and no respecter of persons.[25]

Thus, laughter interrupts, and it does not matter who laughs. The angel who brought the message to Sarah was serious; Sarah, who received the message, is incredulous, and so she laughs! As Adler comments, the traditional focus on Sarah's laughter in this story centers on the idea that Sarah is incredulous at the possibility of conceiving. These commentaries conveniently overlook Sarah's reference to *ednah*—sexual pleasure. So, Sarah gives birth to a son and says, "God has brought me laughter; everyone who hears will laugh with me" (Gen. 21:6). More interesting is the fact that Sarah not only laughs, but even names her child "Isaac" [*Yitzhak*], meaning "one who laughs." Her child becomes the embodiment of the sexual pleasure that Sarah experienced with Abraham. Zornberg adds to this discussion by commenting that Abraham and Sarah "represent the dialectics of laughter."[26] With Isaac, the age of laughter begins.[27] And with the arrival of Isaac, Sarah's motherhood is also tested. She is not aware that her husband has been asked to take her son to Moriah and offer him as a sacrifice.

The *Akedah* ignores Sarah completely, and the very next chapter, *Chayye Sarah*—Life of Sarah—opens with her death. We can only surmise what might have happened. Isaac returned and told his mother that Abraham intended to sacrifice him. Maybe he was rendered speechless and so told his mother nothing. Certainly the relationship between Abraham and Isaac was altered, and certainly Sarah would have noticed. But these are all conjectures. The midrash also conjectures about Sarah's death. The rabbis' concern is precisely that Sarah's death follows on the heels of the aborted sacrifice of Isaac. The rabbis believe that Sarah died of grief upon hearing that Isaac had been sacrificed.[28] There are even variations on how she heard. For example, one version tells us that Satan came to her in a disguise and told her that Abraham had in fact sacrificed Isaac. Rashi's gloss on this version tells us that "Sarah's death was consequent to the Binding of Yitzhak, because upon [hearing] the news of the *Akedah*—that her son had been readied for slaughter and had almost been slaughtered—her soul took flight and she died."[29] In other words, merely hearing the possibility was enough to kill her. We see in this interpretation of Sarah's death a belief that a mother's love is so strong that she would die from heartbreak.

Yet Rashi's reading is more nuanced and more arresting. There are a variety of possibilities of midrashim from which Rashi chooses to develop his own reading. The first interpretation involving Satan has a second variation, in which Satan comes disguised as Isaac. In this version, upon seeing Isaac, Sarah immediately asks, What has your father done to you? The midrash does not focus on this line, but it is interesting that Sarah would immediately know that something was done to Isaac by his father. This midrash recalls Rashi's interpretation that Sarah saw the potential threat of Ishmael to Isaac, and she was able to see this threat because she was Isaac's mother. Satan, disguised as Isaac, tells her what happened and she dies before hearing the end of the story. The second variation on this version has the real Isaac, not Satan disguised as Isaac, telling Sarah himself. In either case, she cannot endure to the end.[30] She does not need to wait to hear the end of the story. She "knows" the "happy" ending: Isaac lives. In spite of that ending, Sarah still dies before Isaac can finish the story. Again, it is too much to bear. This is the version on which Rashi focuses. Zornberg's gloss on this version of the story is worth considering:

> [Sarah] dies not simply because she cannot endure to the end of the story: that would constitute a relatively primitive tragic irony. She dies of the truth of *kime'at shelo nishhat*—of that hair's breadth that separates death from life. . . . No one deceives her, Isaac lives and tells his story, she questions him, she screams six *Teki'ah* notes [Shofar notes] and she *dies before she can finish them.* The profundity of her anguish is suggested in every detail. But what does she not finish, what does she not furnish (*sefeka* is power, means, possibility) to herself or to her world, so that her death becomes an interruption, rather than a conclusion? . . . The problem of Sarah's death is, profoundly, the problem of her life, of *hayyei sarah*—of the contingency of the already born, the all but dead. Her perception of moral vertigo is displaced onto Isaac's *kime'at shelo nishhat* experience. In a real sense, as the Sages put it, "His ashes remain piled on the altar," though he may walk the earth, as large as life. What happened at the Akedah cannot be neutralized, though the sacrifice is not literally consummated. The burden of the "all but" condition is assumed by Sarah, who consummates its meaning in her howls and her death.[31]

Sarah's grief not only illuminates the power of a mother's love, although it does do that; it also tells us of what is not in our control, in particular, the sacrifices that are made beyond our control. Sarah dies, one might say, in place of Isaac. But nothing demanded that she die. Rather, her love for Isaac and the incomprehensibility of how fragile life is, of how she almost lost him, is enough to kill her. Additionally, we see the contrast between

Abraham and Sarah. We do not know what Abraham thought or felt. We get a hint of what he might have thought and felt from Kierkegaard's psychological portrayal of him. We do not know in the end what motivated him to put down the knife, although we can hope it was the face of Isaac. What we see as a common thread in all of the midrashim on Sarah's death is something unique in her relationship to Isaac as his mother. She sees immediately that something was done to him: she knows. She dies from heartbreak. Or, she dies from the mere possibility that her son was to be killed.

Perhaps we could join these two accounts of mothering together: the one who laughs, whose sexual pleasure willingly conceives a child, and the one who would grieve so fiercely for her child that she would die. Sarah's conception of Isaac is not divorced from sexual pleasure. It is Sarah's conception of Isaac that inaugurates "the age of laughter." Isaac marries Rebecca after what some call the first account of love at first sight: Rebecca saw Isaac and "alighted from her camel" (Gen. 24:64). The laughter of Isaac joins the generosity and hospitality of Rebecca. Rebecca manages the household and deceives Isaac so that Jacob receives his blessing—a deception for which she receives praise from the rabbis and from Levinas. Jacob becomes Israel and the rest is, shall we say, history. Sarah's laughter inaugurates a matrilineage.

Additionally, we can recall that Rebecca is remembered for her hospitality, her kindness—in Hebrew, *hesed,* which we also saw in Ruth—when she gives water to Eliezer and to the camel. Zornberg notes that Rebecca actually replaces Sarah and restores to this family the *hesed* that Sarah had furnished. She further notes that when the servant, sent on the mission to find a wife for Isaac, prays that he will succeed in his mission, it is the word *hesed* that recurs in the prayers. The servant knows that the light of kindness needs to be restored to a house that has suffered so deeply. Darkness hangs over this family. Isaac has nearly been killed by his father, and his beloved mother has just died. The servant needs to know that in finding the right girl for Isaac, God is acting rightly both to Isaac and to Abraham. Thus, Rebecca has a huge role to play. And according to the Bible, she fulfills this role: "Isaac loved her and thus found comfort after his mother's death" (Gen. 24:67). According to Zornberg, *hesed* is an end, not a means. She quotes the midrash: "Rebecca represents that essential *hesed* of which *Midrash Rabbah* says: 'Act in hesed *to my master':* . . . Everyone is needy of *hesed,* even Abraham. . . ."[32] Rebecca, then, connects the three generations of Patriarchs: she is the wife of Isaac, who is the son of Abraham and Sarah; and she is the mother of Jacob, who becomes Israel. It is as if she has redeemed both Isaac's near-sacrifice and the death of Sarah that was thought to result from this event.

TRANSFORMING THE VIRILE

Plato's *Phaedo* is often read as an "ode to death": the philosopher's task is to live his life such that he will not fear death. Socrates takes the task one step further. For him, the task is to welcome death. The soul will be liberated and the body will no longer be a hindrance to the knowledge that the soul desires. In addition to this view of death, Plato's *Phaedo* expresses an underlying theme that is often overlooked. At the beginning of this poem about death, Socrates expels his wife, Xanthippe, from the room. As she leaves, she beats her chest in an emotional outburst that appears to make the rest of the men uncomfortable. The excess of emotions is suppressed and quite literally sent away. It seems clear in this dialogue that "womanly" behavior will not be tolerated.

By contrast, *Chayye Sarah* opens with Sarah's death, and in the first few verses we see Abraham not simply mourning her death, but profoundly grieving for her. The image drawn in the Bible is poignant, for it suggests a man who has been weeping with sorrow over the loss of his beloved wife. It is an even more striking image when viewed in contrast to the dismissal of those who would weep at Socrates's death, those who were too "womanlike." The weeping at the death of Socrates illuminates an aspect of death that Heidegger also overlooks.

Levinas concedes Heidegger's point that we cannot know the other's death, that our deaths are our own. However, Levinas does not concede that the dialectic of death can be understood only in terms of being and nothingness, nor does he concede that death is only about knowing death, or knowing what death is. The death of the other cannot be excluded from the analysis of our relation to death; weeping for the other is part of the analysis of death.[33] And why should it not be? Should not an analysis of death that, in a sense, does not allow us to weep for the other be suspect[34]—even if, and maybe especially if, that weeping indicates the feminine element interrupting and possibly transforming the virile? It is worth noting that Socrates does not dismiss the other men who are crying. We might say that Xanthippe, the woman, introduced the emotional aspect of love and death, and now it cannot be completely dismissed. And we might say that Abraham (and the men weeping in the *Phaedo*) had been feminized. And so with the significant acts of the feminine, assorted acts indeed, and with the response of a mother's love for her children, the events of the Bible continue. The maternal motivates the political.

My claims about feminization are not intended to betray my own possible naiveté with regard to the dangers of such a characterization. Certainly, the claim that men "ought" to be feminized is potentially dangerous.

Jewish men were historically viewed *as* feminized. And this view was not positive. The historical context in which we find this characterization reveals the loaded nature of the term. The Jews were characterized as feminine by those—for example, the Nazis—who viewed themselves as virile —and in Levinas's terms, they were virile; they were murderously violent![35] And they were characterized in a historical context in which it was not only negative to be feminine if one was a man, it was also negative to be feminine if one was a woman. Thus, it is not clear if the problem is the feminization of men as much as it is the historical attitude toward women and all the stereotypical attributes ascribed to them.

In his book *The Jewish Derrida,* Gideon Ofrat calls to our attention the various views of the feminine and the Jew, some of which are seemingly contradictory. He reminds us of Derrida's view of the feminine found in *Spurs.*[36] Derrida appropriates Nietzsche's description of woman as something beyond truth. He then incorporates Lacan's view in order to associate truth with phallocentricity. As a consequence of this merger, the feminine becomes the site of an imagined castration, or circumcision—a metaphor for Judaism.

If we follow this train of thought, we can see where Derrida is heading. As Ofrat reads Derrida, "Women and Jews represent the simulacrum of emasculation, and what is emasculation if not circumcision? Is woman the fulfillment of Judaism? As antiphallus, she is the foundation of Derrida's analogy between Jew and woman."[37] And for further support, Ofrat cites Elisabeth Weber's reading of Derrida on this point: "The Jew is merely a woman, the Jew is feminization or femininity of society, a threat to all the virile values reigning in a community, an army, a nation, etc."[38] The twist to this analogy can be seen in the following incomplete syllogism: if woman equals Judaism, and both represent the anti-virile, anti-state, what, then, is the role of woman and the role of the army in Israel? Indeed, what place does Israel have at all? Does this definition of the Jew as woman conflict with Levinas's definition of the feminine found in *Totality and Infinity*? Ofrat recalls that the Jew is normally thought of as the stranger, the guest, or the refugee. And he observes that in Levinas's philosophy, the equation of Jew and woman would render the Jew inclusive and hospitable—the very definition of domesticity. Hence, he reveals the apparent contradiction.

But contrary to how they might appear, these descriptions are not mutually exclusive. First, Judaism does not exclude hospitality, in spite of its status as a religion of "strangers." In fact, if we recall the points made in chapter 1 of this book, to recover the ethical—the response to the other— is, for Levinas, to recover Judaism. And we saw the response to the other and paradigm of hospitality in the actions of Ruth, Boaz, Rebecca, and Sarah. Certainly there are verses in the Bible that accentuate the Jew's responsibility to the Other precisely because the Jew was a stranger for whom God cared.

Second, that Levinas understands the feminine as "not-virile" does not imply that he must also be opposed to Israel. For Levinas, "Sinai" refers not only to the place of the revelation and covenant with God where the Torah was accepted, it also refers to the place of visitation—"visitation as hospitality, opening the great gate to messianic Otherness."[39] Ofrat explains that, "to Levinas, as to Derrida, transcendental hospitality is merely a signpost to mundane hospitality at the level of human fraternity. The command to love the stranger (Deut. 23:8) is an imperative demanding application in all places and at all times."[40] Ofrat maintains that the following quotation from Levinas endorses a view of Israel, and of Jerusalem, that will welcome all, and which will truly signify peace on Earth:

> What is promised in Jerusalem, is a humanity of the Torah . . . a new humanity that is better than a Temple. Our text [his essay begins with a talmudic reading of Deuteronomy 4:22], which began with the cities of refuge, reminds us or teaches us that the longing for Zion, that Zionism, is not one more nationalism or particularism; nor is it a simple search for a place of refuge. It is the hope of a science of society, and of a society, which are wholly human. And this hope is to be found in Jerusalem, in the earthly Jerusalem, and not outside all places, in pious thought.[41]

If we recall that Levinas associates the feminine with hospitality, we can ask if "Jerusalem will fulfill its femininity."[42]

Certainly we can ask after the dangers of Levinas's conception of the feminine as a valorization of stereotypical female attributes. But when we do ask after this danger, we should be careful not to fall into the trap of disparaging the feminine—thus, implying that not only is it bad for men to be like women, it is also bad for women to be like women. In Levinas's view, the tempering of the virile does not deprive men, or women for that matter, of their subjectivity. Levinas finally equates the feminine, in the form of maternity, with the ethical paradigm. Thus, in Levinas's ethical analysis, to become feminized—to respond to the other—is the very contracting of subjectivity. Levinas's contribution to this discussion discloses the significant but silent place of the feminine.

SILENT FOOTSTEPS

One of the most famous examples of King Solomon's wisdom was to decide a case of two women arguing over the custody of a child by offering to split the child in half. One mother consents. The other pleads with Solomon to spare the child. She offers to relinquish her claim on the child if that will save the child's life. Solomon's wisdom tells him that the second woman, who would rather part with her child than have the child killed, must be the real mother. I do not know if Solomon's wisdom is without flaw. Certainly one can imagine a scenario in which a mother believes her child to be in danger of a harm greater than dying—Toni Morrison's novel *Beloved* tells such a story. But the issue here, for Solomon, is not simply whether a child lives or dies. Rather, his concern is to find out who *cares* for the child. The first woman would rather have half a (dead) child, just so she that could have a piece of the child for herself. And his sense of justice tells him that the real mother will reveal herself as the one who cares for the other. Following from Solomon's sense of justice, I view Levinas's turn from a traditional view of Western philosophy as a turn from the ego and the ego's concern for itself toward the other and a focus on the other. This shift illuminates the way in which the ethical is fragile and the maternal, an example of the ethical, even more so. But Levinas's shift to a focus on the other and his reference to the maternal need not leave us with a joyless view of ethics.

Against the familiar view that Levinas is an ascetic thinker, I view him as life-loving. Against the common view that would characterize Levinas as pessimistic, I view him as affirming. How can we not see him this way? He is a survivor of a war in which his wife's family and his own immediate family were murdered. He is a survivor of a war in which one side was determined to extinguish all elements of Judaism and Jewish life. He emerges from this experience with a view of the world that is neither nihilistic nor full of despair. Rather, he offers a phenomenological description of responsibility that cannot be "proven," but which functions for us as proof of the possibility and meaning of ethics.

In contrast to the tired view of much of Western philosophy that sees the search for truth and the willingness to die for that truth as the true test of life, Levinas offers the paradigm of the ethical as the maternal, the possibility to create and sustain new life. It is a turn from the virile paradigm toward the feminine, from the destruction of life toward the priority of the creation and nurturing of life. Like the other figures of the feminine in Levinas's discussions, the maternal is no exception in the little attention it has traditionally received. As in the other cases, the work of the feminine in the role of maternity goes unnoticed, like silent footsteps.

Levinas's conception of the feminine develops from a condition of the possibility of the ethical to the paradigm of the ethical itself. Throughout his books and essays we see a picture of the feminine that displays a variety of characteristics that include hospitality, eros, responsibility, and intelligence. His Jewish roots had a sustained impact on his view of the feminine and of women. This view, while not erasing all the dangers of his conception of the feminine, may give us a different perspective on the feminine. It plays an indispensable role in the formation and sustenance of the ethical relation. The criticisms of Levinas's early books condemned him for leaving the woman out of the ethical relation and characterizing her as simply that which helps the ethical occur. The account of maternity in the later work brings the woman back into the realm of the ethical. However, once the feminine became part of the ethical, the concern arose that the feminine had no role other than one of responsibility. But as I demonstrated, we do not have to view maternity only in its role of responsibility. We have a picture of maternity that is erotic and joyous, even if it is also the exemplar of responsibility. It does seem that filiality usurps the feminine in the role of maternity. But Levinas's point here, and in *Totality and Infinity*, is not that maternity, or the feminine, is replaced. Rather, the political, the third, and, in this case, the community always accompany the ethical.

Finally, the image of maternity may help to alleviate the concern that Levinas offers an essentialist image of women. We may even find it ironic to suggest that the image of maternity is less problematic than merely using the term "the feminine." How can this be? Let us think of it this way. The feminine displays a multitude of attributes. It can be gentle and demure or wild and sexual. But to reduce the feminine to welcoming, habituation, and gentleness may drive us down the road of essentialism. In view of the varied women whom he names in "Judaism and the Feminine," Levinas recognizes that women express a multitude of characteristics. In spite of that, he nonetheless names the feminine, and women, as that which makes a house into a home. There is one trait that nonetheless characterizes the feminine as such.

Maternity, as a physical aspect of women, can be defined only in a specific way. It is already narrowed by its own definition. A woman who is either pregnant or caring for her child is maternal—her body is a maternal body. If this relationship should end in abortion or miscarriage, this woman ceases to be in the maternal state, although we might say that she is still a mother. The relationship emerges from the two who are involved in it. Mothers are a specific group of people, a subset of women, defined by their relationship to a specific kind of other, a gestating fetus or a developing child. The act of nurturing that other is fundamental to the maternal relationship as such. The concept of maternity does not reduce women to a particular aspect of their lives, unless we also advance the normative component that women must be mothers. So as long as this view is not normative—compelling women to become mothers or claiming that all women are like mothers, and so forth—the maternal image remains a powerful example of the ethical relation that applies to all.

The feminine in Levinas's project works silently and yet also indispensably. The feminine provides an image of alterity and mercy, an interruption of ontology's *conatus essendi,* while also providing the model of the ethical itself. Moreover, Levinas did not choose this structure accidentally. For Levinas, this referent applies to both empirical women and the metaphorical status of these attributes in all of us. The feminine, as that which is counter to the virile, is but a fact of history: virility has been the dominant practice such that it is not just the history of events that privileges war; rather the very way we engage intellectually has given priority to death over life. The feminine, the interruption of the virile, resembles Levinas's description of the saying, the interruption of the said. This does not mean that Levinas wants to abolish philosophy—or men!—any more than he wants to do away with the political. Rather, he wants us to be cautious in the philosophical realm and in those other spaces where we—men and women—assume the position of the masculine or virile. The claim that the feminine functions as a metaphor in Levinas's project is correct. But its correctness depends upon two points: (1) the recognition that Levinas derives his characterization of the feminine from empirical women—from women of the Hebrew Bible—and (2) that the feminine functions instructively by teaching us to be attuned to the other—teaching us to be feminine.

Levinas's use of the feminine not only teaches us a great deal about responsibility via the image of maternity; it also teaches us a great deal about maternity, by using this image to express his conception of responsibility. Levinas's image of the ethical—the possibility of "dying for"—reveals the deep and profound unwilled caring for others that subverts the nihilist view of ethics. Profound care for the other is not only possible, it gives meaning to life. Thus, Levinas's project does offer something of use to feminists, but it will not offer it to us easily and it will not be found by applying a straightforward reading of his work motivated by a typical set of feminist concerns. Levinas's work may offer us the opportunity to see feminist concerns in a different light and to see a wider range of what those concerns might be.

In *Totality and Infinity,* Levinas writes, "Life is *love of life,* a relation with contents that are not my being but more dear than my being: thinking, eating, sleeping, reading, working, warming oneself in the sun" (TI 112/ TeI 84). I would add to that series, experiencing the erotic and having children. Contrary to the view that Levinas's philosophy is pessimistic and depressing—too serious because all he does is speak of responsibility—my view is that Levinas's philosophy is life-affirming, and the feminine, as both empirical figure and metaphorical attribute, plays a key role in achieving that end. Maternity—the ethical relation par excellence—unites enjoyment *and* responsibility. Levinas's project reminds us of the possibility of the ethical, and in so doing his project reveals the silent footsteps of the feminine.

NOTES

INTRODUCTION

1. "Ethics and Politics," trans. Jonathan Romney, in *The Levinas Reader,* ed. Seán Hand (London: Blackwell, 1996), 294.

2. There are a couple of stylistic conventions that need to be mentioned before proceeding. Levinas distinguishes between *autre* and *autrui; Autre and Autrui.* Unfortunately, his use of these terms is not always consistent. *Autrui,* lowercase or capitalized, refers to the personal other, while *autre* generally refers to otherness as such—other table, other chair, or alterity—otherness. However, there are several instances where *autre* is capitalized—to indicate its contrast to the Same and occasionally to refer to God, the latter being especially important. For ease of reading, I have, in most cases, left "other" in the lowercase. It should be apparent from the context when I am referring to a personal other, when I am referring to God, and when I am referring to otherness as such.

Again, for ease of reading and to reduce stylistic awkwardness, I occasionally use the masculine pronoun to refer to God. I am aware of the issues surrounding the gendered references to God, but have chosen to follow the standard JPS and Plaut translations here.

3. See, for example, Levinas's essay "Judaism and the Feminine," in which he talks about such concrete women as Rebecca and Sarah, celebrating them for their feminine attributes, but, nonetheless, locating the feminine attributes within concrete women.

4. Levinas does not explicitly equate maternity with the feminine in this work. However, in "Judaism and the Feminine," he says, "'[M]an without woman diminishes the image of God in the world.' And this leads us to another dimension of the feminine—maternity" ("JF" 34/JeF 56).

5. This body of literature is immense. See, for example, the work of Rachel Adler, Judith Baskin, Rachel Biale, Susannah Heschel, Laura Levitt, Miriam Peskowitz, Judith Plaskow, Susan Shapiro, Ellen Umansky, and Laurie Zoloth. See also Hava Tirosh-Samuelson, ed., *Women and Jewish Philosophy* (Bloomington: Indiana University Press, forthcoming). Other collections which take up similar questions include Lynn Davidman and Shelly Tenenbaum, eds., *Feminist Perspectives on Jewish Studies* (New Haven, Conn.: Yale University Press, 1994) and Tamar Rudavsky, ed., *Gender and Judaism* (New York: New York University Press, 1995). Again, the body of literature is immense and the above list is not intended to be exhaustive.

6. See, for example, Jonathan Boyarin and Daniel Boyarin, "Tricksters, Martyrs, and Collaborators: Diaspora and the Gendered Politics of Resistance," in *Powers of Diaspora: Two Essays on the Relevance of Jewish Culture* (Minneapolis: University of Minnesota Press, 2002), 35–102. The Boyarins' thesis supports my position that it is not uncommon for Judaism (and for Jews) to view itself as feminine *and therefore* civilized, while viewing non-Jews as masculine and therefore barbaric.

1. JUDAISM AND THE ETHICAL: RECOVERING THE OTHER

1. Levinas indicates the way in which the original imperative of the face of the other, the ethical relation, turns into something scientific in appearance, by the way we rationalize, universalize, seek knowledge, make decisions, and demand truth.

2. See "A Dialogue with Emmanuel Levinas," in Richard A. Cohen, ed., *Face to Face with Levinas* (New York: State University of New York Press, 1986), 18; and "Interview with François Poirié," in IR, 62.

3. I hesitate to cite Levinas's interviews, since the status of an interview in a philosophical argument is unclear to me. Philosophers say many things, even in interviews. But what they say in an interview does not change the fact that the writing in the project to which they refer might say something other than what they had hoped or believed it to say. My intention in turning to Levinas's interviews is not to verify the philosophical text, but to counter how commentators and readers of his work might have misunderstood what he said elsewhere.

4. Levinas's position is indebted to segments of the Judaic tradition, specifically the modern or rationalist themes that have informed contemporary Judaism. His thought has also been informed by modern Jewish philosophy, such as Martin Buber, *I and Thou*, trans. Ronald G. Smith (New York: Scribner's, 1958) and *Between Man and Man*, trans. Ronald G. Smith (New York: Macmillan, 1965). See also Franz Rosenzweig, *The Star of Redemption*, trans. William W. Hallo (Notre Dame, Ind.: University of Notre Dame Press, 1970).

5. In "The Temptation of Temptation," Levinas tells us that "to receive the gift of the Torah—a Law—is to fulfill it before consciously accepting it" (TT 40/TdT 87). He describes the receiving of the Torah, the doing before hearing, in such a way as to resonate with his conception of responsibility as "more ancient than any recallable past, more ancient than memory." Yet here Levinas wants to make sure that this notion of an adherence prior to examination, prior to temptation, cannot be considered naive (TT 38/TdT 83). According to Levinas, the receiving of the Torah was a free choice. That the choice was "Torah or death" does not alter this free choice. Rather, it indicates that outside the Torah there was only desolation, and in this sense, the choice to choose one or the other was a free one. Moreover, this choice amounts to an acceptance that preceded examination, and practice preceded adherence. By already engaging in a practice, the choice—if choice is the proper word—was outside of the typical opposition between liberty and coercion. By engaging in a set of practices prior to voluntary adherence, the Israelites could have chosen not to accept the Torah. But not to have accepted the Torah would have meant going against the very practice that they had already cultivated. Thus, for Levinas, this sense of responsibility, the responsibility we have to the other, is a responsibility that springs from the acceptance of the Torah. In accepting the Torah, one accepts the responsibility to the other. And yet, in a conventional sense, this responsibility was not chosen. See also Jill Robbins's discussion in *Prodigal Son/Elder Brother* (Chicago: University of Chicago Press, 1991). I will return to this point in chapter 2.

6. I would like to thank Matthew Cousineau for calling to my attention a contemporary example of exactly this conflict that Levinas sees between ethics and politics. In a conversation about the Truth and Reconciliation Commission in South Africa, he reminded me of the act of the Commission. People who come before the commission can confess to committing horrible atrocities during apartheid and receive amnesty. It is supposed that these acts will aid the process of peace and the move to a truly democratic society. The question that concerns Cousineau is the cost of peace: Has justice (and here we might think of justice in both the Levinasian sense and the conventional sense) been compromised in the name of peace?

7. See Llewelyn's discussion of the origin and use of this term in his *Emmanuel Levinas: The Genealogy of Ethics* (London: Routledge, 1995), 4.

8. We can see here how Levinas understands the relationship between philosophy and the pre-philosophical experiences on which philosophy depends. In *Ethics and Infinity*, he is asked about the relationship between the Bible and philosophy. In his response, he emphasizes the significance of the pre-philosophical experiences that give rise to our philosophical positions, whether consciously or not. He refers to the Bible—his relationship to Judaism—

as one example of this pre-philosophical experience. So we can see the circle of betrayal at work: the pre-philosophical experience needs philosophy to express it in terms of the universal. But to do so requires that the pre-philosophical experience be obscured. This is the covering over of religion—or, in Levinas's words, the ethical (see JP).

9. This methodological problem resembles the one that we find in Merleau-Ponty's work. Merleau-Ponty recovers the developmental moments of childhood, moments that existed prior to language. The act of recovering them, of interpreting and talking about them, necessarily means a betrayal of the experience itself. See Maurice Merleau-Ponty, "The Child's Relations with Others," trans. William Cobb, in *The Primacy of Perception,* ed. James M. Edie (Evanston, Ill.: Northwestern University Press, 1964), 96–155.

10. "Rashi" is an acronym made from the initials of Rabbi Shelomo Yitzhaki. He is considered the foremost commentator on the Torah.

11. David Stern, *Midrash and Theory* (Evanston, Ill.: Northwestern University Press, 1996), 15.

12. Ibid., 28.

13. Oona Ajzenstat, *Driven Back to the Text* (Pittsburgh: Duquesne University Press, 2001), 284.

14. Robert Gibbs, *Why Ethics: Signs of Responsibility* (Princeton, N.J.: Princeton University Press, 2001), 298.

15. Ibid., 298.

16. Ibid., 299.

17. David Lachterman, "Torah and Logos," *St. John's Review* 42, no. 2 (1994): 5–26.

18. Gibbs, *Why Ethics,* 302.

19. Ibid. See also Richard A. Cohen, *Ethics, Exegesis and Philosophy* (Cambridge: Cambridge University Press, 2001), especially chapter 7.

2. THE TIME OF CREATION

1. See Martin Heidegger, *Sein und Zeit* (Tübingen: Neomarius Verlag), 1926; trans. John Macquarrie and Edward Robinson under the title *Being and Time* (New York: Harper and Row, 1962).

2. For an interesting reading of Jewish time, see Abraham Joshua Heschel, *Between God and Man,* trans. Fritz A. Rothschild (New York: The Free Press, 1959).

3. That there are two versions of the story of creation further supports Rashi's interpretation that the story of creation cannot be simply a chronological retelling. If it were, there would be much explaining to do with regard to the reversal in the order of things created as well as with regard to the obvious contradictions.

4. References are from W. Gunther Plaut, ed., *The Torah: A Modern Commentary* (New York: Union of American Hebrew Congregations, 1981).

5. The Hebrew word typically translated as "man" (humanity) is *Adam,* which comes from *Adama,* meaning clay or earth. This problem of translation is one to which I will return in chapter 3. Daniel Boyarin translates *Adam* as "earth-creature" in order not to assent to the gender assumption that the first human creature was indisputably, and solely, male. See Daniel Boyarin, "The Politics of Biblical Narratology: Reading the Bible Like/As a Woman," *diacritics* 20, no. 4 (1990): 36.

6. Plaut, *The Torah,* 20.

7. Ibid., 18, editor's note.

8. This passage paraphrases Rashi's gloss, cited in Avivah Gottlieb Zornberg, *The Beginning of Desire: Reflections on Genesis* (New York: Image/Doubleday, 1995), 4. When citing Rashi, I give the original source. However, I have been influenced by Zornberg's reading of Rashi, and so I cite her discussion when relevant.

9. Ibid., 4.

10. Rashi's commentary on Genesis 1:31, in Rashi, *Ariel Chumash: Bereshit to Chaye Sarah* (Jerusalem: United Israel Institutes, 1997).

11. B. Shabbat 88a. See Zornberg's discussion in *Beginning of Desire*, 27.

12. *Pesikta Rabbati*, 21 (citation modified). See Zornberg, *Beginning of Desire*, 27.

13. Deuteronomy 5:4 reads, "Face to Face the Lord spoke to you on the mountain out of the fire" (Plaut, *The Torah*, 1354).

14. This phrase permeates Levinas's work as a way of describing the ethical relation. We should find it no coincidence that the phrase is also used in this ancient Jewish text to describe the relationship between God and the Jewish people when the latter were to receive the Torah—God's ethical commandments—itself.

15. Zornberg, *Beginning of Desire*, 32.

16. Ibid., 31. Translation modified.

17. See Rashi, *Ariel Chumash*, 4. In short, Rashi tells us that if the story of creation were about actual chronology, it would have been written "At first" rather than "In the beginning." The latter simply signifies the beginning of God's creative act. See also Leora Batnitzky, *Idolatry and Representation: The Philosophy of Franz Rosenzweig Reconsidered* (Princeton, N.J.: Princeton University Press, 2000). Batnitzky writes, "In alluding to Isaiah [45:18], Rosenzweig also alludes to the Hebrew *tohu*, the same word that is used in Genesis 1:2 to describe the earth without form. Rosenzweig's point in using the word here is precisely that fundamental difference or diversity is the basis of creation" (124).

18. Rashi, *Ariel Chumash*, 5.

19. Of course we can ask, "What does it mean to be a Jew?" It might mean to speak a common language or practice similar rituals. One might say that it means to have inherited, accepted, or acknowledged a particular history. In addition to these things, one might also say that to be a Jew means to have an inherited history that one does not remember or realize that one has inherited. It is, as Levinas might say, a past more ancient than any past, but a past that has become part of one's present. The claim I wish to make is that the notion of alterity is a Jewish concept that can be traced back to the first line of the book of Genesis in the *Torah*. That is, it is a concept whose roots are older than time itself. I use Rashi's interpretation of the story of creation, and in particular his focus on the significance and uniqueness of water within this account, to make my point. Rashi's reading allows us to see how fundamental the conception of alterity is to Jewish thought. His reading reinforces the strange conception of time that we find in the creation story. On the one hand, the Torah is received at creation. On the other hand, Abraham, the father of Judaism, does not yet have access to the Torah, at least not as a formal code. Judaism does claim that Abraham had to have received the Torah, or at least received it in some sense. If not, we would be forced to ask after what it means to be a Jew without the Torah. This point certainly binds Reform Judaism to Orthodox Judaism: although these two approaches to Judaism differ on their interpretation of the Torah, both believe that Judaism requires the Torah.

20. See Heschel, *Between God and Man*, 214.

21. Ibid., 216.

22. Ibid., 218.

23. A circumcision, commanded to be performed on the eighth day of a baby boy's life, also takes precedence over the observance of the Sabbath if the eighth day falls on the Sabbath.

24. See Rashi, *Ariel Chumash*, 38.

25. Levinas's French and the English translation use "Law" for "Torah." A better translation of Torah is "teaching."

26. See also Levinas's essay "Useless Suffering," in Emmanuel Levinas, *Entre Nous: Thinking-of-the-Other*, trans. Michael B. Smith (New York: Columbia University Press, 1998), 207–218.

27. For Levinas, eros provides the prototype of this relationship.

3. THE INAUGURATION OF SEXUAL DIFFERENCE

1. There is already a grammatical problem with this interpretation that woman is derived from man. The term *Adam,* used as a referent for the created being, is understood to be "pinched" from *Adamah,* the term for earth or clay. Thus, to follow the grammatical pattern would be to say that *Ish* is "pinched" from *Isha,* or man is "pinched" from woman, not vice versa.

2. Simone de Beauvoir, *The Second Sex,* trans. H. M. Parshley (New York: Random House, 1952), xix; *Le Deuxième Sexe* (Paris: Gallimard, 1949), 15.

3. Ibid.

4. De Beauvoir uses *feminine* and *woman* interchangeably. That she equates the two anticipates the problems that we will see in Levinas's own writing—the relationship that *feminine* has to *woman* is precisely the issue in Levinas's work. Moreover, Levinas also uses these terms interchangeably.

5. I need to be careful to distinguish the canon from the Jewish philosophy that Levinas appropriates. On the one hand, these Jewish thinkers are "Western"—that is, European. On the other hand, they are philosophers who are not included in the "traditional" Western canon.

6. De Beauvoir was not the first, and certainly not the only, French thinker to read Hegel's master-slave dialectic in light of male-female relations. See, for example, the work of G. Fessard.

7. Phyllis Trible, "Eve and Adam: Genesis 2–3 Reread," in Kristen E. Dvam, Linda S. Schearing, and Valarie H. Ziegler, eds., *Eve and Adam: Jewish, Christian, and Muslim Readings on Genesis and Gender* (Bloomington: Indiana University Press, 1999), 431–437.

8. In *Totality and Infinity, autrui* signifies the ethical other, which, for Levinas, can only be a human other. It indicates a personal Other, the you, whereas *autre* is translated as other. The distinction between these two terms is not clear in *Time and the Other.*

9. Levinas often uses the word "reciprocal." However, reciprocity is not easily used as an opposite to asymmetry. I believe what Levinas means by asymmetry, although he does not always state it as such, is that the relation is not also reciprocal. I am using symmetry for agreement.

10. For another discussion of Levinas and eros, see Adriaan Peperzak, *Platonic Transformations* (Oxford: Rowman and Littlefield, 1997). Although Peperzak looks at the role of eros in *Totality and Infinity,* he does provide an interesting context—namely, the influence of Plato on Levinas's thought—in which to view Levinas's conception of eros.

11. Rambam is the abbreviated name for the Jewish philosopher and rabbinic scholar Maimonides.

12. Avivah Gottlieb Zornberg, *The Beginning of Desire: Reflections on Genesis* (New York: Image/Doubleday, 1995), 15.

13. Ibid.

14. See also Stella Sandford, *The Metaphysics of Love: Gender and Transcendence* (London: Athlone, 2000), 33–63. Sandford reminds us that any metaphorical meaning of the feminine has purchase only *because of* the meaning already embedded in the term as it would apply to empirical women.

15. Plato, "The Symposium," trans. Michael Joyce, in *The Collected Works of Plato, Including the Letters,* ed. Edith Hamilton and Huntington Cairns (Princeton, N.J.: Princeton University Press, 1961), 526–574.

16. See ibid., 193a–b.

17. For another detailed discussion of this idea see Edith Wyschogrod, *Emmanuel Levinas: The Problem of Ethical Metaphysics* (New York: Fordham University Press, 2000), 127–133.

18. In addition to repeating this point in *Time and the Other,* Levinas makes this point in an essay specifically about Judaism and women. This is the first, but not the last, time that Levinas's philosophical themes will appear, almost verbatim, in his Jewish writings.

19. For an excellent discussion on the relationship between the feminine, female, and *femme,* see Stella Sandford's discussion in *The Metaphysics of Love.* Sandford elucidates the ambiguity in the terms that Levinas employs. I would add to her point by emphasizing the way in which this ambiguity is exacerbated in Levinas's discussion of the feminine in both his philosophical writings and his writings on Judaism. In the latter, he most often refers to the feminine as women, although this ambiguity is certainly present within the philosophical texts alone.

20. Wyschogrod, *Emmanuel Levinas,* 127–133.

21. This version of the story raises questions about the actual separation of woman from an original creature that consisted of both sexes initially. This second version tells us that a rib, which was taken from Adam, was fashioned into a woman, thus implying that man—i.e., male—and woman were created anew from this body part. Regardless of how we understand the creation of woman from man in this version, there is a distinction made between humanity and the rest of the animal kingdom. There was no fitting helpmate for Adam prior to the creation of woman. She is like him, yet different. She is from him, yet distinct—separate and individuated. See Daniel Boyarin, "The Politics of Biblical Narratology: Reading the Bible Like/As a Woman," *diacritics* 20, no. 4 (1990): 36–39.

22. The Hebrew distinguishes between *man* as the referent for humanity, and *man* as the referent for the masculine figure. One possibility is that *Adama,* meaning earth, intends to render man as humanity.

23. The citation that Levinas gives in his text, Isaiah 29:6, appears to be a misprint.

24. *Midrash Rabbah,* Genesis, VIII.1, in Rabbi Moshe Weissman, ed., *The Midrash Says: The Book of Beraishis* (Brooklyn: Benei Yakov Publications, 1980), 33.

25. According to the rabbis, the interpretation of the duality as hermaphroditic rather than androgynous is significant. The rabbis believe that this duality emphasizes the creation of two bodies in one rather than one being with ambiguous or dual genitalia; see Rabbi Dr. H. Freedman, trans., *Midrash Rabbah* I, Genesis, VIII.1 (London: Soncino, 1983), 54. Although the rabbis also conjecture that the taking of the rib indicates that woman is a separate creation, the taking of the rib could be interpreted as simply the separation of the two bodies. The rabbis use the term "bisexual" to indicate not dual sexual orientation but rather, I presume, the presence of two sexes within one being. However, there is debate over whether God took a rib or a side—the taking of a side supports the position that the bodies were independent but attached. Finally, another midrash interprets the creation of woman this way: "While Adam slept, [God] severed the female body that was attached to Adam's back and replaced the missing part with flesh" (Freedman, *Midrash Rabbah,* Genesis, VIII.1).

26. Freedman, *Midrash Rabbah,* Genesis, VIII.1.

27. See Susan Shapiro, "On Thinking Identity Otherwise," in Laurence Silberstein, ed., *Mapping Jewish Identities* (New York: New York University Press, 2000), 299–323.

28. In "Judaism and the Feminine," Levinas cites one interpretation that claims there were "two distinct acts of creation . . . necessary for Adam—the one for the man in Adam, the second for the woman," and that this interpretation affirms a rabbinic text (JF 34/ JeF 57). I develop my discussion of Derrida's critique in chapter 5.

29. Judith Plaskow, *Standing Again at Sinai: Judaism from a Feminist Perspective* (San Francisco: Harper and Row, 1990).

30. Ibid., 245n44.

31. Trible's reading can be supported by Rashi's reading. See Rashi, *Ariel Chumash: Bereshit to Chaye Sarah* (Jerusalem: United Israel Institutes, 1997) on the issue of jealousy in the act of creation.

32. See Boyarin, "The Politics of Biblical Narratology," for another interpretation of the change in versions of the creation of the sexes, a change that appears to move from equity between the sexes to a hierarchy of one over the other. Boyarin cites a passage from Mieke Bal's book *Lethal Love: Feminist Readings of Biblical Love Stories* (Bloomington: Indiana University Press, 1987), in which Bal criticizes the explanation that Robert Alter gives for this change. Alter claims that the original version, which presents the sexes equally, was altered when the narrator, who lived in a society where there was no gender equity, had to account for the disparity. Thus, the version that presents the creation of the sexes unequally was introduced.

33. Bal, *Lethal Love,* 115. At first glance, it seems that Bal, and Levinas, if the theory applies to him, assumes a heterosexual (heterosexist) framework. The interpretation of the creation story that claims that male and female are created as two totalities that only need to be separated from each other could lend itself to a framework that supports a homosexual relationship. That each is a totality unto itself could signify that each contains an aspect of male and female, and that each is other to the other solely by virtue of being a totality to another totality. See also Boyarin's discussion in "Politics of Biblical Narratology," 37.

34. Bal, *Lethal Love,* 113.

35. The discussion of the discrepancy in the number of *yods* in the spelling of a creature may help us understand why Levinas will insist later that the face of the other is a human face. One interpretation argues that two *yods* in the spelling refers to that which is human and that which is divine. Thus, the Hebrew word for creature, when it refers to non-human things, may indicate that they lack a certain element of the divine. This is not to say that we do not have an ethical obligation to non-human animals (or non-human other things), but rather that our first experience of alterity, which gives rise to the ethical in the first place, originates from another human. Thus, any obligation that we have to animals would derive first from the initial ethical experience that we have toward other humans. For an interesting discussion of the place of non-human animals within a Levinasian framework, see John Llewelyn, "Am I Obsessed by Bobby? (Humanism of the Other Animal)," in Robert Bernasconi and Simon Critchley, eds., *Re-Reading Levinas* (Bloomington: Indiana University Press, 1991), 234–245.

36. It is worth pointing out that the "mystery" of the feminine for Levinas corresponds to the "mystery" of the Other in general. The Other cannot be known by me. Unfortunately, Levinas was unaware of the connotations for referring to the feminine as such. Such references rightly raise concerns for feminists reading his work. However, if we understand the relationship between the feminine and the Other, then the sense of mystery should be understood in that context.

37. For more on this topic, see Tina Chanter, "The Alterity and Immodesty of Time: Death as Future and Eros as Feminine in Levinas," in David Wood, ed., *Writing the Future* (New York: Routledge, 1990), 137–154.

38. See Emmanuel Levinas, "Reality and its Shadow," in *Collected Philosophical Papers,* trans. Alphonso Lingis (Dordrecht: Kluwer Academic Publishers, 1987), 1–13, for a discussion on the relationship between eros, art, and ethics.

39. Georg Wilhelm Friedrich Hegel, *Hegel's Phenomenology of Spirit,* trans. A. V. Miller (New York: Oxford University Press, 1977), 111–119.

40. The future also has a metaphorical significance. Rather than the future being the individual son, it could also signify Israel, or the continuation of Israel. Thus, woman's maternity is less about her role in giving her husband a replica of himself, in which she is merely the vehicle for this event, than it is about the role she plays in the birth and continuation of the messianic age. See "Judaism and the Feminine" for a further discussion of this point.

41. Sandford also argues this point in *The Metaphysics of Love.* However, her argument hinges on her claim that the relationship between eros, the feminine, and fecundity is the

key to understanding Levinas's conception of metaphysics, and that this understanding of metaphysics, one that is connected to transcendence, is not a vision of the world that is useful to feminists. Sandford's book is illuminating in a number of ways, most notably for the way she tracks the ambiguity of Levinas's own terminology. Although I agree with her on a number of her points—for example, the transcendental function of the feminine—I ultimately disagree with her conclusion that Levinas's project is not useful to feminist readers of him. For another discussion of a similar theme—the use of Levinas to feminists and the role of the feminine in Levinas's analysis—see Tina Chanter, *Time, Death, and the Feminine: Levinas with Heidegger* (Stanford, Calif.: Stanford University Press, 2001).

42. *"Que dirait Eurydice? What would Eurydice say?," Emmanuel Levinas en/in conversation avec/with Bracha Lichtenberg-Ettinger* (Paris: BCE Atelier, 1977), 27.

43. Levinas's discussion of "dying in giving life, in bringing life into the world" is no doubt disturbing, certainly if we understand him to mean that he is advocating that women give their lives in childbirth. Although I will raise this issue again later, a few remarks here are warranted. Rather than advocating death in childbirth, it seems Levinas has instead identified the very real risk in childbirth. Every time a woman goes to full term and gives birth she assumes a risk, a life-threatening risk, and it seems to be this point that Levinas finds interesting. Women risk their lives for the possibility to create a future. It seems that Levinas, rather than advocating that women should give their lives, has identified what few men—and, for that matter, women—see: although childbirth is seen as completely mundane, women in fact *do* risk their lives in pregnancy, labor, and childbirth. And that individuals, in this case women, might find the life of an other worth the sacrifice of their own lives indicates the possibility of ethics—the for-the-other.

44. See TO 361/TA 14.

45. An interview with Jean Wahl added to the end of Wahl's *A Short History of Existentialism,* trans. Forrest Williams and Stanley Maron (New York: Philosophical Library, 1949), 52.

4. THE HOSPITALITY OF THE FEMININE

1. For an extended discussion of this theme, see Catherine Chalier, "Ethics and the Feminine," in Robert Bernasconi and Simon Critchley, eds., *Re-Reading Levinas* (Bloomington: Indiana University Press, 1991), 119–129.

2. The rabbis also emphasize woman's silence when, in response to their wonder about why Eve was created from Adam's rib, they surmise that God's other choices would have led to non-virtuous traits in women. The midrash commentary tells us that woman was not created from God's eye, "lest she [woman] be a coquette; nor from the ear, lest she be an eavesdropper; nor from the mouth, lest she be a gossip." Despite all of God's efforts to create a woman who had only virtuous traits, and much to the dismay of the rabbis, woman still managed to acquire all the qualities God tried to prevent. Besides giving us examples of the biblical woman who possess these non-virtuous traits, the Talmud relates the less-than-positive view that "Ten measures of speech descended to the world; women took nine and men one" (Kid. 49b). Although woman, concrete woman, obviously speaks, her silence is preferred.

3. See also Richard Cohen's discussion of this ambiguity in *Elevations: The Height and the Good in Rosenzweig and Levinas* (Chicago: University of Chicago Press, 1994), 195–204. Cohen provides a nuanced reading of this problem by drawing a distinction between "gendered metaphysics" and "gendered metaphors." Although I disagree with his characterization of the feminist response to Levinas's work, Cohen's reading of this topic is quite helpful.

4. Adriaan Peperzak, *To the Other* (West Lafayette, Ind.: Purdue University Press, 1993), 129.

5. Stella Sandford, *The Metaphysics of Love* (London: Athlone, 2000), 47.

6. Ibid., 47.

7. DF 30–37/DL 50–62.

8. B. Yoma, 43b.

9. In his essay, Levinas refers only to the Book of Numbers. But it is clear that he is referring to the rabbinic reading of Numbers. Numbers itself is not very sympathetic to women, even if one can show that it improves on other ancient treatment of women who committed adultery. For an extended discussion on the rabbinic reading, see Judith Hauptman, *Rereading the Rabbis: A Woman's Voice* (Boulder: Westview, 1998), 17–29.

10. For example, in the ancient Greek vision of the world, women are responsible for burial rights while men are responsible for the state. See, for example, Sophocles's *Antigone*.

11. From this exemption emerges the prayer that men say in the morning when they thank God for not having been born a heathen, a slave, or a woman. The apologetic interpretation of the prayer claims that it emphasizes the responsibility men have to uphold all of the 613 commandments—this obligation is an honor—rather than insinuating that it is inherently bad to be a woman.

12. This structure, wherein woman/the home provides the condition of possibility for men to go out into the world, is not unlike the structure that we see in Hegel's *Philosophy of Right,* trans. T. Knox (Oxford: Clarendon, 1967). For Hegel, the distinction between the life of transcendence and the world that makes such a life possible is a distinction between the family life, which Hegel confines to the home, and the life in civil society, to which the home provides access. Women, in both cases, are confined to a life that makes possible men's transcendence.

13. Charlotte Fonrobert, *Menstrual Purity: Rabbinic and Christian Reconstructions of Biblical Gender* (Stanford, Calif.: Stanford University Press, 2000), 65.

14. Ibid., 67.

15. What they share is an aversion to violence. It is interesting that Levinas does not name Judith.

16. Feminist readers of Levinas often charge that he presents an essentialist view of women. It is not clear that he escapes the charge of essentialism with regard to the feminine in these two related descriptions—"The Dwelling" and "Judaism and the Feminine." It is also not clear that an essentialist view is entirely unavoidable or necessarily bad. But more importantly, what interests Levinas about the women whom he names is their active role in propelling the events in the Bible, a role to which little attention is paid. These women, working behind the scenes, are—not *should be*—responsible for making the world habitable. Do we condemn him for noticing their contributions, or would we also condemn him if he ignored this detail?

17. For a more detailed discussion of this topic, see David Biale, *Eros and the Jews* (New York: Basic Books, 1992).

18. Jean-Paul Sartre, *Being and Nothingness,* trans. Hazel Barnes (New York: Washington Square Books, 1953). Specifically, this theme can be found on page 491, although it is present in the entire subheading "First Attitude toward Others: Love, Language, Masochism" contained within the larger section "Concrete Relations with Others."

19. Although we can wonder if the birth of a son is a reflection of the fecundity of a male writer, it seems more than coincidental that Judaism has a less than positive attitude toward the birth of a daughter. Even filial piety is more often talked about as son to his parents, as if there is no daughter present. One might also wonder if Levinas is hoping to avoid the possible ambiguity of an erotic relationship that would corrupt the parental relationship as ethical—again, if this is the case, it would also be presupposing a heterosexual (and Freudian!) framework. For an interesting discussion of paternity in *Totality and Infinity* and the question of the daughter, see Kelly Oliver, "Paternal Election and the Absent Father," in

Tina Chanter, ed., *Feminist Interpretations of Levinas* (University Park: Penn State Press, 2001), 224–240.

20. See the discussion of this topic in the previous chapter. In another interpretation consistent with his view that the leitmotif of separation and individuation weaves through the text, Rashi offers an interesting gloss on God's punishment of Eve through the pains of childbirth. Quoting the Talmud, Rashi offers the interpretation that the punishment was not about childbirth per se, but rather about the "pains of raising children" (B. Eruvin 100b). Anyone who has had a child knows that with each milestone the child reaches, there is joy mixed with sorrow. The child grows and becomes independent. The parents must watch their child stumble and fall, but they must also watch the child separate from them. This growth is not easy for anyone involved!

21. It is not clear why Levinas writes with a masculine pronoun here. This section seems very clearly to be about erotic love, which culminates in the birth of a child, and thus, for Levinas, the author, a love that is with a woman. There are places in the essay where he specifically refers to the feminine, and where language to describe the beloved seems to be feminine language. Thus, the ambiguity makes unclear whether Levinas intends this discrepancy.

22. Although "virgin" and "virginity" are certainly correct translations of *vierge* and *virginité,* I think we could also think of these words in terms of their connotation of purity rather than of sexual inexperience.

23. This discussion of love resonates with the analysis that Levinas gives of the feminine and the erotic in *Time and the Other.*

24. The relationship is outside of time. Cf. EE 93. It is a means of escaping temporality.

25. See Levinas's description in *Time and the Other.*

26. Echoing Sartre, Levinas states that "if to love is to love the love the Beloved bears me, to love is also to love oneself in love, and thus to return to oneself" (TI 266/TeI 244). Voluptuosity in love does not transcend itself. It is in this description that we see what Levinas means by a return to the self. As a dual solitude, love remains sealed unto itself. The love relationship in Levinas's analysis is directed toward a future. He makes this point repeatedly. The love relation is the juncture between present and future. It is being that is also a "being not yet" (TI 257/TeI 234). "It manifests itself at the limit of being and non-being" (TI 256/TeI 233). We find a similar analysis in *Time and the Other.*

27. See Alphonso Lingis, *Libido: The French Existential Theories* (Bloomington: Indiana University Press, 1985).

28. For another discussion of Levinas and eros, see Alphonso Lingis, "Phenomenology of the Face and Carnal Intimacy," in *Libido,* 58–73. For other discussions of Levinas and Rosenzweig on love, see Cohen, *Elevations,* in particular the section on the "Metaphysics of Gender," in which Cohen discusses regions of being. See note 64 of chapter 1 of *Elevations.*

29. Craig Vasey, "Faceless Women and Serious Others: Levinas, Misogyny, and Feminism," in Charles Scott and Arlene Dallery, eds., *Ethics and Danger* (Albany: SUNY Press, 1992), 317–330.

5. EROS, SEXUAL DIFFERENCE, AND THE QUESTION OF ETHICS

1. Jacques Derrida, "Choreographies: An Interview between Jacques Derrida and Christine V. McDonald," trans. Christine V. McDonald, *diacritics* (Summer 1982): 73. Reprinted in Jacques Derrida, *Points . . . ,* ed. Elisabeth Weber (Stanford, Calif.: Stanford University Press, 1992), 102.

2. If we interpret woman as taken from part of man, then she is viewed as man's partner or man's wife, or she is identified with the womb—that is, identified as a mother. See Derrida, "Choreographies," 101.

3. We will focus on the talmudic reading "And God Created Woman" and on Levinas's essay "Judaism and the Feminine."

4. Luce Irigaray, "Questions to Emmanuel Levinas," in *The Irigaray Reader,* ed. Margaret Whitford (Oxford: Blackwell, 1991), 178–189.

5. Ibid., 180.

6. Luce Irigaray, "The Fecundity of the Caress," in *An Ethics of Sexual Difference,* trans. Carolyn Burke and Gillian Gill (Ithaca: Cornell University Press, 1993), 185–217.

7. For a detailed discussion of Irigaray's relationship with and debt to Levinas, see Tina Chanter, *Ethics of Eros: Irigaray's Rewriting of the Philosophers* (New York: London, 1995).

8. See Chanter, *Ethics of Eros,* 218.

9. Irigaray also underscores the ambiguity of the erotic as a relation that is at once sated and insatiable and therefore resembles both finite need and the infinity of ethics.

10. Irigaray, "The Fecundity of the Caress," 202.

11. Ibid.

12. Ibid.

13. Irigaray capitalizes "Father." One cannot help noticing the allusion to Christianity's trinity and the role that Mary played as bridge between God, the Father, and the birth of Jesus Christ. And it is precisely this reading of Levinas, one that implicitly assumes a Christian perspective, that I wish to confront. My point is not that Irigaray is necessarily mistaken in her criticism of Levinas. Rather, I wish to call attention to how Irigaray might be overlooking elements of Levinas's thought by viewing him through Christianity, even if this view is unintended.

14. Irigaray, "The Fecundity of the Caress," 203.

15. It is often claimed in Judaism that women are not required to study Torah because they are already ethical, they are already closer to God. One can see both the positive and negative in this view. Historically, women have been denied both rights and privileges because they (women) were thought to be more moral. Ironically, women were initially denied the vote in the United States because politics was deemed too dirty for them to touch; they then acquired the vote because it was thought that their moral character would improve the lot of politics. Unfortunately, the non-requirement to study Torah was transformed into a prohibition among the more Orthodox segments of the Jewish religion. One cannot help wondering how this view of women being more ethical, being closer to God, could be woven into Levinas's analysis.

16. Irigaray, "The Fecundity of the Caress," 194.

17. Ibid., 204.

18. We could also take Chanter's title, *Ethics of Eros,* as a cue.

19. Alison Ainley takes issue with such an interpretation, arguing instead that the dwelling that Levinas calls forth here is more like a community of reconciliation. However, as I mentioned previously, one must still account for Levinas's explicit exclusion of the erotic from the ethical. As long as woman is in the role of the beloved, she is excluded from the ethical—at least in relationship to her lover. See Ainley's "Amorous Discourses: 'The Phenomenology of Eros' and Love Stories," in Robert Bernasconi and David Wood, eds., *The Provocation of Levinas* (London: Routledge, 1988), 70–82.

20. The role of the mother changes when Levinas renames the feminine as "maternity" in *Otherwise than Being.*

21. Irigaray, "Questions to Emmanuel Levinas," 182.

22. Ainley also makes this point. She claims that Levinas is self-conscious about his use of sexual difference and the role that each, feminine and masculine, plays for him and his analysis. See Ainley, "Amorous Discourses."

23. Although Levinas seems aware of this standpoint, this awareness does not exonerate him with regard to the way he conceives his analysis. Irigaray calls our attention to the fact that "what Levinas does not see is that the locus of paternity, to which he accords the privilege of ethical alterity, has already assumed the place of the genealogy of the feminine, has already covered over the relationships between mothers and daughters, in which formerly transmission of the divine was located" (Irigaray, "Questions to Emmanuel Levinas," 182).

24. Irigaray, "Questions to Emmanuel Levinas," 181–182.

25. It is not clear how much Judaism, or which Jewish views, Levinas appropriates in his view of love and sexuality. But, to be sure, Levinas is no ordinary man, and he is no ordinary Jewish man. He is heavily steeped in the Hebrew and talmudic traditions, both of which have much to say about love, family, and sexuality. Thus, we can be sure that he is aware of these writings.

26. See David Biale, *Eros and the Jews* (New York: Basic Books, 1992), for an extensive study in this complex and rich relationship.

27. Biale, *Eros and the Jews,* 53–54. Irigaray questions Levinas on the notion of God, asking him where God is in the act of sexuality. Irigaray wants to know what happened to God in carnality, and she wonders if "monotheistic religions cannot claim to be ethical unless they submit themselves to a radical interrogation relative to the sexual attribution of their paradigms, whether these be God, the ways in which God is referred to (in particular the masculine gender used by language, when he is not represented pictorially), God's commandments, etc." ("Questions to Emmanuel Levinas," 185). I share Irigaray's discomfort with the way Levinas portrays the role of the woman—as beloved, passive, non-subject. However, in the passage I quoted above, her criticisms seem more relevant to Christianity in general than to Levinas in particular. Jews, for example, do not pictorially represent God. The rabbis claim that Moses seeing only the back of God indicates God's brilliance, but also serves to keep God from being described and thus limited. It also indicates that each individual has a personal relationship with God that would be disrupted by an individual's pictorial representation. And in Hebrew, the word for God is often in the plural, indicating that God is both masculine and feminine. This same theme is also found in the Kabbalah. Thus, what does Irigaray mean when she asks "Where is God in sexuality?" To which God—to whose God—is she referring?

28. Biale, *Eros and the Jews,* 54.

29. Ibid., 91.

30. Ibid.

31. Ibid., 95.

32. Ibid., 96.

33. At certain points in its history, Judaism believed that a woman's sexual pleasure was needed for procreation to take place. The rabbis report a theory that when a woman reached orgasm a "little white thing" was released that aided in pregnancy. Consequently, rabbinic interpretations emerged that claimed that Judaism's generous view of sexual pleasure was linked to the need to procreate. However, the rabbis also make clear that the laws of *onah* apply to women who cannot have children, including women who have experienced menopause and are thus beyond childbearing years. This point indicates that while there is tension in Judaism's view of sexuality, the right to sexual gratification for its own sake has priority over whatever sexual pleasure might have to do with procreation.

34. Biale, *Eros and the Jews,* 44.

35. See E. Wyschogrod, *Emmanuel Levinas: The Problem of Ethical Metaphysics* (New York: Fordham University Press, 2000), for a discussion on this theme. The relationship be-

tween father and son is also characterized as a relationship of pupil to student—a relationship that Levinas uses to characterize the Messianic experience.

36. Philo, *On the Creation of the World,* trans. F. H. Colson and G. H. Whitaker (Cambridge, Mass: Harvard University Press, 1929), as reprinted in Daniel Frank, Oliver Leaman, and Charles Manekin, eds., *The Jewish Philosophy Reader* (New York: Routledge, 2000), 19.

37. Ainley contends that Levinas accounts for such a possibility and thus the universal status remains unchallenged by sexual difference, that the dwelling to which Levinas refers "expresses a desire for a community of reconciliation" ("Amorous Discourses," 74). However, if the erotic relationship is explicitly excluded from the ethical, then, at the very least, insofar as woman takes the role of the beloved within the erotic, the ethical does not apply to her. What, then, are we to say about its universal status?

38. Derrida, "Choreographies," 89.

39. Ibid., 98.

40. Derrida makes this point in a number of his essays. For example, he claims that *Totality and Infinity* could not have been written by a woman. See his "Violence and Metaphysics," in *Writing and Difference,* trans. A. Bass (London: Routledge and Kegan Paul, 1978), 79–153; "At This Moment in This Very Work Here I Am," in Robert Bernasconi and Simon Critchley, eds., *Re-Reading Levinas* (Bloomington: Indiana University Press, 1991), 11–48; and "Choreographies."

41. Derrida, "At This Moment," 39–40.

42. See Kelly Oliver, "Paternal Election and the Absent Father," in Tina Chanter, ed., *Feminist Interpretations of Levinas* (University Park: Penn State Press, 2001), 224–240.

43. If we take into account the Judaic interpretation of the ethical and its relation to gender, our choices are limited: it is not only that the future must be a son because the author is male, and thus if the author were female the future would be a daughter; I think, in this case, the author must be male.

44. Derrida, "At This Moment, 40."

45. Ibid.

46. Derrida, "Choreographies," 102.

6. RUTH; OR, LOVE AND THE ETHICS OF FECUNDITY

1. Quoted in Seyla Benhabib, *Situating the Self* (New York: Routledge, 1992), 156. For the full quotation, see Thomas Hobbes, "Philosophical Rudiments Concerning Government and Society," in *The English Works of Thomas Hobbes,* ed. W. Molesworth (Darmstadt: Wissenschaftliche Buchgesellschaft, 1966), vol. 2, 109.

2. Martin Buber, *I and Thou,* trans. Ronald G. Smith (New York: Scribner's, 1958), 3.

3. See ibid., part 1.

4. Ibid., 7.

5. See Jean-Paul Sartre, *Being and Nothingness* (New York: Washington Square Books, 1966).

6. Little has been written on the relationship between Levinas and Buber, but there are a few places one can look. See Robert Gibbs, *Correlations in Rosenzweig and Levinas* (Princeton, N.J.: Princeton University Press, 1992); Richard Cohen, *Elevations: The Height and the Good in Rosenzweig and Levinas* (Chicago: University of Chicago Press, 1994); and Robert Bernasconi, "'Failure of Communication' as a Surplus: Dialogue and Lack of Dialogue between Buber and Levinas," in Robert Bernasconi and David Wood, eds., *The Provocation of Levinas* (New York: Routledge, 1988), 100–135.

7. Emmanuel Levinas, "Martin Buber and the Theory of Knowledge," in *Proper Names,* trans. Michael B. Smith (London: Athlone, 1996), 32.

8. For Levinas's writings on Rosenzweig, see "'Between Two Worlds' (The Way of Franz Rosenzweig)," in DF 181–201, and "Franz Rosenzweig: A Modern Jewish Thinker," in *Outside the Subject,* trans. Michael B. Smith (London: Athlone, 1993), 49–66.

9. Robert Gibbs also outlines these themes, and though I develop these points on my own, I need to acknowledge Gibbs's *Correlations.*

10. Rosenzweig says, "Not until he is married does he become a true member of his people. . . . To learn the Torah and to keep the commandments is the omnipresent basis of Jewish life. Marriage brings with it the full realization of this life, *for only then do the 'good works' become possible*" (*The Star of Redemption,* trans. William Hallo [Notre Dame, Ind.: University of Notre Dame], 326, emphasis added).

11. Gibbs, *Correlations,* 26.

12. See, for example, Levinas's essays in *In the Time of the Nations.*

13. See *Totality and Infinity* for this discussion.

14. In Derrida's view, the assumed sexual difference, and demarcation, in this text is striking (Jacques Derrida, "At This Moment in This Very Work Here I Am," in Robert Bernasconi and Simon Critchley, eds., *Re-Reading Levinas* [Bloomington: Indiana University Press, 1991], 11–48). In his own response to the question of whether Levinas has assumed sexual difference in his writing, Derrida references his comment in a footnote to "Violence and Metaphysics," his essay on *Totality and Infinity:* "Let us observe in passing that *Totality and Infinity* pushes the respect for dissymmetry to the point where it seems to us impossible, essentially impossible, that it could have been written by a woman. The philosophical subject of it is man" ("At This Moment," 40). In an interview with Bracha Lichtenberg-Ettinger, Levinas claims that he is subordinating not woman but sexual difference to alterity. See Emmanuel Levinas, *"Que dirait Eurydice? What would Eurydice say?," Emmanuel Levinas en/in conversation avec/with Bracha Lichtenberg-Ettinger* (Paris: BCE Atelier, 1977). However, in light of the stance that Levinas takes as author, the other is marked by sexual difference, and then disguised as a neutral other. The wholly other, who is not supposed to be marked by sexual difference, is found already to be marked by masculinity (Derrida, "At This Moment," 40). See my discussion in chapter 5.

15. Rosenzweig, to be sure, was not a feminist. He believed in gendered relations and that gendered behavior was fundamental to culture, but he also believed that with regard to love, the roles of giver and receiver of love go back and forth. For purposes of phenomenological description, Levinas separates the two. See Franz Rosenzweig, *The Star of Redemption,* trans. William Hallo (Notre Dame, Ind.: University of Notre Dame Press, 1970). In "Questions to Emmanuel Levinas," Irigaray recalls the Song of Songs to illustrate a contrast to Levinas's discussion of love. She does indicate that she is aware of a connection between Levinas's discussion of love and the one in this biblical poem.

16. See Rachel Adler, *Engendering Judaism: An Inclusive Theology and Ethics* (Boston: Beacon, 1998), 133–148. Adler tells us that in the Song of Songs, the woman's voice and her declaration of love are noted. The Song of Songs is "one canonical source whose perspective is unarguably antipatriarchal . . . and it is atypical, moreover, because it celebrates mutuality" (135).

17. Although gender is not to be underestimated, particularly for Rosenzweig—women hold a special privilege in Rosenzweig's view of revelation. See Cohen's chapter "The Metaphysics of Gender" in *Elevations,* in which he discusses "regions of being."

18. Levinas's connection should not necessarily be an indication that he thinks that every sexual act ought to *end* in maternity, or even be *intended* to end in maternity. We must be careful to avoid a logic that reverses the necessary relation between sexuality and fecundity. Factually, fecundity requires sexuality, though sexuality does not require fecundity. In terms of his ethical analysis, however, Levinas does privilege sexual activity that ends in fecundity. Yet, even if we acknowledge the priority that Levinas assigns to a love that results in

a child, we must also acknowledge that he allows for a sexuality that intends pleasure for its own sake. If we take note of his Jewish roots, then the remarks that Judaism makes about sexuality are significant. Finally, Levinas refers to the Virgin Mary as an example of what he does *not* mean by love. Thus, ultimately he distinguishes his conception of love from a Christian conception of love.

19. The *ketubah,* the Jewish marriage contract, states that a husband is responsible to his wife for three things: food, clothing, and sexual gratification. Although Judaism considers a marriage that produces no children after ten years grounds for granting an annulment, Judaism does not require a childless couple to dissolve their marriage. Levinas writes, "[L]ove [which] becomes its own end, where it remains without any 'intentionality' that spreads beyond it, a world of voluptuousness or a world of charm and grace, one which can coexist with a religious civilization, is foreign to Judaism" (JF 36–37/JeF 60). This point, according to Levinas, is not intended to mean that women are to get pregnant and be confined to the home; nor is it about Judaism's prudish attitude toward sexuality. Rather, Levinas tells us, this view of love is due to "the permanent opening up of the messianic perspective—of the immanence of Israel, of humanity reflecting the image of God that can carry on its face" (JF 37/JeF 60).

20. Edith Wyschogrod, *Emmanuel Levinas: The Problem of Ethical Metaphysics,* 2nd ed. (Boston: Fordham University Press, 2000), 133. Levinas gives a similar argument for this point in *Time and the Other.*

21. See Rosenzweig, *Star of Redemption.* For Rosenzweig, creation is the past and redemption is the future. These three moments of past, present, and future —creation, revelation, and redemption—correspond to Man, God, and World.

22. Rosenzweig, *Star of Redemption,* 204. See also Leora Batnitzky, *Idolatry and Representation: The Philosophy of Franz Rosenzweig Reconsidered* (Princeton, N.J.: Princeton University Press, 2000), 116–119.

23. Rosenzweig, *Star of Redemption,* 205.

24. See Susan Handelman, *Fragments of Redemption* (Bloomington: Indiana University Press, 1991), 266–267. Handelman's discussion links the notion of love in Rosenzweig's reading of the Song of Songs to the "Here I am" (*hineni*) that we find in the biblical response of Abraham, Noah, and others, the response that indicates subjectivity.

25. Rosenzweig, *Star of Redemption,* 64.

26. Ibid., 326. Catherine Chalier makes a similar claim in "Exteriority and the Feminine," in Tina Chanter, ed., *Feminist Interpretations of Emmanuel Levinas* (University Park: Penn State Press, 2001), 171–179. Chalier argues that it is the feminine that gives meaning to male ethical and spiritual life. She tells us that without the feminine, without woman (Chalier's equivocation), "without her weakness [*défaillance*] and the intimacy of her home, man would know 'nothing of what transforms his natural life into ethics'" (Chalier, "Exteriority," 173, although the last few quoted words are from Levinas JF 34/JeF 50).

27. Ainley also takes up this point. She claims that while Levinas wants to give us an account of love that contains within it the "beyond it" and makes maternity possible, he does not want to make it a determining factor ("Amorous Discourses," 76). However, Ainley also realizes and takes issue with the assumed heterosexual framework that Levinas assumes by taking such a position ("Amorous Discourses," 78).

28. The topic of sexual relations within the Jewish tradition is not obscure. It is not a topic that Levinas would have had to search for in order to come across the writings on it. Because the Talmud governs all aspects of life, discussions on marriage and family not only are included, but are discussed at length.

29. See the section "The Infinity of Time" (TI 285/TeI 261), in which Levinas ends with the question of messianism.

30. Gibbs, *Correlations,* 238.

31. The House of Ruth is the name of the shelter for battered women in Baltimore, Maryland, and Washington, D.C. It takes its name from Ruth's character as a helper, particularly to other women.

32. Elie Wiesel, "Ruth," in *Sages and Dreamers* (New York: Touchstone, 1991), 51.

33. Ruth 1:16–17.

34. Ruth 2:6.

35. Ruth 2:10.

36. Ruth 2:11.

37. It is worth noting that it is not Boaz who approaches Ruth. Rather, Ruth approaches Boaz, while he is sleeping, and Naomi encourages her to do so.

38. The rabbis ask, "How can one rob from the poor?" The answer: we rob from the poor when we do not give them what we are obliged to give them: gleanings, the forgotten sheaves, the corner of the field, and the poor man's tithe. We rob them when we fail in our obligation to them.

39. In modern times, it is used also in reference to one who has converted to Judaism.

40. I am tracing a theme that can also be found in the work of Julia Kristeva and Elie Wiesel, who both provide illuminating discussions of the relationship between alterity and conversion. See Kristeva, *Strangers to Ourselves,* trans. Leon S. Roudiez (New York: Columbia University Press, 1991), and Wiesel, "Ruth."

41. *Midrash Rabbah,* Ruth, ch. VIII, p. 92.

42. Wiesel, "Ruth," 53. The Jewish faith views loyalty as a strong ethical duty. This value informs the legal view that forbids fathers from testifying against their sons in a court of law. It is precisely the role that partiality plays, that of knowing someone, which gives rise to the ethical call to loyalty. We can see even in the Jews' relationship to God that the relationship is one of loyalty. Judaism understands the term "chosen people," to reflect the involuntary choice of the Jews to enter into the covenant. In this context, "chosen," means "election." The Jews are elected to responsibility. Nonetheless, their entry into the covenant gives rise to their loyalty to God. God proclaims, "I am the Lord thy God which have brought thee out of the land of Egypt, out of the house of bondage" (Exodus 20:2). See also George Fletcher, *Loyalty: An Essay on the Morality of Relationships* (New York: Oxford, 1993), 37.

43. Kristeva, "Strangers to Ourselves," 71.

44. Mieke Bal, *Lethal Love: Feminist Readings of Biblical Love Stories* (Bloomington: Indiana University Press, 1987), 72.

45. Adler, *Engendering Judaism.*

46. Ibid., 155.

47. See ibid., 149–155. Adler gives a fascinating description of *hesed:* "It is a mode of relation directed toward the other that is nevertheless independent of the other. It can sustain itself when the other is too empty, too bitter, or too grieved to reciprocate" (149).

48. See Levinas's use of *hesed* in several interviews. In particular, see his interviews with François Poirié (IR 69) and Salomon Malka (IR 99–100).

49. If Irigaray is right, then Levinas's analysis does not allow for a relationship between women—sexual or otherwise.

50. For a detailed analysis of this theme, see Judith A. Kates and Gail Twersky Reimer, eds., *Reading Ruth: Contemporary Women Reclaim a Sacred Text* (New York: Ballantine Books, 1994). For another reading of the Book of Ruth, also inspired by Levinas's work, see Laurie Zoloth, *Health Care and the Ethics of Encounter* (Chapel Hill: University of North Carolina Press, 1999).

7. CAIN AND THE RESPONSIBILITY OF CHOICE

1. Levinas takes up this same theme in "The Temptation of Temptation," in which he provides his own reading of the receiving of the Torah. See the discussion of this theme in

chapter 2. For Levinas, the receiving of the Torah does not present the multitude of options with which Christianity tempts us. In contrast to Christianity, the offering of the Torah presented only two options: truth or death. But, similar to the view that I suggested, Levinas claims that we can interpret these options as something other than God threatening to condemn the Hebrews to death. Levinas suggests that by not accepting the Torah, one is not accepting education—Jewish education. And a life outside of Judaism could lead only to catastrophe and death. Since the accepting of the Torah still precedes the rationale of what accepting the Torah means, Levinas accepts the Hebraic notion of "doing before hearing," where "hearing" means "understanding." One does, and then one understands. One accepts the Torah before one knows it. For Levinas, the Torah provides the way beyond ontology. See also E. Wyschogrod, *Emmanuel Levinas: The Problem of Ethical Metaphysics* (New York: Fordham University Press, 2000), on this point. For an interesting analysis of how this expression—ethics before cognition—is intertwined into Levinas's analysis, see E. Wyschogrod, "Doing before Hearing," in François Laruelle, ed., *Textes pour Emmanuel Lévinas* (Paris: Jean-Michel Place, 1980), 179–202.

2. See "God and Philosophy, 70–71."

3. Levinas contrasts the view that he offers with the one put forth in Heidegger's *Being and Time,* in which *Dasein*'s concern appears as a concern only for *Dasein*'s own projects, not for the other. On the other hand, this concern for its own projects is not enjoyment. *Dasein* does not seem to partake in projects for the sake of itself, for the sake of enjoying. One eats for-the-sake-of . . . , rather than eating to enjoy.

4. In "A Religion for Adults," Levinas observes that "reciprocity is a structure founded on an original inequality. For equality to make its entry into the world, beings must be able to demand more of themselves than of the Other, feel responsibilities on which the fate of humanity hangs, and in this sense pose themselves problems outside humanity" (RA 22/ RdA 39).

5. The term "stranger" is translated from the Hebrew word *ger.* This word can also be translated as "convert," or it can refer to someone who simply resides somewhere. Thus, the English translation does not capture the ambiguity of the Hebrew word. One midrash commentary tells us that the stranger in the Torah is a non-Jew. This is to say that from the Jew's vantage point, the stranger is the individual who does not share race, ethnicity, or kinship with him or her. See my discussion in the previous chapter.

6. "Intention, Event, and the Other" (IR 145). Handelman reminds us that "turning toward" is a prime root of the Hebrew word for "face (*panah, panim*)" (Susan Handelman, *Fragments of Redemption* [Bloomington: Indiana University Press, 1991], 268).

7. The ambiguity of the face of the other—that it both compels me not to kill it and yet also elicits a murderous desire in me—is transformed in *Otherwise than Being* into the face that persecutes me. The languages of hostage and of persecutor are inverted in this text. See Robert Bernasconi, "Only the Persecuted . . . : Language of the Oppressor, Language of the Oppressed," in Adriaan T. Peperzak, ed., *Ethics as First Philosophy: The Significance of Emmanuel Levinas for Philosophy, Literature and Religion* (New York: Routledge, 1995), 77–86.

8. As Jill Robbins remarks in her essay "Visage, Figure: Speech and Murder in Levinas's *Totality and Infinity,*" the rest of this sentence is absent. The Hebrew word *vayommer* is translated as "said unto" rather than "spoke to" or "told to," indicating that what was said is somehow significant (in Cathy Caruth and Deborah Esch, eds., *Critical Encounters: Reference and Responsibility in Deconstructive Writing* [New Brunswick, N.J.: Rutgers University Press, 1994], 292).

9. The original story used the Hebrew names Hevel and Kayin for Abel and Cain. I changed the names to the Anglicized version for ease of reading and consistency.

10. For the speculative dialogue, see Rabbi Moshe Weissman, ed., *The Midrash Says: The Book of Beraishis* (Brooklyn: Benei Yakov Publications, 1980). Another rabbinic inter-

pretation likens this point to "two athletes who wrestle before the king; had the king wished he could have separated them. But he did not so desire and one overcame the other and killed him, he [the victim] crying out [before he died], 'let my cause be pleased before the king!'" Rabbi Dr. H. Freedman, trans., *Midrash Rabbah,* Genesis I (New York: Soncino, 1983), 189. This interpretation is derived from God's own claim that Abel's blood cries out against Him, God.

11. Nahum M. Sarna, *JPS Torah Commentary,* commentary on Genesis (Philadelphia: Jewish Publication Society, 1989), 34.

12. This line also indicates the significance of being created from one human species. There is no hierarchy, since no one can claim a different ancestry. But also, to kill one human is as if one killed the entire world. See Sarna, *JPS Torah Commentary,* 13.

13. John Llewelyn, *Emmanuel Levinas: The Genealogy of Ethics* (London: Routledge, 1995), 119–120.

14. Sarna, *JPS Torah Commentary,* 34.

15. Rabbi A. M. Silberman, trans., *Chumash and Rashi,* Bereshit (Jerusalem: Feldheim, 1934), 19.

16. Simon Wiesenthal, *The Sunflower* (New York: Schocken, 1976); 1st ed., Paris: Opera Mundi, 1969.

17. The symposium following the story comprises a wide range of commentaries. The commentators range from Herbert Marcuse and Cynthia Ozick to Gabriel Marcel and Jacques Maritain.

18. I say "foreshadows" only because the essays in *Difficult Freedom* were compiled in the years following the liberation of France after World War II, and thus they predate *Totality and Infinity,* which was first published in 1961.

19. This theme evokes the Hebraic notion "to do and to hear." This expression recalls the discussion in chapter 2 of this book, in which Rashi recounts the fear and trembling in the receiving of the Torah.

20. See Myra Bookman and Mitchell Aboulafia, "Ethics of Care Revisited: Gilligan and Levinas," in *Philosophy Today* 44 (2001), SPEP Supplement 2000, vol. 26, 169–174.

21. Carol Gilligan, *In a Different Voice* (Cambridge, Mass.: Harvard University Press, 1982).

22. See, for example, Nancy Chodorow, *The Reproduction of Mothering* (Berkeley: University of California Press, 1978).

23. Too many theorists have written about essentialism and its problems to list them all here. For a few references, see, e.g., Tina Chanter, *Ethics of Eros: Irigaray's Rewriting of the Philosophers,* which includes a chapter devoted to this topic and an extensive accompanying bibliography (London: Routledge, 1995). See also the classic by Diana Fuss, *Essentially Speaking* (Princeton, N.J.: Princeton University Press, 1989).

8. ABRAHAM AND
THE TEMPERING OF VIRILITY

1. Søren Kierkegaard, *Fear and Trembling,* trans. Alistair Hannay (London: Penguin, 1985).

2. I use "Kierkegaard" and "de Silentio" interchangeably, since Levinas does not make this distinction.

3. In other words, the story takes place as such, with the circumstances as such. But what if the absurdity were not present? What if there was nothing in God's relationship to Abraham that made it absurd that he would ask for Isaac's life, but only horrifying? One cannot help but wonder what Kierkegaard's reading of the story would be if the covenant had not been promised through Isaac. Is the teleological suspension of the ethical only an

issue because of the promise of Canaan? What would we think of a God who had no reason to return the son to the father? What would we think of the father who was willing to sacrifice his son under that circumstance? Would faith still be a possibility? If so, what would it be like?

4. Rabbi Dr. H. Freedman and Maurice Simon, trans., *The Midrash Rabbah,* Genesis, L.VI. 8 (New York: Soncino, 1977), 498.

5. The Hebrew reads *V'ha-a-lay-hu* (and offer him up), *sham* (there) *l'olah* (as an offering). See Gunther Plaut, ed., *The Torah: A Modern Commentary* (New York: Union of American Hebrew Congregations, 1981).

6. I am indebted to Susan Handelman for first alerting me to this midrash. See also Sandor Goodhart's work.

7. See Franz Rosenzweig, *The Star of Redemption,* trans. William W. Hallo (Notre Dame, Ind.: University of Notre Dame Press, 1970), 266.

8. We could contrast this view with Descartes's in *Meditations on First Philosophy* (Indianapolis: Hackett, 1993). For Descartes, God must be a being that does not deceive, and the avoidance of error comes precisely when he follows God's will.

9. See Merold Westphal, "Levinas's Teleological Suspension of the Religious," in Adriaan T. Peperzak, ed., *Ethics as First Philosophy: The Significance of Emmanuel Levinas for Philosophy, Literature, and Religion* (London/New York: Routledge, 1995), 151–160, for another perspective on the relationship between Levinas and Kierkegaard. In Westphal's view, Levinas makes a parallel move to the one made by Kierkegaard. Where Kierkegaard suspends the ethical, Levinas suspends the religious, if we think of what is suspended as that which is derivative of something higher than it. The problem with Westphal's view is that he fails to take into account the places where Levinas tells us that religion is equated with ethics, as in "On Jewish Philosophy." After failing to take this point into account, Westphal then assumes that we would need to synthesize Levinas and Kierkegaard in order to have a complete picture of the ethical, one which combines the ethical and the religious. However, Levinas already assumes this point. To hear the call of the other is to respond to the trace of God, the infinite, in the other. These things, the ethical and the religious, are not mutually exclusive. Although Levinas owes a debt to Kierkegaard, he does not need Kierkegaard, here, to save the religious from its suspension by the ethical. But we might say, as I am arguing in this chapter, that Levinas's view comes from assuming implicitly what Kierkegaard makes explicit—that Abraham did raise his knife. Thus, in light of how horrifying that is, the fact that he put it down needs to be explained. For a similar reading of this view, see Jill Robbins, "Tracing Responsibility in Levinas's Ethical Thought," in Peperzak, *Ethics as First Philosophy,* 173–183. Robbins suggests that "if God can be understood as 'not contaminated by being,' as Levinas puts it, that is, in accordance with what can be called a 'Judaic' *non*ontotheological theology, then perhaps the nonmanifestation of the revelation of God can be understood otherwise, as a differential constitution of (textual) traces, as the other-trace. Then perhaps we can begin to think God, in Levinas's work, as the *name*—unpronounceable if you like—for the difficult way in which we are responsible *to* traces" (182).

10. Jean-Paul Sartre, *Existentialism,* trans. Bernard Frechtman (New York: Philosophical Library, 1947), 23–24.

11. The Jews admire Abraham for his treatment of the stranger, and because he argued with God to save the few pious who might be in Sodom.

12. In the *Midrash Rabbah,* the rabbis ask, "Where was the knife? Tears had fallen from the angels upon it and dissolved it. 'Then I will strangle him,' said he [Abraham] to Him. 'LAY NOT THY HAND UPON THE LAD' was the reply. 'Let us bring forth a drop of blood from him,' he pleaded. 'NEITHER DO THOU ANY THING TO HIM,' He answered. . . ." (Freedman, *Midrash Rabbah,* Genesis, LVI. 7-8). Even the midrash gives the impression of Abraham that he was bound and determined to sacrifice Isaac. I discuss this further in this chapter.

13. See Jill Robbins, *Prodigal Son/Elder Brother: Interpretation and Alterity in Augustine, Petrarch, Kafka, Levinas* (Chicago: University of Chicago Press, 1991), for another claim of the importance of Kierkegaard's reading of the Akedah. In fact, Robbins repeats the question that Levinas asks in *Difficult Freedom:* "Can one still be Jewish without Kierkegaard?" Does this question mean to imply that it is Kierkegaard who has taught us how to read the text in the first place?

14. And could we not say that this distance from obedience, this sensitivity to hearing a second voice—if there was one—is precisely what the Nazis lacked? Such a view can be seen in some of the speeches that Himmler gave to the SS, speeches of encouragement so that they would continue with their duty in spite of their own horror at the Nazi activities. That the Nazis were able to squelch whatever response they had to the other in order to carry out Hitler's plan is the cause for Himmler's praise. Himmler himself saw his actions as a conflict between will and obligation; see William Lawrence Shirer, *The Rise and Fall of the Third Reich* (New York: Simon and Schuster, 1960), 937–938.

15. All generations to come will have men like Abraham and men like Jacob, Moses, and Samuel. They represent philanthropy, service to God, study of Torah, and civil justice, respectively.

16. See Rashi, *Ariel Chumash: Bereshit to Chaye Sarah* (Jerusalem: United Israel Institutes, 1997), 138.

17. Isaiah, 65:24, as cited in OTB 150/AE 235.

18. We could say that Abraham's actions are akin to the Hebrew Teshuva, the word used for repentance. But this word also means to turn, as if to turn back or to be reconnected with that from which one became disconnected, such as from the ethical. We might recall the Hebrew name of the story: *Akedah*—binding. How is Isaac—or is it Abraham—being bound, and to whom?

19. See Kenneth Seeskin, *Autonomy in Jewish Philosophy* (Cambridge: Cambridge University Press, 2001). Seeskin argues, in contrast to the popular view, that Judaism is a religion of autonomy, not a religion of blind obedience to rules and laws. Among other examples, he cites Abraham, who argues with God about the righteous in Sodom. This is why it is so interesting that Abraham walks up the mountain with Isaac, without so much as a "Why?"

20. See Handelman's discussion in *Fragments of Redemption* (Bloomington: Indiana University Press, 1991), 275–282.

21. See James Hatley, *Suffering Witness* (Albany: SUNY Press, 2000).

22. Levinas has a similar concern about the relationship between National Socialism and the kind of reading that Kierkegaard gives us of Abraham. See PN 76.

23. See Hannah Arendt, *The Origins of Totalitarianism* (New York: Harcourt Brace Jovanovich, 1973).

24. Jan Patočka, *Heretical Essays in the Philosophy of History,* trans. Erazim Icohák, ed. James Dodd (Chicago: Open Court, 1996).

25. Jacques Derrida, *The Gift of Death,* trans. David Wills (Chicago: University of Chicago Press, 1995), 2.

26. Ibid., 10.

27. Ibid., 24.

28. Ibid.

29. Ibid., 32.

30. Ibid., 61.

31. Ibid.

32. Ibid., 68.

33. Ibid., 85.

34. Ibid., 86.

35. See also David S. Stern, "The Bind of Responsibility: Kierkegaard, Derrida, and the *Akedah* of Isaac," *Philosophy Today* (forthcoming).

36. Rosenzweig, *Star of Redemption,* 175–176.

37. In a personal correspondence, Merold Westphal rightly asks me if I am being generous enough to Abraham in my phrasing this sentence in such a way. For Westphal, everything Levinas speaks of with regard to the Other—revelation, teaching beyond recollection, and height—occurs in the Abraham story, although Westphal does realize the important difference that the Other is God. In Westphal's view, Abraham represents the opposite of the *conatus essendi,* he is "anything but the masculine psychism whose ego is or tries to be unconstrained." Westphal's comments are instructive, and I appreciate that he wants to be more charitable to Abraham. But I would maintain that the "important difference" that the Other is God is not simply important but essential. Levinas's reading of the story "Yosl Raskover Talks to God," found in his essay "Loving the Torah More than God," illustrates precisely his worry when the Other becomes God at the expense of the human Other. My point is that while Abraham may have struggled with the decision to raise the knife, he still raised the knife. What I want to commend Abraham for is putting the knife down. As I will discuss in the next chapter, certainly it is the case that women kill their children. I wish to maintain that the image of maternity nonetheless heightens our awareness such that when mothers kill their children we are horrified. For interesting work on Kierkegaard and Levinas, see Westphal's "The Transparent Shadow: Kierkegaard and Levinas in Dialogue," in Martin J. Matustik and Merold Westphal, eds., *Kierkegaard in Post/Modernity* (Bloomington: Indiana University Press, 1995), 151–160.

9. MATERNITY, SACRIFICE, AND SARAH'S CHOICE

1. See Levinas, PP.

2. Zornberg, *The Beginning of Desire: Reflections on Genesis* (New York: Image/Doubleday, 1995), 134–135.

3. Ibid., 135.

4. For a different account of this event, see the poem "Sarah's Choice" by Eleanor Wilner. In this poem, Wilner inverts the story to read God asking Sarah rather than Abraham to sacrifice Isaac. Sarah immediately decides against this action and in fact gathers Hagar and the two children and leaves. See Eleanor Wilner, *Reversing the Spell* (Port Townsend, Wash.: Copper Canyon, 1998). I wish to thank Emily Grosholz for this reference.

5. We might even want to contrast the skin images here: the too-tight skin could be maternity, the figure of a pregnant woman, while the skin that is too loose, the skin that is wrinkled, is that of someone in need. One cannot help thinking of the concentration-camp victims in World War II, who were not much more than skin and bones.

6. Levinas makes an interesting shift in his discussion of corporeality from *Totality and Infinity* to *Otherwise than Being.* Kelly Oliver notes in her essay "Paternal Election and the Absent Father" that in spite of Levinas's transformation of paternity from threat to love, he still has the problem of the absent body of the father (in Tina Chanter, ed., *Feminist Interpretations of Emmanuel Levinas* [University Park: Penn State Press, 2001], 224–240). In addition to replacing the father with the mother, the move to the maternal body in *Otherwise than Being* also introduces a strong element of the corporeal. Not only is the mother's body present, but Levinas talks in terms of her fleshly body: skin, bread from the mouth, gestation, and so on. This concern resembles Alison Ainley's in "Levinas and Kant: Maternal Morality and Illegitimate Offspring" (in Chanter, *Feminist Interpretations,* 203–223). Ainley argues that the representation of the image of maternity raises questions with regard

to, among other things, how women philosophers, readers of Levinas, are to understand themselves in relationship to this image. Again, the problem turns on how to understand the image: as metaphor, representation, literal referent, and so on.

7. The philosophical literature in this area is quite rich. See Cynthia Willett, *Maternal Ethics and Other Slave Moralities* (New York: Routledge, 1995) and Kelly Oliver's many books and essays, including *Reading Kristeva: Unraveling the Double Bind* (Bloomington: Indiana University Press, 1993); *Womanizing Nietzsche* (New York: Routledge, 1995); and *Family Values* (New York: Routledge, 1997).

8. One wonders if Levinas's reference here to the skin as limit, and to the face of the other, is a reference to Moses seeing the back of God, and only the back of God. To put "skin" on God would be to thematize God, to define God, and therefore, to limit God. God would be "weighted down" with skin. Because Moses sees only the back of God, God's alterity remains undisturbed.

9. Stella Sandford, "Masculine Mothers? Maternity in Levinas and Plato," in Chanter, ed., *Feminist Interpretations of Levinas,* 180–201.

10. Ibid., 185.

11. Emmanuel Levinas, "No Identity," in *Collected Philosophical Papers,* trans. Alphonso Lingis (Dordrecht: Kluwer Academic Publishers, 1993), 147n6; originally published as "Sans Identité," in *Humanisme de l'autre homme* (Montpellier: Fata Morgana, 1972), 83–101.

12. See Sandford, "Masculine Mothers?" 202n56.

13. See Richard A. Cohen, *Ethics, Exegesis and Philosophy* (Cambridge: Cambridge University Press, 2001), especially the chapter titled "Maternal Body/Maternal Psyche."

14. See Robert Gibbs, *Why Ethics* (Princeton, N.J.: Princeton University Press, 2000) and James Hatley, *Suffering Witness* (Albany: SUNY Press, 2000), especially chapter 5.

15. This transformation continues with the birth of the child, when the mother's body produces milk—the only sustenance that the child needs for the first six to eight months of its life. This stage serves as a link between the body that is unwilled responsibility and the choices that a mother must make. The mother's body produces milk on its own. But the mother must take steps to feed the baby. Finally, the mother must wean the baby with the hope that the baby will not turn its frustration onto the mother. Levinas might have found interesting the four stories of "weaning" in the "Attunement" section of *Fear and Trembling.* The narratives illustrate the trauma of freedom. The mother, in the process of weaning, must help the child become independent of her without the effect of the child turning away from her completely.

16. Chalier, "Ethics and the Feminine." Similar to my interpretation of Ruth, Chalier offers the biblical character of Rebecca, whose excessive fulfillment of the feminine moves her from beyond the ethical to the very example of the ethical. Levinas also cites this story as an example of response to the other at the beginning of his essay "The Bible and the Greeks" in *In the Time of the Nations.* For an interesting discussion of Chalier's view, see Richard Cohen's comments in *Elevations,* 96. As my discussion indicates, I disagree with Cohen's claim that maternity is simply a condition of ethics rather than naming the ethical relationship itself.

17. Chalier, "Ethics and the Feminine," 126–127.

18. See Daniel Boyarin's fine essay "Justify My Love," in Miram Peskowitz and Laura Levitt, eds., *Judaism since Gender* (New York: Routledge, 1997), 131–137.

19. Sandford, "Masculine Mothers?" 199.

20. See Kelly Oliver's work on the cultural view of the relationship between the mother and child and how that changing view paralleled the change in our care and treatment of both mothers and fetuses. See Oliver's work also for an interesting discussion on the placenta—for example, *Family Values: Subjects between Nature and Culture* (New York: Routledge, 1997), 27–29.

21. Laurie Zoloth, "Into the Woods: Killer Mothers, Feminist Ethics, and the Problem of Evil," in Hava Tirosh-Samuelson, ed., *Women and Gender in Jewish Philosophy* (Bloomington: Indiana University Press, forthcoming).

22. See Toni Morrison's moving novel *Beloved* (New York: Penguin, 1987) for a fictional account of such a discussion.

23. In the historical novel *The Angel of Darkness* (New York: Random House, 1997), Caleb Carr explores precisely this question as it may have appeared at the turn of the nineteenth century. The focus of the novel is the birth and rise of forensic science. The main character is a forensic psychologist, practicing when psychology is viewed with suspicion. He is investigating a series of kidnappings/murders in which the perpetrator turns out to be a woman. Throughout the story, no one can believe that a woman could commit such a horrible crime and not be considered "sick."

24. The most recent case to hit the media was the Andrea Yates case in Texas (May 2001). Yates systematically killed her five children by drowning them. They ranged in age from seven years to five months. Granted, to die by drowning is traumatic no matter how we choose to look at it. However, certainly one can see how the evil of this act is amplified in two different scenarios: we can imagine a child running from his mother because he has just seen what she has done to his siblings and he sees that he is about to suffer the same fate (as was the case with the oldest child); or we can imagine being one of the younger children and knowing that it is your mother, to whom you would run for protection, who is committing this action against you.

25. *"Que dirait Eurydice? What would Eurydice say?," Emmanuel Levinas en/in conversation avec/with Bracha Lichtenberg-Ettinger* (Paris: BCE Atelier, 1977), 27.

26. Franz Rosenzweig, *The Star of Redemption,* trans. William W. Hallo (Notre Dame, Ind.: University of Notre Dame Press, 1970), 202. In "Mourir Pour," Levinas responds to Heidegger's view that death is what separates us. For Levinas, it is, precisely, death, and my concern for the other's death, that connects us (DFo 215/MP 262). In death, relations with others are not dissolved. But in his reference to the biblical story of King Saul and his son Jonathan, Levinas does not refer to, nor does he think the narrator of the story points to, a life "after death." Rather, the love that exists between the two is "stronger than death" and lives on after death. Sacrifice, for Levinas, is not a losing oneself; rather, it is a giving oneself in the other. See DFo 215–217. Finally, although Levinas does refer to women dying in childbirth as an example of the possibility of dying for another (see the quotation from the interview with Bracha Ettinger-Lichtenberg in chapter 2 of this book), it is worth noting that in the above example, Levinas uses the story in which it is two men each giving his self in the other.

10. THE SILENT FOOTSTEPS OF REBECCA

1. For Levinas, maternity functions as an icon. However, I would hesitate to use such a word in light of its linguistic/symbolic connotations.

2. The Babylonian Talmud, *Yevamot* 65b.

3. "The Torah freed the woman from the religious obligation to 'be fruitful and multiply' [because] . . . the woman endangers her life in pregnancy and childbirth [and hence cannot be obligated to have children]." Rabbi Simkha of Dvinsk, *Meshech Hokhmah,* commenting on Genesis 9:1 as quoted in Rabbi Joseph Telushkin, ed., *Jewish Wisdom* (New York: William Morrow and Co., 1994), 143. So again we have the rabbinic corrective to the Torah. However, this issue appears less complex and easier to resolve than it actually is. For an illuminating discussion on this topic, see Judith Hauptman, *Rereading the Rabbis: A Woman's Voice* (Boulder: Westview, 1998), 132 ff.

4. Ironically, the rabbis, who were men, had enough insight and sensitivity not only to recognize this risk but also to exempt women from the commandment to procreate, while

Simone de Beauvoir did not recognize the risk that women took in procreation—or at least did not count that risk as authentic. See Simone de Beauvoir, *The Second Sex*, trans. H. M. Parshley (New York: Vintage, 1974), in particular, chapter 4, "The Nomads."

5. Ewa Ziarek addresses this point, along with addressing the general limits of a Levinasian ethics for a feminist framework. By reading Levinas through a Kristevan lens, Ziarek expands the possibilities of Levinas's work for women. See her "Kristeva and Levinas: Mourning, Ethics, and the Feminine," in Kelly Oliver, ed., *Ethics, Politics and Difference in Julia Kristeva's Writing* (New York: Routledge, 1993), 62–78.

6. Erika Duncan, "The Hungry Jewish Mother," in Susannah Heschel, ed., *On Being a Jewish Feminist* (New York: Schocken, 1983), 28.

7. Ibid., 28.

8. Ibid.

9. See Tina Chanter's introduction in Tina Chanter, ed., *Feminist Interpretations of Emmanuel Levinas* (University Park: Penn State Press, 2001), 26n10, and her discussion in her *Time, Death, and the Feminine* (Stanford, Calif.: Stanford University Press, 2001).

10. Although we commonly speak of a woman who died in childbirth, people often forget that pregnancy itself produces a risk to a woman's health and life. See note 14, below.

11. See Richard Cohen, *Ethics, Exegesis and Philosophy* (Cambridge: Cambridge University Press, 2001), 199–200.

12. These two positions in the abortion debate are antipodes that often end up, on the one hand, eliminating the mother as human being ("pro-life") and, on the other, foreclosing the possibility of mourning the loss by denying that the fetus has any nascent humanity (pro-choice). Levinas's ethics provides us an extraordinary perspective from which to view both of these positions critically, because he concentrates on the relationship between mother and child as a primordial togetherness.

13. Deliberation and choice belong to a domain of reason, which for Levinas arises only with the moment of the third party. This is the same moment when consciousness pulled back from the face-to-face and actively represented for itself that the other also had others. That is why it is always erroneous to seek in Levinas's thought answers to political questions, or to those questions that lie on the line between the ethical and the political, as though his ethics belonged to a virtue ethics, a utilitarian calculus, or a Kantian deontology.

14. My point here is not to claim that Levinas would support abortion rights, personally, philosophically, or ethically. First, I do not know what his view on abortion would be, nor do I know how he would respond to rights language in general. *Halachah*, or Jewish law, is, at the very least, ambivalent on this topic. There is evidence in the Torah that Judaism can support the precedence of the life of the mother over the life of the fetus, especially if the woman already has children for whom she is caring. Although this point could be read as "your life is only valuable as a caretaker," it could also be understood to recognize the familial bonds that are already in place. Additionally, although "life" is sometimes broadly construed to include emotional well-being, this interpretation would certainly be a liberal reading. My point here is that Levinas's conception of maternity, even in spite of himself, might actually be useful for understanding why the abortion issue is so complex and for making an argument in favor of maintaining women's safe and legal access to this procedure.

15. It might seem to some that more than a single line on this topic is warranted. However, I do not want to give the appearance of protesting too much. The "thou shalt not murder" needs to be understood as such: opposition to murder, to unjustified killing. Levinas is not opposed to war or killing, if the justification is in place. Certainly he recognizes the conflict between ethics and justice. The conflict exists because political events sometimes render justice necessary. Levinas's ethics, though they speak of passivity, do not yield a life of pacifism.

16. We can extend Levinas's discussion of maternity to the care of a child once born. Maternity illustrates the "passivity," the unwilled responsibility. But certainly Levinas would not think that responsibility ended with the birth of a child. In fact, we can import the dis-

cussion of the father-son relationship discussed in *Totality and Infinity* into this conversation. The mother's nurturing of the child reveals the fluidity of the care and responsibility directed toward that child.

17. Julia Kristeva and Catherine Clément, *The Feminine and the Sacred,* trans. Jane Marie Todd (New York: Columbia University Press, 2001). This book is interesting in that it is a series of letters exchanged between Julia Kristeva and Catherine Clément.

18. Ibid., 57.

19. Ibid.

20. It is worth noting the opposing positions with regard to the relationship, or lack of relationship, that Levinas indicates in his texts. On the one hand, Irigaray is concerned that, in *Totality and Infinity,* fecundity is connected to eros, and she thus claims that Levinas's analysis implies that the only "good" sexual encounter is one that intends a child. On the other hand, Chanter is concerned that eros drops from the discussion when maternity enters it in *Otherwise than Being,* giving us a conception of maternity that is without sex. Although both concerns have merit, if read together they leave Levinas in a precarious position—either he joins eros and fecundity, in which case Irigaray is critical, or he does not, in which case Chanter is. Moreover, it is not clear that either of these relationships must be read negatively. Could we not read the connection in *Totality and Infinity* as eros joined to fecundity—that is, not that fecundity must accompany eros, but rather that eros does accompany the means to fecundity? In the case of the maternal body, could it not be the case that Levinas's focus on responsibility and the maternal body itself precludes the discussion of eros in this capacity—but not in all dimensions of maternity? Although it is not clear that Levinas's conception of maternity needs to be rendered as one that is opposed to eros, I do find it interesting that Levinas, even when giving opposite accounts of this relationship, is unable to give us a relationship between eros and childbearing that is satisfactory to feminist theorists. Though the concerns are important with regard to Levinas's project, what I find more significant is that this opposition points to the underplayed discussion of motherhood in feminist theory. These concerns point to the larger question, "How are we to think of the relationships between motherhood and feminism, sexuality and childbirth, women and responsibility?"

21. See Tina Chanter, *Ethics of Eros: Irigaray's Rewriting of the Philosophers* (New York: London, 1995), which is excellent on the topic of the feminine. In particular, see chapter 5, 197–207.

22. Rachel Adler, *Engendering Judaism: An Inclusive Theology and Ethics* (Boston: Beacon, 1998), 107. For another interesting discussion, see the chapter on Sarah, "Du rire à la naissance," in Catherine Chalier, *Les Matriarches: Sarah, Rebecca, Rachel et Léa* (Paris: Cerf, 2000).

23. See Brian Schroeder, "Abraham's Odyssey," in Melvyn New, ed., with Robert Bernasconi and Richard Cohen, *In Proximity: Levinas and the 18th Century* (Lubbock: Texas Tech University Press, 2001), 91–110. In this essay, Schroeder, also concerned with the perception (accurate or not) of Levinas as not playful enough, weaves views from Levinas's texts and reads them through Fielding's work. He gives, in the end, a life-affirming view of Levinas.

24. Adler, *Engendering Judaism,* 105.

25. Ibid., 106.

26. Avivah Gottlieb Zornberg, *The Beginning of Desire: Reflections on Genesis* (New York: Image/Doubleday, 1995), 113.

27. Ibid., 112.

28. *Midrash Rabbah,* LVIII 5.

29. Rashi, *Ariel Chumash: Bereshit to Chaye Sarah* (Jerusalem: United Israel Institutes, 1997), 23: 2.

30. *Pirkei d'Rabbi Eliezer,* ch. 32. See Zornberg, *Beginning of Desire,* 124.

31. Zornberg, *Beginning of Desire,* 127–128.

32. *Midrash Rabbah* (Bereshit) 60: 2, quoted in Zornberg, *Beginning of Desire,* 140.

33. This scene gives us a fascinating contrast to the biblical scene and the midrashic commentary on Abraham mourning the death of Sarah.

34. For a clear discussion of Levinas's critique of Heidegger, see GDT/DMT.

35. The literature in this area is both fascinating and abundant. For a good place to begin, see the work of Sander Gilman and Daniel Boyarin. For an interesting analysis on the feminization of the Jew in Nazi Germany, see Klaus Theleweit. *Male Fantasies,* vol. 2, trans. Erica Carter and Chris Turner (Minneapolis: University of Minnesota Press, 1989).

36. Gideon Ofrat, *The Jewish Derrida,* trans. (from the Hebrew) by Peretz Kidron (Syracuse: Syracuse University Press, 2001).

37. Ibid., 50.

38. Ibid.

39. Ibid., 145.

40. Ibid., 144.

41. Ibid., 131. See also Emmanuel Levinas, *Beyond the Verse: Talmudic Readings and Lectures,* trans. Gary D. Mole (Bloomington: Indiana University Press, 1994), 52; *L'Au-delà du verset: Lectures et discours talmudiques* (Paris: Minuit, 1982), 70.

42. Ibid., 130.

WORKS BY EMMANUEL LEVINAS

"A Propos of 'Kierkegaard vivant.'" In *Proper Names,* trans. Michael B. Smith, 75–79. London: Athlone, 1996. Originally published as "A Propos de 'Kierkegaard vivant,'" in *Nom propres,* 111–115.

"And God Created Woman." In *Nine Talmudic Readings,* trans. Annette Aronowicz, 161–177. Bloomington: Indiana University Press, 1990. Originally published as "Et Dieu créa la femme," in *Du sacré au saint: Cinq nouvelles lectures talmudiques* (Paris: Minuit, 1977), 122–148.

"Between Two Worlds (The Way of Franz Rosenzweig)." In *Difficult Freedom,* trans. Sean Hand, 181–201. Baltimore: Johns Hopkins University Press, 1990. Originally published as "Entre deux mondes," in *Difficile Liberté: essais sur le judaïsme* (Paris: Albin Michel, 1963 and 1976), 253–281.

Beyond the Verse: Talmudic Readings and Lectures. Translated by Gary D. Mole. Bloomington: Indiana University Press, 1994. Originally published as *L'Au-delà du verset: Lectures et discours talmudiques* (Paris: Minuit, 1982).

"The Bible and the Greeks." In *In the Time of the Nations,* trans. Michael B. Smith, 133–135. Bloomington: Indiana University Press, 1994. Originally published as "La Bible et les Grecs," in *A l'heure des nations* (Paris: Minuit, 1988), 155–158.

Collected Philosophical Papers. Translated by Alphonso Lingis. Dordrecht: Kluwer Academic Publishers, 1987.

"Damages Due to Fire." In *Nine Talmudic Readings,* trans. Annette Aronowicz, 178–197. Bloomington: Indiana University Press, 1990. Originally published as "Les dommages causés par le feu," in *Du Sacré au saint* (Paris: Minuit, 1977), 149–180.

"Dialogue with Martin Buber." In *Proper Names,* trans. Michael B. Smith, 36–39. London: Athlone, 1996. Originally published as "Noms propres: Dialogue avec Martin Buber," in *Noms propres,* 51–55.

"Dieu et la philosophie." In *De Dieu qui vient à l'idée,* 93–127. Paris: Vrin, 1986.

"Dying for . . . " In *Entre Nous: Thinking-of-the-Other,* trans. Michael B. Smith, 207–218. New York: Columbia University Press, 1998. Originally published as "Mourir Pour," in *Heidegger: Questions Ouvertes* (Paris: Collège International de Philosophie, 1988).

Ethics and Infinity. Translated by Richard Cohen. Pittsburgh: Duquesne University Press, 1985. Originally published as *Ethique et infini: dialogues avec Philippe Nemo* (Paris: Librairie Arthème Fayard and Radio-France, 1982).

"Ethics and Spirit." In *Difficult Freedom,* trans. Sean Hand, 3–10. Baltimore: Johns Hopkins University Press, 1990. Originally published as "Ethique et Esprit" in *Difficile Liberté: essais sur le judaïsme* (Paris: Albin Michel, 1963 and 1976), 13–23.

Existence and Existents. Translated by Alphonso Lingis. Dordrecht, Boston, and London: Kluwer Academic Publishers, 1978; reprinted in 1988. Originally published as *De l'existence à l'existant* (Paris: Vrin, 1981; 1st ed. 1947).

"Freedom and Command." In *Collected Philosophical Papers,* 15–24.

God, Death, and Time. Translated by Bettina Bergo. Stanford, Calif.: Stanford University Press, 2000. Originally published as *Dieu, la mort et le temps* (Paris: Éditions Grasset et Fasquelle, 1993).

"Intention, Event, and the Other." In *Is It Righteous to Be? Interviews with Emmanuel Levinas,* 140–157.

Interview with Salomon Malka. In *Is It Righteous to Be? Interviews with Emmanuel Levinas,* 93–102.

Is It Righteous to Be? Interviews with Emmanuel Levinas. Edited by Jill Robbins. Stanford, Calif.: Stanford University Press, 2001.

"Judaism." In *Difficult Freedom,* trans. Sean Hand, 24–26. Baltimore: Johns Hopkins University Press, 1990. Originally published as "Judaïsme," in *Difficile Liberté: essais sur le judaïsme* (Paris: Albin Michel, 1963 and 1976), 43–46.

"Judaism and the Feminine." In *Difficult Freedom,* trans. Sean Hand, 30–37. Baltimore: Johns Hopkins University Press, 1990. Originally published as "Le judaïsme et le féminin," in *Difficile Liberté: essais sur le judaïsme* (Paris: Albin Michel, 1963 and 1976), 51–62.

"Kierkegaard: Existence and Ethics." In *Proper Names,* trans. Michael B. Smith, 66–74. London: Athlone, 1996. Originally published as "Kierkegaard: Existence et Éthique," in *Noms propres,* 99–109.

"Loving the Torah More Than God." In *Difficult Freedom,* trans. Sean Hand, 142–145. Baltimore: Johns Hopkins University Press, 1990. Originally published as "Aimer la Thora plus que Dieu," in *Difficile Liberté: Essais sur le judaïsme* (Paris: Albin Michel, 1963 and 1976), 201–206.

"Martin Buber and the Theory of Knowledge." In *Proper Names,* trans. Michael B. Smith, 17–35. London: Athlone, 1996. Originally published as "Martin Buber et la théorie de la connaissance," in *Noms propres,* 29–50.

"No Identity." In *Collected Philosophical Papers,* 141–151. Originally published as "Sans Identité," in *Humanisme de l'autre homme* (Montpellier: Fata Morgana, 1972), 83–101.

Nom propres. Montpellier: Fata Morgana, 1976.

"On Jewish Philosophy." In *In the Time of the Nations,* trans. Michael B. Smith, 167–183. Bloomington: Indiana University Press, 1994. Originally published as "Sur le philosophie juive," in *A l'heure des nations* (Paris: Minuit, 1988), 197–215. Reprinted in *Is It Righteous to Be? Interviews with Emmanuel Levinas,* 239–254.

"On the Jewish Reading of the Scriptures." In *Beyond the Verse,* 101–115. Originally published as "De la lecture juive des Ecritures," in *L'Au-delà du verset: Lectures et discours talmudiques,* 125–142.

Otherwise than Being; or, Beyond Essence. Translated by Alphonso Lingis. The Hague: Martinus Nijhoff, 1981. Originally published as *Autrement qu'être, ou, Au-delà de l'essence* (Dordrecht: Martinus Nijhoff, 1974).

Outside the Subject. Translated by Michael B. Smith. London: Athlone, 1993. Originally published as *Hors sujet* (Montpellier: Fata Morgana, 1987).

"Peace and Proximity." In *Emmanuel Levinas: Basic Philosophical Writings,* ed. Adriaan T. Peperzak, Simon Critchley, and Robert Bernasconi, 161–170. Bloomington: Indiana University Press, 1996. Originally published as "Paix et proximité," in *Les Cahiers de la nuit surveillée: Emmanuel Levinas,* no. 3 (Paris: Editions Verdier, 1984), 339–346.

"Que dirait Eurydice? What Would Eurydice Say?" Emmanuel Levinas en/in conversation avec/with Bracha Lichtenberg-Ettinger. Paris: BLE Atelier, 1977.

"A Religion for Adults." In *Difficult Freedom,* trans. Sean Hand, 11–23. Baltimore: Johns Hopkins University Press, 1990. Originally published as "Une religion d'adultes," in *Difficile Liberté: Essais sur le judaisme* (Paris: Albin Michel, 1963 and 1976), 24–42.

"Revelation in the Jewish Tradition." In *Beyond the Verse,* 129–150. Originally published as "La Révélation dans la tradition Juive," in *L'Au-delà du verset,* 158–181.

"The Temptation of Temptation." In *Nine Talmudic Readings,* trans. Annette Aronowicz, 30–50. Bloomington: Indiana University Press, 1990. Originally published as "La tentation de la tentation," in *Quatre lectures talmudiques* (Paris: Minuit, 1968), 65–110.

Time and the Other. Translated by Richard Cohen. Pittsburgh: Duquesne University Press, 1987. Originally published as *Le Temps et l'autre* (Montpellier: Fata Morgana, 1979; 1st ed. 1947).

Totality and Infinity. Translated by Alphonso Lingis. Pittsburgh: Duquesne University Press, 1969. Originally published as *Totalité et infini: Essai sur l'exteriorité* (The Hague: Martinus Nijhoff, 1971; 1st ed. 1961).

"Toward the Other." In *Nine Talmudic Readings,* trans. Annette Aronowicz, 12–29. Bloomington: Indiana University Press, 1990. Originally published as "Envers autrui," in *Quatre lectures talmudiques* (Paris: Minuit, 1968), 27–64.

"Useless Suffering." In *Entre Nous: Thinking-of-the-Other,* trans. Michael B. Smith, 207–218. New York: Columbia University Press, 1998.

GENERAL BIBLIOGRAPHY

Adler, Rachel. *Engendering Judaism: An Inclusive Theology and Ethics.* Boston: Beacon, 1998.
Ainley, Alison. "Amorous Discourses: 'The Phenomenology of Eros' and Love Stories." In Robert Bernasconi and David Wood, eds., *The Provocation of Levinas,* 70–82. London: Routledge, 1988.
———. "Levinas and Kant: Maternal Morality and Illegitimate Offspring." In Chanter, ed., *Feminist Interpretations of Levinas,* 203–223.
Ajzenstat, Oona. *Driven Back to the Text: The Premodern Sources of Levinas's Postmodernism.* Pittsburgh: Duquesne University Press, 2001.
Arendt, Hannah. *The Origins of Totalitarianism.* New York: Harcourt Brace Jovanovich, 1973.
Bal, Micke. *Lethal Love: Feminist Readings of Biblical Love Stories.* Bloomington: Indiana University Press, 1987.
Batnitzky, Leora. *Idolatry and Representation: The Philosophy of Franz Rosenzweig Reconsidered.* Princeton, N.J.: Princeton University Press, 2000.
Beauvoir, Simone de. *Le Deuxième Sexe.* Paris: Gallimard, 1949. Translated by H. M. Parshley under the title *The Second Sex* (New York: Random House, 1952).
Benhabib, Seyla. *Situating the Self.* New York: Routledge, 1992.
Benso, Silvia. "Levinas—Another Ascetic Priest." *Journal of the British Society for Phenomenology* 27, no. 2 (1997): 137–156.
Bergo, Bettina. *Levinas between Ethics and Politics: For the Beauty that Adorns the Earth.* Dordrecht: Kluwer Academic Publishers, 1999.
Bernasconi, Robert. "'Failure of Communication' as a Surplus: Dialogue and Lack of Dialogue between Buber and Levinas." In Robert Bernasconi and David Wood, eds., *The Provocation of Levinas,* 100–135. New York: Routledge, 1988.
———. "Only the Persecuted . . . : Language of the Oppressor, Language of the Oppressed." In Peperzak, ed., *Ethics as First Philosophy,* 77–86.
———. "Who Is My Neighbor? Who Is the Other? Questioning 'The Generosity of Western Thought.'" In *Ethics and Responsibility in the Phenomenological Tradition,* 1–31. Ninth Annual Symposium of the Simon Silverman Phenomenology Center. Pittsburgh: Duquesne University Press, 1992.
Biale, David. *Eros and the Jews.* New York: Basic Books, 1992.
Bookman, Myra, and Mitchell Aboulafia. "Ethics of Care Revisited: Gilligan and Levinas." *Philosophy Today* 44 (2001): 169–174. SPEP Supplement 2000, vol. 26.
Boyarin, Daniel. "Justify My Love." In Peskowitz and Levitt, eds., *Judaism since Gender,* 131–137.
———. "The Politics of Biblical Narratology: Reading the Bible Like/As a Woman." *diacritics* 20, no. 4 (1990): 31–42.
Boyarin, Jonathan, and Daniel Boyarin. "Tricksters, Martyrs, and Collaborators: Diaspora and the Gendered Politics of Resistance." In *Powers of Diaspora: Two Essays on the Relevance of Jewish Culture,* 35–102. Minneapolis: University of Minnesota Press, 2002.
Buber, Martin. *Between Man and Man.* Translated by Ronald G. Smith. New York: Macmillan, 1965.
———. *I and Thou.* Translated by Ronald G. Smith. New York: Scribner's, 1958.

Carr, Caleb. *The Angel of Darkness.* New York: Random House, 1997.

Chalier, Catherine. "Ethics and the Feminine." In Robert Bernasconi and Simon Critchley, eds., *Re-Reading Levinas,* 119–129. Bloomington: Indiana University Press, 1991.

———. "The Exteriority of the Feminine." Translated by Bettina Bergo. In Chanter, ed., *Feminist Interpretations of Emmanuel Levinas,* 171–179. Originally published in Chalier, *Figures du féminin.*

———. *Figures du féminin.* Paris: La Nuit surveillée, Collection Questions, 1982.

———. *Les Matriarches: Sarah, Rebecca, Rachel et Léa.* Paris: Cerf, 2000.

Chanter, Tina. "The Alterity and Immodesty of Time: Death as Future and Eros as Feminine in Levinas." In David Wood, ed., *Writing the Future,* 137–154. New York: Routledge, 1990.

———. *Ethics of Eros: Irigaray's Rewriting of the Philosophers.* New York: Routledge, 1995.

———. *Time, Death, and the Feminine.* Stanford, Calif.: Stanford University Press, 2001.

Chanter, Tina, ed. *Feminist Interpretations of Emmanuel Levinas.* University Park: Penn State Press, 2001.

Chapman, Helen. "Levinas and the Concept of the Feminine." *Warwick Journal of Philosophy* 1, no. 1 (1988): 65–83.

Chodorow, Nancy. *The Reproduction of Mothering.* Berkeley: University of California Press, 1978.

Clément, Catherine, and Julia Kristeva. *The Feminine and the Sacred.* Translated by Jane Marie Todd. New York: Columbia University Press, 2001.

Cohen, Richard A. *Elevations: The Height of the Good in Rosenzweig and Levinas.* Chicago: University of Chicago Press, 1994.

———. *Ethics, Exegesis and Philosophy.* Cambridge: Cambridge University Press, 2001.

Cohen, Richard A., ed. *Face to Face with Levinas.* Albany: SUNY Press, 1986.

Critchley, Simon. *The Ethics of Deconstruction.* Oxford: Blackwell, 1992.

Derrida, Jacques. "At This Moment in This Very Work Here I Am." Translated by Ruben Berezdivin. In Robert Bernasconi and Simon Critchley, eds., *Re-Reading Levinas,* 11–48. Bloomington: Indiana University Press, 1991.

———. "Choreographies: An Interview between Jacques Derrida and Christine V. McDonald." Translated by Christine V. McDonald. *diacritics* (Summer 1982): 178–189. Reprinted in *Points . . . Interviews 1974–1994,* ed. Elisabeth Weber, trans. Peggy Kamuf, 89–108. Stanford, Calif.: Stanford University Press, 1995.

———. *The Gift of Death.* Translated by David Wills. Chicago: University of Chicago Press, 1995.

———. "Violence and Metaphysics." In *Writing and Difference,* translated by A. Bass, 79–153. Chicago: University of Chicago Press, 1978.

Descartes, René. *Discourse on Method; and Meditations on First Philosophy.* Translated by Donald A. Cress. Indianapolis: Hackett, 1993.

Duncan, Erika. "The Hungry Jewish Mother." In Susannah Heschel, ed., *On Being a Jewish Feminist,* 27–39. New York: Schocken, 1983.

Fackenheim, Emil. *Jewish Philosophers and Jewish Philosophy.* Edited by Michael Morgan. Bloomington: Indiana University Press, 1996.

Fletcher, George. *Loyalty: An Essay on the Morality of Relationships.* New York: Oxford, 1993.

Fonrobert, Charlotte. *Menstrual Purity: Rabbinic and Christian Reconstructions of Biblical Gender.* Stanford, Calif.: Stanford University Press, 2000.

Freedman, Rabbi Dr. H., trans. *Midrash Rabbah,* I. Genesis. London: Soncino, 1983.

Fuss, Diana. *Essentially Speaking.* New York: Routledge, 1989.

Gibbs, Robert. *Correlations in Rosenzweig and Levinas.* Princeton, N.J.: Princeton University Press, 1992.

———. *Why Ethics? Signs of Responsibilities.* Princeton, N.J.: Princeton University Press, 2000.

Gilligan, Carol. *In a Different Voice.* Cambridge, Mass.: Harvard University Press, 1982.
Handelman, Susan. *Fragments of Redemption.* Bloomington: Indiana University Press, 1991.
Hatley, James. *Suffering Witness.* Albany: SUNY Press, 2000.
Hauptman, Judith. *Rereading the Rabbis: A Woman's Voice.* Boulder: Westview Press, 1998.
Hegel, G. W. F. *Phenomenology of Spirit.* Translated by A. V. Miller. New York: Oxford University Press, 1977.
———. *Philosophy of Right.* Translated by T. Knot. Oxford: Clarendon, 1967.
Heidegger, Martin. *Sein und Zeit.* Tübingen: Neomarius Verlag, 1926. Translated by John Macquarrie and Edward Robinson under the title *Being and Time.* New York: Harper and Row, 1962.
Heschel, Abraham Joshua. *Between God and Man: An Interpretation of Judaism.* Edited by Fritz Rothschild. New York: Free Press, 1959.
———. *The Sabbath.* New York: Farrar, Straus, Giroux, 1951.
Irigaray, Luce. "The Fecundity of the Caress." In *An Ethics of Sexual Difference,* trans. Carolyn Burke and Gillian Gill, 185–217. Ithaca, N.Y.: Cornell University Press, 1993.
———. "Questions to Emmanuel Levinas." In *The Irigaray Reader,* ed. Margaret Whitford, 178–189. Oxford: Blackwell, 1991.
Kates, Judith A., and Gail Twersky Reimer. *Reading Ruth: Contemporary Women Reclaim a Sacred Text.* New York: Ballantine Books, 1994.
Katz, Claire. "'For Love Is as Strong as Death': Taking Another Look at Levinas on Love." *Philosophy Today* 45, no. 5 (2001): 124–132.
———. "From Eros to Maternity: Love, Death, and the Feminine in the Philosophy of Emmanuel Levinas." In Tirosh-Samuelson, ed., *Women and Gender in Jewish Philosophy.*
———. "Raising Cain: The Problem of Evil and the Question of Responsibility." *Studies in Practical Philosophy,* forthcoming.
———. "Re-Inhabiting the House of Ruth: The Work of the Feminine in *Totality and Infinity.*" In Chanter, ed., *Feminist Interpretations of Emmanuel Levinas,* 145–170.
———. "The Responsibility of Irresponsibility: Taking Another Look at the *Akedah.*" In Eric Nelson, Antje Kapust, and Kent Still, eds., *Addressing Levinas.* Evanston: Northwestern University Press, forthcoming.
———. "The Voice of God and the Face of the Other." *Journal of Textual Reasoning* 1, no. 2, forthcoming.
Kavka, Martin. "Saying Kaddish for Gillian Rose, or on Levinas and *Geltungsphilosophie.*" In Clayton Crockett, ed., *Secular Theology: American Radical Theological Thought,* 104–129. London: Routledge, 2001.
Kayser, Paulette. *Emmanuel Levinas: La trace du féminin.* Paris: PUF, 2000.
Kearney, Richard. "A Dialogue with Emmanuel Levinas." In Cohen, ed., *Face to Face with Levinas,* 13–34.
Keenan, Dennis King. *Death and Responsibility: The "Work" of Levinas.* Albany: SUNY Press, 1999.
Kierkegaard, Søren. *Fear and Trembling.* Translated by Alistair Hannay. London: Penguin, 1985.
Kristeva, Julia. *Strangers to Ourselves.* Translated by Leon S. Roudiez. New York: Columbia University Press, 1991.
Lachterman, David. "Torah and Logos." *The St. John's Review* 42, no. 2 (1994): 5–26.
Lingis, Alphonso. *Libido: The French Existential Theories.* Bloomington: Indiana University Press, 1985.
Llewelyn, John. "Am I Obsessed by Bobby? (Humanism of the Other Animal)." In Robert Bernasconi and Simon Critchley, eds., *Re-Reading Levinas,* 234–245. Bloomington: Indiana University Press, 1991.
———. *Emmanuel Levinas: The Genealogy of Ethics.* London: Routledge, 1995.

Merleau-Ponty, Maurice. "The Child's Relations with Others." Translated by William Cobb. In James M. Edie, ed., *The Primacy of Perception,* 96–155. Evanston: Northwestern University Press, 1964.

Morrison, Toni. *Beloved.* New York: Penguin, 1987.

Novak, David. "Election of Israel." In Daniel Frank, Oliver Leaman, and Charles Manekin, eds., *The Jewish Philosophy Reader,* 126–127. New York: Routledge, 2000.

Ofrat, Gideon. *The Jewish Derrida.* Translated by Peretz Kidron. Syracuse, N.Y.: Syracuse University Press, 2001.

Oliver, Kelly. *Family Values: Subjects between Nature and Culture.* New York: Routledge, 1997.

———. "Paternal Election and the Absent Father." In Chanter, ed., *Feminist Interpretations of Levinas,* 224–240.

Patočka, Jan. *Heretical Essays in the Philosophy of History.* Translated by Erazim Icohák, edited by James Dodd. Chicago: Open Court, 1996.

Peperzak, Adriaan T. "Judaism and Philosophy in Levinas." *International Journal for Philosophy of Religion* 40 (December 1966): 125–140.

———. *Platonic Transformations.* Oxford: Rowman and Littlefield, 1997.

———. *To the Other.* West Lafayette, Ind.: Purdue University Press, 1993.

Peperzak, Adriaan T., ed. *Ethics as First Philosophy: The Significance of Emmanuel Levinas for Philosophy, Literature, and Religion.* New York and London: Routledge, 1995.

Pesikta Rabbati. Volume 1. Translated by William Braude. New Haven: Yale University Press, 1968.

Peskowitz, Miriam, and Laura Levitt, eds. *Judaism since Gender.* New York: Routledge, 1997.

Plaskow, Judith. *Standing Again at Sinai: Judaism from a Feminist Perspective.* San Francisco: Harper and Row, 1990.

Plato. "Phaedo." In *The Collected Dialogues including the Letters,* ed. Edith Hamilton and Huntington Cairns, 40–98. Princeton, N.J.: Princeton University Press, 1961.

———. *Republic.* Translated by Allan Bloom. New York: Basic Books, 1968.

———. "Timaeus." In *Timaeus and Crito,* trans. Desmond Lee. London: Penguin Classics, 1977.

Plaut, Gunther, ed. *The Torah: A Modern Commentary.* New York: Union of American Hebrew Congregations, 1981.

Robbins, Jill. *Altered Readings.* Chicago: University of Chicago Press, 1999.

———. "Circumcising Confession: Derrida, Autobiography, Judaism." *diacritics* 25, no. 4 (Winter 1995): 20–38.

———. *Prodigal Son/Elder Brother: Interpretation and Alterity in Augustine, Petrarch, Kafka, Levinas.* Chicago: University of Chicago Press, 1991.

———. "Tracing Responsibility in Levinas's Ethical Thought." In Peperzak, ed. *Ethics as First Philosophy,* 173–183.

———. "Visage, Figure: Speech and Murder in Levinas's *Totality and Infinity.*" In Cathy Caruth and Deborah Esch, eds., *Critical Encounters: Reference and Responsibility in Deconstructive Writing,* 275–298. New Brunswick, N.J.: Rutgers University Press, 1994.

Rosenzweig, Franz. *The Star of Redemption.* Translated by William W. Hallo. Notre Dame, Ind.: University of Notre Dame Press, 1970.

Rötzer, Florian. *Conversations with French Philosophers.* Translated by Gary E. Aylesworth. Atlantic Highlands, N.J.: Humanities, 1995.

Rousseau, Jean-Jacques. *Emile.* Translated by Allan Bloom. New York: Basic Books, 1979.

Rudavsky, Tamar. *Gender and Judaism.* New York: New York University Press, 1995.

Samuelson, Norbert. *The First Seven Days: A Philosophical Commentary on the Creation of Genesis.* Atlanta: Scholars Press, 1992.

Sandford, Stella. "Masculine Mothers? Maternity in Levinas and Plato." In Chanter, ed., *Feminist Interpretations of Levinas,* 180–201.

————. *The Metaphysics of Love: Gender and Transcendence in Levinas.* London: Athlone, 2000.

Sarna, Nahum M. *JPS Torah Commentary.* Genesis. Philadelphia: Jewish Publication Society, 1989.

Sartre, Jean-Paul. *L'être et néant.* Paris: Gallimard, 1943. Translated by Hazel Barnes under the title *Being and Nothingness* (New York: Washington Square Books, 1966).

————. *Existentialism.* Translated by Bernard Frechtman. New York: Philosophical Library, 1947.

————. *Notebooks for an Ethics.* Translated by David Pellauer. Chicago: University of Chicago Press, 1992.

Schroeder, Brian. "Abraham's Odyssey." In Melvyn New, ed., with Robert Bernasconi and Richard Cohen, *In Proximity: Emmanuel Levinas and the Eighteenth Century,* 91–110. Lubbock: Texas Tech University Press, 2001.

Seeskin, Kenneth. *Autonomy in Jewish Philosophy.* Cambridge: Cambridge University Press, 2001.

Shapiro, Susan. "A Matter of Discipline: Reading for Gender in Jewish Philosophy." In Peskowitz and Levitt, eds., *Judaism since Gender,* 158–173.

————. "On Thinking Identity Otherwise." In Laurence Silberstein, ed., *Mapping Jewish Identities,* 299–323. New York: New York University Press, 2000.

————. "Toward a Postmodern Judaism: A Response." In Steven Kepnes, Peter Ochs, and Robert Gibbs, eds., *Reasoning after Revelation,* 77–92. Boulder: Westview, 1998.

Shirer, William Lawrence. *The Rise and Fall of the Third Reich.* New York: Simon and Schuster, 1960.

Silberman, Rabbi A. M., trans. *Chumash and Rashi.* Bereshit. Jerusalem: Feldheim, 1934.

Simkha of Dvinsk, Rabbi. *Meshech Hokhmah.* Commentary on Genesis cited in *Jewish Wisdom.* Edited by Rabbi Joseph Telushkin. New York: William Morrow and Co., 1994.

Srajek, Martin. *In the Margins of Deconstruction: Jewish Conceptions of Ethics in Emmanuel Levinas and Jacques Derrida.* Pittsburgh: Duquesne University Press, 2000. First published in hard copy by Kluwer Academic Publishers, 1998.

Stern, David. *Midrash and Theory.* Evanston, Ill.: Northwestern University Press, 1996.

Stern, David S. "The Bind of Responsibility: Kierkegaard, Derrida, and the *Akedah* of Isaac." *Philosophy Today,* forthcoming.

Stone, Ira. *Reading Talmud/Reading Levinas.* Philadelphia: Jewish Publication Society, 1998.

Theleweit, Klaus. *Male Fantasies,* vol. 2. Translated by Erica Carter and Chris Turner. Minneapolis: University of Minnesota Press, 1989.

Tirosh-Samuelson, Hava, ed. *Women and Gender in Jewish Philosophy.* Bloomington: Indiana University Press, forthcoming.

Trible, Phyllis. *Texts of Terror: Literary-Feminist Readings of Biblical Narratives.* Philadelphia: Fortress, 1984.

Vasey, Craig. "Faceless Women and Serious Others: Levinas, Misogyny, and Feminism." In Arleen B. Dallery and Charles E. Scott, eds., with P. Holley Roberts, *Ethics and Danger: Essays on Heidegger and Continental Thought,* 317–330. Albany: SUNY Press, 1992.

Wahl, Jean. An interview added to the end of Jean Wahl's *A Short History of Existentialism.* Translated by Forrest Williams and Stanley Maron. New York: Philosophical Library, 1949.

Ward, Graham. "On Time and Salvation: The Eschatology of Emmanuel Levinas." In Sean Hand, ed., *Facing the Other: The Ethics of Emmanuel Levinas,* 153–172. Richmond, Surrey: Curzon, 1996.

Weissman, Rabbi Moshe, ed. *The Midrash Says: The Book of Beraishis.* Brooklyn: Benei Yakov Publications, 1980.

Westphal, Merold. "Levinas's Teleological Suspension of the Religious." In Peperzak, ed., *Ethics as First Philosophy,* 151–160.

———. "The Transparent Shadow." In Martin J. Matustik and Merold Westphal, eds., *Kierkegaard in Post/Modernity,* 265–282. Bloomington: Indiana University Press, 1995.

Wiesel, Elie. "Ruth." In *Sages and Dreamers,* 50–64. New York: Touchstone, 1991.

Wiesenthal, Simon. *The Sunflower.* New York: Schocken, 1976. First published by Operal Mundi in Paris, 1969.

Wilner, Eleanor. *Reversing the Spell.* Port Townsend, Wash.: Copper Canyon, 1998.

Wyschogrod, Edith. "Doing before Hearing." In François Laruelle, ed., *Textes pour Emmanuel Lévinas,* 179–202. Paris: Jean-Michel Place, 1980.

———. *Emmanuel Levinas: The Problem of Ethical Metaphysics.* New York: Fordham University Press, 2000.

———. "God and 'Being's Move' in the Philosophy of Emmanuel Levinas." *Journal of Religion* 62 (1982): 145–155.

Ziarek, Ewa. "Kristeva and Levinas: Mourning, Ethics, and the Feminine." In Kelly Oliver, ed., *Ethics, Politics and Difference in Julia Kristeva's Writing,* 62–78. New York: Routledge, 1993.

Zoloth, Laurie. *Health Care and the Ethics of Encounter.* Chapel Hill: University of North Carolina Press, 1999.

———. "Into the Woods." In Tirosh-Samuelson, ed., *Women and Gender in Jewish Philosophy.*

Zornberg, Avivah Gottlieb. *The Beginning of Desire: Reflections on Genesis.* New York: Image/ Doubleday, 1995.

INDEX

Claire Elise Katz is an assistant professor of philosophy, Jewish studies, and women's studies at Penn State University. She is the editor of *Emmanuel Levinas: Critical Assessments*.